THE IMAGE OF THE JEW
IN EUROPEAN LIBERAL CULTURE,
1789-1914

Parkes-Wiener Series on Jewish Studies
Series Editors: David Cesarani and Tony Kushner
ISSN 1368-5449

The field of Jewish Studies is one of the youngest, but fastest growing and most exciting areas of scholarship in the academic world today. The selection of publications reflects the international character and diversity of Jewish Studies; it ranges over Jewish history from Abraham to modern Zionism, and Jewish culture from Moses to post-modernism.

Relevant books in the series:

Forging Modern Jewish Identities
Michael Berkowitz, Susan Tanenbaum and Sam Bloom (eds.)

Cultures of Ambivalence and Contempt:
Studies in Jewish-Non-Jewish Relations
Siân Jones, Tony Kushner and Sarah Pearce (eds.)

The Berlin Haskalah and German Religious Thought:
Orphans of Knowledge
David Sorkin

The Jewish Immigrant in England 1870–1914 (3rd edn)
Lloyd P. Gartner

Scenes and Personalities in Anglo-Jewry 1800–2000
Israel Finestein

Claude Montefiore: His Life and Thought
Daniel R. Langton

An English Jew: The Life and Writings of Claude Montefiore
(2nd revised and enlarged edn)
Edward Kessler (ed.)

The Image of the Jew
in
European Liberal Culture,
1789–1914

Editors

Bryan Cheyette
Nadia Valman

VALLENTINE MITCHELL
LONDON • PORTLAND, OR

First published in 2004 in Great Britain by
VALLENTINE MITCHELL
Suite 314 Premier House, 112–114 Station Road,
Edgware, Middlesex HA8 7BJ

and in the United States of America by
VALLENTINE MITCHELL
c/o ISBS, 920 N.E. 58th Street, Suite 300
Portland, Oregon 97213-3786

Website http://www.vmbooks.com

Copyright © 2004 Vallentine Mitchell

British Library Cataloguing in Publication Data

The image of the Jew in European liberal culture, 1789–1914
1. Jews in literature 2. Antisemitism in literature
3. European literature – 19th century – History and criticism
I. Cheyette, Bryan II. Valman, Nadia
809.9'3352296

ISBN 0 8530 3518 0 (cloth)
ISBN 0 8530 3517 2 (paper)
ISSN 1368-5449

Library of Congress Cataloging-in-Publication Data:

The image of the Jew in European liberal culture, 1789–1914 / editors
Bryan Cheyette, Nadia Valman
    p.cm. – (Parkes-Wiener series on Jewish studies, ISSN
1368-5449)
"This group of studies first appeared in a special issue of Jewish
Culture and History ... vol. 6, no. 1 (summer, 2003) published by
Frank Cass and Co. Ltd."
Includes bibliographical references and index.
ISBN 0-8530-3518-0 (cloth) – ISBN 0-8530-3517-2 (paper)
1. Jews in literature. 2. Antisemitism in literature. 3. English
literature–19th century–History and criticism. 4. French
literature–19th century–History and criticism. 5. Italian
literature–19th century–History and criticism. 6. German
literature–19th century–History and criticism. I. Cheyette, Bryan.
II. Valman, Nadia. III. Series.
    PN56.3.J4143 2004
    809'.933529924'009034–dc22
                                                    2003025083

This group of studies first appeared in a special issue of Jewish Culture and History [ISSN
1462-169X], Vol.6, No.1 (Summer, 2003)
published by Vallentine Mitchell & Co. Ltd.

Printed in Great Britain by Antony Rowe Ltd., Chippenham, Wiltshire

Contents

Introduction:
Liberalism and Anti-semitism

BRYAN CHEYETTE and NADIA VALMAN

In this introduction, we consider not only the specific national contexts of representations of the Jews in the long nineteenth century but also the ways these intersected with broader currents in modern Europe that transcend the particular nation-states discussed. As well as considering a range of national concepts – Britain, Germany, France and Italy – the contributions highlight racialised images of Jews in both Jewish and non-Jewish literature and consider the operation of an equivalent Semitic discourse in the work of Jews and non-Jews alike. Some contributors compare different kinds of racial discourse in the nineteenth century with Semitic racial discourse, and others focus on the formation of a European Jewish literary canon in different countries. As will become clear, the field of comparative Jewish literary studies in Europe is still in the nascent stages of scholarly development in contrast to the growing number of books comparing British and American-Jewish literature. While most welcome, such studies inadvertently privilege an Anglo-American, as opposed to a European, context for the understanding of the literary image of the Jew and the growth of Jewish literature.[1]

The volume seeks to highlight the tension between the particularity of a specific literature and culture and some of the broader, effectively transnational, transformations in the long nineteenth century – such as the fracturing and revival of Christian influence, the growth of European liberalism and the rise of scientific race-thinking. Many of the individual authors addressed in our collection had a transnational reach and set of influences which resonated well beyond the borders of their national affiliations. These include Walter Scott, Heinrich Heine, Edmund Burke, Matthew Arnold, Thomas Carlyle, Ernest Renan, George Eliot, Theodore Fontane, Gustav Freytag, Amy Levy, Cesare Lombroso, Max Nordau, Charles Péguy, Marcel Proust and Israel Zangwill.

The relationship between national and European contexts has repeatedly shaped representations of the Jew. As demonstrated in the essay by Nils Roemer, this question was initially addressed by the proponents of *Wissenschaft* Judaism in the first half of the nineteenth century, which defined Jewish history and culture in such a way that it encompassed 'the world' (that is, Europe) as a whole. Half a century later, the Jewish critics of these *Wissenschaft* ideals aimed above all to locate Jewish literature within particular nation-states as a bulwark against the rise of anti-semitism. That this tension is still with us can be seen in the recent debate between David Feldman and Zygmunt Bauman on the relationship of Western modernity to its Jewish citizens.

This debate concerns the nature of liberal anti-semitism and the related issue of whether modernity can be viewed as complicit with the history of European anti-semitism. In nineteenth-century France, Germany and Italy, liberal nation-building was the condition for the formal emancipation of the Jews. But in Bauman's overarching thesis, anti-semitism is built into the project of modernity. European nation-states, he argues, generated an homogenising impulse that emancipated and unified their diverse citizens but suppressed alternative collectivities, local and diasporic loyalties. The Jews 'were the epitome of incongruity: a non-national nation, and so cast a shadow on the fundamental principle of modern European order: that nationhood is the essence of human destiny'.[2] Feldman, however, notes the congruence of Bauman's postmodern critique of modernity with a tradition of Jewish nationalism, which rejected the Enlightenment ideals of *Wissenschaft* Judaism and instead regarded liberal tolerance as a sham.[3] He argues instead that the power of modern states to purge themselves of ethnic, religious and cultural diversity has been overestimated, and points to the continued reshaping of Jewish identities throughout Europe in this period.[4] In this view, anti-semitic political strategies in late nineteenth-century Britain, France and Germany were all driven not by the modern nation-state but by 'attempts to create a democratic, demagogic and anti-socialist politics' at a time when old elites were being challenged in a new age of mass political participation.[5] But Feldman also insists on the different trajectories and outcomes of such strategies in these respective countries. What is at stake in the dispute between Bauman and Feldman is the nature of liberalism and modernity and the extent to which these supposedly inclusive formations should be placed at the heart of the history of European and Western oppression or, instead, located in particular national contexts.

To take the example of Anglo-Jewry, the historiography has tended to split along two main faultlines when discussing liberal forms of oppression. Todd M. Endelman and David Feldman reinforce a British exceptionalism – not unlike its American counterpart – and argue that while British liberalism may be compatible with a native anti-semitism, it has nonetheless offered Jews opportunities which they could not have found elsewhere (apart from the United States). These historians tend to stress the changing nature of British liberalism – its mainly non-violent response to Anglo-Jewry – and they note the genuinely inclusive character of the British welfare state.[6] Their approach is implicitly comparative especially in relation to the continent of Europe and the Russian Empire.

Endelman, for example, compares patterns of conversion to Christianity in late nineteenth-century England and Germany. The high incidence of Jewish conversion in Germany and the vehemence with which it was denounced by Jewish communal leaders can be compared with an atmosphere of relative indifference towards the threat of apostasy in England. The dissimilarity of Jewish responses to the pressure to convert reflects the distinctive political cultures and social systems of these states:

> In politically illiberal Germany, unsure of its own national identity and unhappy about the passing of an older social and economic order, there was no room for cultural and religious pluralism, particularly when those who wished to be tolerated had lived previously as degraded outsiders and were now competing successfully for wealth, status and honors. In England, by contrast, a mature industrial society well before 1870, the values of liberal individualism were sufficiently enshrined and a sense of national confidence sufficiently established that Jewish integration into the mainstream hardly appeared threatening to the national well-being.[7]

This argument depends on a dismissal of the ways that in England too, 'Caricaturists, novelists, and dramatists employed unflattering stereotypes of Jews in their work; preachers, politicians, and journalists disparaged Jews as sharpers and cheats, aliens and outsiders, and even as the traditional blaspheming enemies of Christianity'. Endelman argues that such expressions of hostility lacked political resonance; they were not 'linked to more profound or potentially divisive questions about the basic structure of state and society' and did not breed anti-semitic campaigns to reverse the tide of integration as in Germany.[8] His approach leads to the conclusion that the rise of anti-semitism in late nineteenth-century Europe was typically an expression of anti-modernism. Anti-semitism held most political power in those states, Germany and Austria, and to a lesser extent France, where opposition to capitalism, urbanisation, state intervention and democracy became a dominant sentiment; in England anxieties about the erosion of tradition was similarly projected onto the Jews who were seen as its main beneficiaries, but in its more liberal climate this had less political impact.

Less celebratory of the virtues of Victorian liberalism, a different historiographical approach contends that far from being the antithesis of anti-semitism, liberalism has always been ambivalent towards Jews (and all ethnic minorities) not least in its anti-immigration policies. David Cesarani, Tony Kushner and Bill Williams have argued that Anglo-Jews have been coerced into transcending their own cultural difference and, in the name of liberal tolerance, have been forced to conform to a homogeneous Britishness. Jews have been the object of violent attacks in the United Kingdom throughout history and, most crucially, they contend, anti-semitism has taken a particular liberal form in Britain.[9] Williams, for example, in his groundbreaking article, 'The Anti-Semitism of Tolerance: Middle-Class Manchester and the Jews 1870-1900', argued that the influx of eastern European immigrants in the late nineteenth century disturbed the precarious balance of tolerance that had governed the integration of Jews into the Manchester bourgeoisie. It revealed that 'the equilibrium between Christian middle-class goodwill and Jewish middle-class achievement' was 'an alliance of convenience' that failed to guarantee 'either the validation of the Jewish identity per se or the demise of older anti-Semitic traditions, which continued to travel freely along the informal channels of communication and which were readily absorbed into the pages of the new literary press and into early debates centring on the desirability of the immigrant Jewish poor'.[10] The revival of mediaeval notions of clannish, acquisitive and devious Jews, illustrated starkly in the essay by Estelle Pearlman in this volume, provided racialised images of immigrants who implicitly rejected the ameliorative influence of emancipation. Such representations appeared in the publications of an aspiring middle class insecure of its own cultural identity, and operated within the broader bourgeois consensus that anti-semitism was disreputable and that 'alien' immigrants could be distinguished from respectable Anglicised Jews – thus ultimately underlining the premise of liberal tolerance.[11] This account, in terms which Zygmunt Bauman was later to echo, emphasises not the breakdown of Enlightenment values in the *fin de siècle*, or their relative weakness, but instead the continuation of their profound ambivalence towards Jews.

That the progressive ideology of liberalism could encompass more retrogressive 'prejudice' has been demonstrated by a number of historians. In revolutionary and First Empire France, Frances Malino argues, the spectre of the usurious Jew reappeared in discussions of Jewish citizenship, indicating 'how easily the prejudices of the old regime could be fitted into the new'.[12] In the case of the German states in the early nineteenth century, as Reinhard Rürup has shown, Liberal politicians who supported Jewish emancipation conceived it 'as a long-term process of remoulding Jewry with a view to bringing about their assimilation to the society and culture of the Christian-German majority of the population'.[13] The underlying assumption in German liberal policy was that 'Jews could only be granted legal equality as part of a gradual process, and that their "civil improvement" was a prerequisite for, rather than a consequence of, legal equality'.[14] Similarly, in France emancipation was pursued with the objective of 'modernising' the Jews through state intervention – such that the image of the Jew as particular and alien was preserved by and interwoven with revolutionary universalism, religious freedom and the application of the constitution to all residents of France.[15] If the mission for Jewish regeneration was taken up more informally in Italy and in Britain, it was no less coercive in intention. In Italian Jewish communities, civil equality was established alongside Jewish communal institutions designed to discourage traditional occupations and promote model citizenship.[16] Emancipation was linked not only to the Jews' obligations as citizens but to their identification with the nation. For, as Feldman has demonstrated in the British case, 'Whigs, radicals and nonconformists not only promoted the rights of rational, propertied individuals to exercise the vote, to sit in Parliament regardless of their particular religious beliefs; they also promoted a particular view of English national identity... liberalism and Jewish emancipation were concerned not only with the rights of individuals but also with an image and account of the national community to which the Jews were being admitted'.[17] It is with such images and accounts that this volume is concerned.

A number of critics who work within Anglo-Jewish literary studies have added to the historiographical debate by focusing on the discourses of religious and/or secular conversion which only 'tolerates' Jews when they are seen to be good citizens who have transcended their difference. But this liberal formulation of anti-semitism always has a Jewish Other in reserve (in stark contrast to 'his' benevolent counterpart) who is deemed not to conform to the dominant norms of society. This approach views the figure of 'the Jew' through the lens of certain dominant discourses – whether they be nation, religion or race – and therefore perceives racial representations of Jews as a microcosm of broader concerns.[18] 'By encompassing the unruly "Jew" – an age-old outcast from history as well as Christian theology,' argues Bryan Cheyette, 'the efficacy of a civilizing liberalism, or an all-controlling Imperialism, or a nationalizing socialism, could be established beyond all doubt'.[19] That the theme of the transcendence of Jewish difference was ubiquitous in nineteenth-century culture is also the focus of the work of Michael

Ragussis. Literature in this period, he argues, was saturated with the 'ideology of conversion'; at the same time, however, this ideology was contested by a 'revisionary' counter-narrative which revealed and critiqued English intolerance.[20] Ragussis rightly regards with suspicion the philo-semitism of British conversionists. Yet, in distinguishing between conversionist and revisionist narratives, rather than considering their structural similarities, he reinscribes the division between anti-semitic and liberal discourses. Other critics working in this field tend to focus on the conventional historiography of anti-semitism and stress mainly hostile negative images and violent acts against Jews.[21] Anti-semitism, in these terms, is essentially illiberal and unBritish.

What is clear from these debates is that the question of liberal anti-semitism has a complex and contested history which cannot be reduced either to a lethal teleology (culminating in the Shoah) or a benign assimilation (culminating in the astonishing success story of pre-war German Jewry or post-war Anglo-American Jews). By focusing on the exceptional nature of a particular culture – whether the exceptional tolerance of Britain and Italy or the exceptional intolerance of Germany or France – these more general questions concerning liberalism and modernity are obscured. *The Image of the Jew in European Liberal Culture* provides a number of case studies in British, French, Italian and German literature that draw on a minimalist approach to Jewish literature and culture; at the same time, this introduction seeks to situate them in terms of the complex interchange of ideas, individuals and political ideologies across national cultures.

It is, in fact, in these broader terms that a comparative approach is defended by Till van Rahden, in the recent volume *Two Nations: British and German Jews in Comparative Perspective*, arguing that new research on nineteenth-century England and Germany has above all revealed the tensions within the liberal tradition itself:

> Although liberals did support individual rights and tolerance, they also subscribed to a vision of a homogeneous, Christian nation-state. Their unwillingness to accept cultural pluralism, to include a right to be different in the liberal canon of individual rights, came to be the Achilles heel of liberalism with regard to antisemitism. It is this contradiction which explains why liberals revealed some ambivalence or sympathy towards antisemitism and were willing to place Jews outside the 'Circle of the "We"'.[22]

Indeed, Stephan Wendehorst notes that in both Britain and Germany 'the Christian state, as opposed to the early modern confessional state, was a nineteenth-century novelty' that provided a coherent underpinning ideology for a mixed Catholic and Protestant population – 'a coherence that was based on the exclusion of the Jews'.[23] In the context of competing versions of the nation, liberalism could encompass anti-semitism. As David Cesarani suggests, following Zygmunt Bauman, 'Ambivalence towards Jewish particularity, rather than unequivocal hostility, is probably a more useful category with which to explore such a spectrum of attitudes'.[24]

This formulation takes in not only the many expressions of anti-semitism that have been so well documented but also the equally problematic philo-semitic strains in nineteenth-century culture that are more often overlooked. As we will see, many of the essays in this volume reject the entrenched historiography which distinguishes absolutely between 'anti-semitism' and 'philo-semitism'. Literary texts produce many moments when 'anti-semitism' and 'philo-semitism' become indistinguishable and there is instead an interplay between these supposed irreconcilable states. The German novelist Theodore Fontane, for example, has recently been described as a 'Philosemitic Antisemite', as Florian Krobb notes in his essay, but this term could easily be applied to many of the figures discussed in this collection. At this point, however, the conventional critical vocabulary clearly breaks down, as Edward Hughes shows with regard to Proust. If 'anti-semitism' is essentialised hostility that exists only on the margins of liberal society then it is, by definition, a pathological form of expression that has little or no impact on a supposedly humanising liberal culture. In contrast to this approach, the representation of 'Jewish' or Semitic difference *within* an apparently benevolent liberalism is what brings together the various national literatures in this collection.

After Enlightenment: Race, Nation and Gender

While the essay by Nils Roemer does not deal explicitly with racial constructions of Jews in European literature, it shows the ways that Jewish literary canon-formation shifts radically – at the beginning and the end of the nineteenth century – in relation to the growth of racial anti-semitism in Europe in the 1870s and 1880s. Whereas Enlightenment-inspired *Wissenschaft* scholars wanted to 'dislodge German Jews and Anglo-Jews from particular national contexts', those who opposed the *Wissenschaft* project 'replaced global perceptions of Jewish history and literature with a focus on the history and literature of particular Jewish communities'. Ludwig Strauss, for instance, argued with reference to German literature that when studying Goethe 'one finds one's Jewish substance'.[25] The opposition to more 'global' definitions of Jewish literature was evidently a result of the racialised definition of Jews which made the nation-state, as opposed to the diaspora, the primary determinant of Jewish identity.

What is clear from Roemer's account is the double-edged nature of the construction of the Jews in *Wissenschaft* discourse as a world-historical (or at least transnational) people. As Pearlman and Hughes show in their essays, the 'cosmopolitan Jew' was a central feature of Edouard Drumont's virulent *La France juive* (1886) and popular anti-semitic culture. It was precisely this extraterritorial representation of Jews – what Roemer felicitously calls 'Diaspora nationalism' – that proved so threatening to many Jewish thinkers at the end of the nineteenth century, who instead wished to locate a 'distinct Jewish literature within the framework of pre-existing German and English literary canons'. To this end, the influential work of Matthew Arnold played a pivotal role with regard to the location of Jewish literature within a specific national culture. Roemer notes that one of the main proponents of this nation-centred view of Jewish literature is Edward Nathan Calisch who in his *The Jew in English Literature as Author and Subject* (1909) argues that English literature is, on occasion, 'permeated with the Jewish spirit'. These terms, as Michael Galchinsky indicates in his essay, are taken directly from Arnold's *Culture and Anarchy: An Essay in Political and Social Criticism* (1869). In Calisch's words, 'the Hellenic and Hebraic spirit are not antipodes, they are supplementary to each other'. As is well known, the opposition between 'Hebrew and Hellene' is at the core of Arnold's seminal definition of 'culture' or *Bildung*, which in turn is taken from Heine and Renan.[26]

Arnold's synthesis of Renan's racial discourse (which distinguished between 'Aryans and Semites') and Heine's efficacious distinction between 'Hebrew and Hellene' gives a strong sense of how French, German and English understandings of 'culture' or *Bildung* were brought together in relation to the cosmopolitan or extraterritorial construction of the Jew. The anxiety, especially in the second half of the nineteenth century, concerning whether culture or *Bildung* was to be linked with the nation-state, or was, in a more humanistic definition, to transcend mere national characteristics, was often embodied in the figure of the Jew. It was in these terms that Jews personified liberal anxieties concerning the power and efficacy of culture insofar as Jews were considered to be part of the nation while exceeding national categories. Arnold, for instance, identified strongly with unbounded cosmopolitans such as Heine, Spinoza and the actress Rachel but also held up the liberal nation-state as the means for institutionalising culture. The figure of the Jewish cosmopolitan (both Hebrew and Semite) was, therefore, always double-edged as they embodied the ideal of culture and, at the same time, threatened to exceed the only vehicle deemed suitable to institutionalise this ideal.[27]

In contrast to the location of the figure of the 'Jew' at the centre of the Enlightenment ideal of European culture, Michael Galchinsky argues that racial discourse concerning Jews in England was, in the first half of the nineteenth century, somewhat marginal compared to the widespread debates at the time concerning a range of other racialised minorities. Galchinsky rightly rejects a teleological approach to literary anti-semitism and replaces it with a 'relational methodology' where 'the meaning of both Englishness and Jewishness alters depending on which [racialised] group Jews are compared to'.[28] George Eliot, for instance, writing in February 1848, compares Jews and Africans in the following terms:

> Extermination up to a certain point seems to be the law for the inferior races – for the rest, fusion both for physical and moral ends. ...The negroes certainly puzzle me – all the other races seem plainly destined to extermination or fusion not excepting even the 'Hebrew-Caucasian'. But the negroes are too important physiologically and geographically for one to think of their extermination, while the repulsion between them and the other races seems too strong for fusion to take place to any great extent.[29]

While this letter obviously predates *Daniel Deronda* by nearly three decades, many of its propositions, as we will see below, remain at the heart of George Eliot's last novel, not least the construction of the racial destiny of Jews and Africans represented in the starkest of terms as the choice between 'extermination or fusion'. A strangely incongruous but revealing authorial aside about halfway into *Daniel Deronda* – 'And one man differs from another, as we all differ from the Bosjesman [Bushman]' – seems to confirm the status of the African as the ultimate unassimilable other.[30] In Galchinsky's reading, Jews are metonyms for various Enlightenment discourses whether it be Jacobinism (in the case of Edmund Burke) or liberalism (in the case of Thomas Carlyle) whereas other racialised minorities stand outside of these discourses and are therefore a greater cause for concern.

As Florian Krobb argues, Jews in Germany were similarly associated with the discourse of 'progress' in the 'bourgeois realist' fiction of Theodor Fontane and Gustav Freytag. Both of these writers worked within the 'consensus of bourgeois society' which Krobb associates specifically with the genre of literary realism. The work of Freytag, in particular, has been compared with that of Charles Dickens in relation to their equivalent constructions of 'good' and 'bad' Jews or figures who both uphold and stand outside of a dominant liberal discourse.[31] According to Krobb, Jews are 'seen as forces of change... a new elite' and also represent an 'older nobility'. To this extent, the metonymic position of Jews as symbols of progress places them at the centre of intellectual debates concerning the nature of German society in the mid-nineteenth century. That 'the Jew' could figure the terms of the realist novel in both England and Germany points to the relationship between liberalism and literary discourse rather than the exceptionalism of a particular national culture.

The question of genre is also crucial in this regard. If literary realism is a child of the Enlightenment – with its faith in the rational perception and understanding of society – the historical novel displayed a more evident problem with placing Jews within a narrative of liberal progress. Jefferson Chase, in these terms, highlights the struggle between 'romantic-essentialism' and 'liberal-constitutionalism' in Germany and relates this to the difficulties in representing Jews in the genre of German historical fiction. On the one hand, the instability of the German-nation state until 1870 meant that 'Germany had to be invented via literature in order to exist at all'. On the other, as in the case of Freytag and Dickens, Chase demonstrates the enormous influence of Sir Walter Scott on the genre of German historical fiction, which works against the case for German particularity. Scott's novel *Ivanhoe* (1819) created a powerful foundational myth in imagining the medieval origins of the English nation in the reconciliation of and compromise between the ruling Norman race and the oppressed Saxon race. If such a myth spoke eloquently to the social instability of contemporary England, racked by rioting, recession and Regency rule, it was equally usable in nineteenth-century Germany – and, for that matter, the United States.[32]

In Scott's novel the new nation would be defined in liberal terms, as transcending the prejudice, barbarism and corrupt aristocratic culture that fuelled both domestic racial conflict and bloodthirsty crusades. The conclusion signals a reversal of the dispossession that has afflicted King Richard, the Saxons, and the disinherited knight Ivanhoe; similarly, the nation's future benevolence is indicated in the relaxation of persecution against the Jewish figures, the moneylender Isaac of York and his noble and beautiful daughter Rebecca. Yet the conclusion of *Ivanhoe* is also fraught with ambivalence, since the restoration of civil order leaves the Jews without a livelihood and their refusal to convert to Christianity leaves them without a place in the nation. The tension between tolerance and exclusion that marks Scott's novel is replicated in his German imitators.

The key element of *Ivanhoe* that resonates through these texts is, as Chase points out, the figure of the beautiful Jewess who is 'both a source of dangerous instability and ...a sympathetic victim'. The victimisation of the Jewess offers opportunities for the authors to demonstrate liberal tolerance. Rebecca's nobility, argues Michael Ragussis in his deconstructive reading of *Ivanhoe*, provides the novel with its critique of anti-semitism. In the failed attempts to convert Rebecca, Scott 'attempts to enlist the sympathies of his English readers for the broadest basis of cultural diversity by suggesting that the project to convert the Jews (and to erase the Scots) has its parallel in the attempted genocide of the Saxons during the Norman Conquest'. Rebecca, who remains an object of desire for Ivanhoe despite his marriage, 'represents the religious and racial question that England cannot solve' and thus exposes the fissures in the myth of national unity. Her memory is 'at once the scar of unfulfilled erotic desire and the scar of unresolved historical guilt'.[33]

Such contradictions remain subtextual in Chase's reading of Grillparzer, Spindler and Hauff. Esther Ben-David's surrender to a Jewish destiny of exclusion and dispossession in *The Jew* (1827), for example, is an aspect of Spindler's 'more radical impetus towards separation' than a liberal critique *of* Jewish separation. If the Jewess's nobility in this text, and in Hauff's *The Jew Süß* (1827), resides in her voluntary renunciation of the gentile hero, the effect is not so dissimilar from that of Grillparzer's *The Jewess of Toledo* (1839/72) in which the Jewish heroine is rather less noble. In each, as in *Ivanhoe*, the outcome of the plot suggests that the resolution of conflict and the establishment of a stable national community is dependent on the exclusion of the Jew(ess). What Chase clearly demonstrates is the way that the conflict between 'romantic-essentialism' and 'liberal-constitutionalism' is enacted through narratives of sexual transgression. In this way, the unplaceable figure of the Jew(ess) exposes the limits of tolerance within Enlightenment thinking.

Fin de Siècle Jews

Our collection begins with the turn of the nineteenth century and ends with the turn of the twentieth century, and it is the self-representation of a number of influential secularised and assimilated Jewish writers and intellectuals at the *fin de siècle* that is the subject of this section of the book. In the previous section, we have seen the extent to which assimilated or acculturated Jews in Britain and Germany became metonyms for Enlightenment ideals of progress through self-cultivation, or *Bildung*. It is now an established orthodoxy that the self-image of acculturating German Jews in the first decade of the nineteenth century was uniquely defined by the ideal of *Bildung*. As Steven Aschheim has recently argued, 'according to this paradigm, it was the peculiar nature and ideals of German culture in the age of emancipation that provided the substance of German-Jewish identity'.[34]

In teleological terms, it is argued that German Jewry 'most stubbornly clung on to its liberal-humanist precepts: the belief in the progressive powers of reason, the ... insistence on the primacy of culture, self-cultivation and the critical mind'.[35] Acculturated German-Jewish intellectuals, above and beyond their European counterparts, are said to have been the main advocates of these values. In the light of the Holocaust, these ideals are recorded with an understandable pathos not least by the Weimar generation of German-Jewish intellectuals such as Franz Rosenzweig and Walter Benjamin. Rosenzweig wrote poignantly in 1924 that 'The liberal German-Jewish position, which has been the meeting ground for almost the whole of German Jewry for nearly a century, has obviously dwindled to the size of a pin-point'.[36] However, it would be a mistake to over-determine the exceptionality of the German-Jewish commitment to *Bildung*, versions of which were surely no less valued by acculturating Jews in England, France and Italy. The middle-class educated Italian Jews described in David Forgacs' essay, for example, were deeply committed to the humanist ideals of intellectual and scientific enquiry, through which they strove to further the cause of the Italian state in the post-unification period.

Conversely, by the 1890s the rejection of Enlightenment values was also a phenomenon that transcended particular national cultures. One of its most striking manifestations was the prevalent discourse of racial science, which replaced the universal brotherhood of man with the notion of different races, whose physical, moral and intellectual capacities could be measured from the body.[37] German racial science, in particular, sought to demonstrate the continuity of the Jewish race across time and space as an argument against the efficacy of emancipation and assimilation. Moreover, as recent research has shown, 'Jews too began appropriating the methods and ideas of racial science and making them a part of particular political and ideological programmes. By the turn of the century ... Jewish social scientists – among others within the Jewish community – were fully engaged in discussions and debates about racial identity and difference, purity and impurity, superiority and inferiority.'[38] Thus Zionists, as well as anti-semites, could embrace the notion of racial identity in order to confirm 'the insufficiency of the liberal, emancipationist definition of Jewry as solely a religious or faith community'. At the same time, the Anglo-Jewish social scientist Joseph

Jacobs used the empirical methodology of racial science 'to demonstrate that the Jews' racial purity made them perfectly suitable for survival and success in Victorian Britain ... social scientific research signaled a direct correspondence between emancipation, integration and eugenic health'.[39] Race science could serve both liberal and anti-emancipatory arguments. Revealing the proximity of these two possibilities, Lombroso, in David Forgacs' account, both writes against the idea of the Jews as a race and at the same time reattributes familiar negative traits to unassimilated Jews, who become the antithesis of his own commitment to science, secularism and progress.

Lombroso and his student Max Nordau were two enormously influential figures in the 1890s who contributed to the avalanche of texts defining the 'degeneration' of European culture at the turn of the century. In other accounts, Jews were a key aspect of this diagnosis. In England, for example, Jewish immigrants were represented as better equipped to win the battle of survival in competition with the indigenous working class. The ascendancy of the Jewish immigrant demonstrated, according to the Earl of Dunraven, 'the superiority of the lower order over the higher order of organism – the comparative indestructibility of lower forms of animal life' that threatened to contaminate the national stock.[40] In French and German medical literature, Jews were frequently associated with psychopathology and physical debility.[41] Such thinking haunts the work of both Lombroso and Nordau. In the case of Lombroso, unassimilated Jews were deemed to be commercially untrustworthy, neurotic, atavistic, of weak character and arrogant. Although Nordau wrote Jews out of his bestselling account of degeneration, it is clear, as Marilyn Reizbaum notes, that the spectre of the 'degenerate Jew' preoccupies his thinking. Indeed, his celebrated call in 1900 for 'muscle Jews' was based on the presumption of the degeneration of the Jewish body in the ghetto. Both Nordau and Lombroso, as well as Amy Levy, Cecily Sidgwick and Leonard Merrick, in Nadia Valman's account, display what Forgacs describes as 'a wider pattern in this period of Jewish disidentification, or, if one prefers, Jewish self-hatred. The "ridicule and repugnance" which Lombroso describes certain Jews as arousing is that typically experienced by the assimilated and secularised Jew, the rationalist or scientist, towards the practices of religious Jews.' Like other Jewish scientists across Europe, as John Efron and Sander Gilman have shown, Nordau and Lombroso were necessarily responding to a discourse which constructed Jews as 'unable to undertake the task of science because of [their] inherently pathological nature'.[42]

Thus, both use the language and methodology of scientific thinking to distance themselves, in Forgacs' words, from 'those aspects of Jewish culture which were tied to the past, to dogma, superstition and ritual'. This was not only a self-hating Jewish position, but also a liberal position. The British Liberal polemicist Goldwin Smith, writing in 1881, for example, politicised the language of ethnography to argue that intramarriage, circumcision and social exclusivity amongst orthodox Jewry – 'a vast relic of primaeval tribalism, with its tribal mark, its tribal separatism, and its tribal God' – constituted a threat to liberal culture, and disqualified the Jews from the rights of emancipation. Their clandestine loyalties he saw as 'one of the new social diseases of the present day'.[43] Not unlike Israel Zangwill, Lombroso in his account of contemporary European anti-semitism bifurcated Jews into those who are irredeemably ghettoised (either literally or culturally) and those who are capable of assimilating into the mainstream so as to form a transcendent 'new religion'. In contrast, as Reizbaum argues, Nordau's legacy 'reflects the continuities between the new and the old, despite what is apprehended as a bifurcated sensibility'. In an example of Galchinsky's 'relational methodology', Reizbaum demonstrates the extent to which James Joyce in *Ulysses* (1922) was to apply Nordau's Zionist construction of the 'new Jew' to the context and history of Irish nationalism. In bringing together Siegfried Sassoon and Leopold Bloom, Reizbaum demonstrates the centrality of cosmopolitan or hybrid Jews to a post-Enlightenment depiction of European culture.[44]

It was not only in the discourse of science that Jews were constructed as retrogressive. Nadia Valman's essay examines the representation of Judaism in a number of 'marriage problem' novels of the 1890s. Taking their cue from Amy Levy's feminist novel *Reuben Sachs* (1888), other Jewish-born writers diagnosed the degenerate aspects of Anglo-Jewish and German-Jewish society specifically in their treatment of women. In their work, we can see the convergence of the popularly disseminated scientific accounts of Jewish degeneration with feminist writing. Like Lombroso, who saw Jewish ritual traditions as 'savage', these authors suggest that gender relations in Jewish society are archaic; like Nordau, they regard Jewish men as pusillanimous. Thereby, they project their own position as progressive. But, as Valman shows, the liberal emphasis on the freedom of the individual that underlies this perspective is in unstable tension with the vocabulary of racial and religious determinism that lends authority to the authors' polemics.

On the one hand, the idea of Jewish degeneracy is a secularised version of the Christian tradition of seeing Judaism as fallen and irredeemable. In this sense, the structure of nineteenth-century scientific thought remained underpinned by Christian theology. On the other hand, as Daniel Pick powerfully argues, 'The language of degeneration should be understood in relation to a long and complex process of political definition and redefinition in European culture and society'. For example, in the widespread reconfiguration of liberalism in late-Victorian and Edwardian England, according to Pick, 'The notion of degeneration was used at once to signify the urgency of intervention and, still more alarmingly, the potential impossibility of constituting the nation from society in its entirety'. As David Glover also shows in his essay, these notions found one form of expression in the Royal Commission on Alien Immigration of 1903, followed by the 1905 Aliens Act, in which 'Englishness' came to be defined 'in a double movement of inclusion and exclusion, ideological assimilation and expulsion'.[45]

After Dreyfus: Whither Liberalism?

The authors in this section all wrote in the light of the Dreyfus affair and the heightened anti-semitism and anti-anti-semitism that circulated during and after the ordeal of Alfred Dreyfus. The essays are organised so as to characterise all shades of popular and literary representations of Jews after the Dreyfus affair. These range from the high cultural ambivalence towards liberal values in the fiction of Marcel Proust, through the middlebrow adherence to these values in the work of Charles Péguy, Israel Zangwill and Herbert Samuel, to the complete rejection of liberalism in the mass circulation picture postcards of Edwardian Britain. Here the contrast between low, high and middlebrow culture helps to illustrate a wider set of social and political issues.[46] As David Feldman argues, when discussing the impact of anti-semitism in different national cultures (France, Britain and Germany) it is crucial to understand why at certain times 'Jew-hatred found political expression and leadership. And beyond this, why it was the case that in some national contexts this political expression was defeated and why in others antisemitism was incorporated within the mainstream of politics.'[47] What the literary and cultural representations under discussion show us is that they were largely the same either in (according to the mythology) exceptionally intolerant Germany and France or exceptionally tolerant Britain and Italy. The various accounts of Semitic discourse under discussion, therefore, are determined finally by the differing ways that liberalism was institutionalised within these national cultures.

It is in these terms that the role of popular or mass representations of anti-liberal Jew-hatred – such as the Edwardian postcards discussed by Estelle Pearlman – is a crucial backdrop to our collection. Undeniably, post-Enlightenment European liberal culture was saturated with the most illiberal images and discourses about Jews. But what is at stake is the extent to which the interests of European nation-states, under the severest pressure, coincide with the liberal incorporation of Jewish immigrants and indigenous Jewish populations. At the time of the Dreyfus affair,

> Jew-hatred re-emerged as a powerful political presence at the same moment as manhood suffrage, or something close to it, was introduced across western and central Europe. Elites were faced with the challenge of maintaining existing property relations within these new conditions and also of sustaining their own political primacy. The possibility of doing so by building a mass democratic constituency united by a populist and exclusive nationalism, in which antisemitism played a central role, was one path open to the political elites in Germany, France and Britain.[48]

Edward Hughes shows in his essay that the complex fiction of Marcel Proust is able to interrogate the full political and social panoply of cultural representations concerning Jews after Dreyfus: from the popular racial anti-semitism of Edouard Drumont, to the Jewish disidentification of Bloch, to the Biblical figure of Esther and the Jewish prostitute, Rachel. As in Reizbaum's account of Joyce's *Ulysses*, the crucial issue here is Proust's construction of a range of competing discourses about Jews, the conflicts of which produce an overwhelming ambivalence. As Bryan Cheyette has argued elsewhere, there is danger in deploying a theory of ambivalence as an all-embracing category irrespective of the specific historical or social context in which a literary text is produced.[49] In the case of Proust, Hughes shows that ambivalence is utilised specifically in relation to monolithic constructions (and self-constructions) of Jewishness in post-Dreyfus France. By focusing on the social exclusions and inclusions of Proust's Jews, Hughes argues that 'ambiguity becomes a strategy with an entirely unambiguous function, which is to resist cultural homogenisation'. Unlike Joyce, where textual ambivalence helps to disrupt the dominant discourses of gender, race, nation and religion, Proust in this reading is concerned above all with undermining notions of ethnic specificity.

To this end, the question of gender and sexuality plays an important role in Proust's *A la recherche du temps perdu*, not least in the Biblical figure of Esther who provides a paradigm of 'tribal survival through assimilation' and the Jewish prostitute Rachel who subversively merges the sacred and the profane, Judaism and Christianity. Hughes' emphasis on the Esther motif recalls that of Eve Kosofsky Sedgwick, for whom it is 'a model for a certain simplified but highly potent imagining of coming out and its transformative potential'.[50] Sedgwick reads the scene of

Esther's revelation of her hidden Jewish identity, as reworked by Racine, as a counter-example to the epistemological drama of gay coming out. Unlike the disclosure of homosexuality, the scene of Esther's revelation is not complicated with proliferating uncertainties, since for both Esther and Assuérus there is 'no suggestion that identity might be a debatable, a porous, a mutable fact'.[51] Hughes, in contrast, argues that for Proust Esther is a profoundly hybrid figure who calls all certainties into question: 'Working between Jewess and Persian, Jewess and Christian, mother and son, supplicating Queen and powerful King, Old Testament and Racine, Proust celebrates those interstitial spaces and frontiers around which identities and power relations are being negotiated'.

The most famous French Jewesses of the nineteenth century, the actress Rachel and her successor Sarah Bernhardt, were figures both of exotic genius and degraded commerce.[52] Proust's Jewish prostitute 'Rachel quand du Seigneur' similarly evokes the thrill of veneration and desecration. Rachel is an unreadable figure, an impenetrable 'mystery', her immobile face 'held in equilibrium by two infinites which converged on her without meeting'. To the Narrator, she is a disposable commodity, to Robert Saint-Loup a sublime object of desire. Like Proust's writing itself, Hughes argues, Rachel's face 'holds in tension the rival value-systems of Judaism and Christianity'. Invoking the intertext of Halévy's *La Juive*, Proust recalls the imbrication of Jewish and Christian identities in the opera's heroine – also called Rachel – a Jewess finally revealed to be the daughter of a Catholic cleric. The echoes of *La Juive* are used to emphasise 'that fiction, misrecognition, and inaccuracy lie at the heart of ... fanatically held convictions about race, religion, vice, and virtue'.

Hughes' reading of *A la recherche du temps perdu* as a 'drama of tribal assimilation' echoes, as Nelly Wilson outlines, Charles Péguy's anti-modernist understanding of a unique 'Jewish voice'. As with Proust, Péguy believed that the mission of the Jews was to provoke 'inquiétude'. This 'inquiétude' resulted from the perceived particularism of French Jewry in contradistinction to the universalising values of the Enlightenment. In purely literary terms, as Hughes subtly explores, Proust's writing is able to reconstruct in great detail the ambivalent position of Jews within a liberal culture which excludes and includes ethnic minorities at the same time. In the first decades of the twentieth century, the very fact that Jews retained a strong public identity was perceived to be a sign of the failure of liberalism. Péguy's anti-modernist philo-semitism, in Wilson's terms, welcomed this failure and argued that a 'barbaric' anti-semitism would only die out in a 'Republic of equal citizens' – an argument that Jean-Paul Sartre would take up again in *Anti-*

Semite and Jew (1948). Unlike Proust, who pointedly relativises both religious and racial discourse, Péguy is characterised in Wilson's reading by the primacy of religion – especially his conversion to Catholicism in 1908. Péguy's anti-modern philo-semitism is finally replaced by a Catholic philo-semitism which views Christianity as completed Judaism.

Wilson gives an interesting account of the impact on Péguy of Israel Zangwill's story 'Chad Gadya', which was translated into French for the first time in 1904 in his journal, *Cahiers de la Quinzaine*. Zangwill published 'Chad Gadya' in his *Dreamers of the Ghetto* (1898), a fictionalised history made up of a group of heterodox Jews – Uriel Acosta, Disraeli, Heine, Ferdinand Lassalle, Spinoza, Sabbatai Zevi – converts, revolutionaries, or false messiahs. These figures represent what Zangwill called 'the middle path', somewhere between Judaism and Christianity.[53] As Wilson notes, the conflict between modernity and tradition in 'Chad Gadya' ultimately results in the suicide of the alienated Jewish intellectual who falls into despair at his abiding nostalgia for the ghettoised Judiasm of his youth. Zangwill, for much of *Dreamers of the Ghetto*, sees his disruptive and unplaceable *Luftmenschen* in these tragic terms. For this reason, he eventually came to champion the 'melting pot' as the only possible means of Jews transcending their plight in Western Europe (living the contradictions of liberalism) or Eastern Europe (facing the violence of anti-semitism). In fact, the pressing needs of Jews in the Pale of the Settlement led Zangwill to champion Jewish territorialism in a bid to form a Jewish state in a supposedly redundant location – ranging from Uganda to Galveston, Texas – which might act as a refuge from the pogroms.

As David Glover has argued, Zangwill's global vision, at its most creatively cosmopolitan in *Dreamers of the Ghetto*, echoes interestingly with the liberal imperialism of Herbert Samuel. Glover rightly relates Samuel's 'imperial approach to race and citizenship' to Zangwill's own globalised solution to the 'Jewish Question' in the first decades of the twentieth century. Here again we have a 'relational' reading, where the 1905 Aliens Act is understood in the language of Britain's imperial vision. Zangwill's stories, in this interpretation, act as a disruptive commentary on the essentially complacent version of Liberalism that Samuel promoted. The ordering pretensions of modernity, as Bauman has long since argued, have always been challenged and qualified by modernist culture.[54] It was in these terms that Zangwill implicitly contested Samuel's technocratic liberalism where Jews had, *par excellence*, an untroubled role within a facile modernity. In Weimar Germany, as Walter Benjamin famously noted, aesthetics and politics were not so neatly demarcated. Elsewhere an anti-semitic politics was beginning to move to the top of the political agenda, but in Britain the liberal nation-state held firm and anti-semitism, finally, 'worked against the grain of democracy, not with it'.[55]

Cosmopolitan Texts

Nineteenth-century texts frequently functioned in transnational as well as national contexts. *Ivanhoe*, as we have seen, was as popular and influential in emergent European nation-states as it was in Britain; Victor Hugo called it 'le véritable épopée de notre âge' [the true epic of our time].[56] Jewish conversion narratives were translated from German for use by British missionaries. Amy Levy's novel of Anglo-Jewry, *Reuben Sachs* (1888) was translated into German by Eleanor Marx, while Israel Zangwill's *Chad Gadya* had an even greater impact on French Jewry than it did on British Jews. Nordau and Lombroso as well as Weininger were read by physicians and intellectuals across Europe, and their work was popularised in political polemic and literary culture, disseminating a Semitic discourse that was not confined to national borders. Perhaps the most transnationally celebrated nineteenth-century text of Jewish identity was George Eliot's *Daniel Deronda* (1876), constructed from painstaking research in German sources, published almost simultaneously in English and German in 1876 and translated into Russian, Lithuanian and Hebrew during the 1880s as an aid to the Zionist cause.

Widely received by contemporary readers as a corrective to anti-semitic representation, *Daniel Deronda* has largely been read as an exemplary liberal text.[57] In these terms, Eliot's letter to Harriet Beecher Stowe explaining her motive for writing the novel is often quoted:

> not only towards the Jews, but towards all oriental peoples with whom we English come in contact, a spirit of arrogance and contemptuous dictatorialness is observable which has become a national disgrace to us. There is nothing I should care more to do, if it were possible, than to rouse the imagination of men and women to a vision of human claims in those races of their fellow-men who most differ from them in customs and beliefs. But towards the Hebrews we western people who have been reared in Christianity, have a peculiar debt and, whether we acknowledge it or not, a peculiar thoroughness of fellowship in religious and moral sentiment.[58]

Eliot's invocation of the 'human claims' of other races and of the Jewish roots of Christian culture looks back both to Enlightenment humanism and to early nineteenth-century Christian philo-semitism. In her novel,

Daniel Deronda reverses his mother's hostility to her Jewish heritage, and, inspired by the mystic Mordecai, dedicates himself to redeeming the Jewish nation. The novel's representation of Judaism as, in Mordecai's words, 'the heart of mankind... the core of affection which binds a race and its families in dutiful love' offers a universalised account of the Jewish mission that positions it as a paradigm for national renewal.[59]

Mordecai's organicist view of Judaism can, however, be read within the context of contemporary British politics, in which Eliot's work appears in a distinctly less liberal light. Bernard Semmel has linked Mordecai's vision of a nation that fuses 'religion and law and moral life' with Disraeli's pronouncements in the 1860s and 1870s on the need 'to preserve the British national inheritance from both a divisive and alienating individualism and a cosmopolitanism that denied the bonds of a shared past'. Despite her earlier disdain for Disraeli's Jewish chauvinism, Eliot was increasingly aligning herself not with Gladstone's liberal cosmopolitanism but with Disraeli's nationalism.[60] Rather than the racial 'fusion' she anticipated in the 1848 letter to John Sibree cited above, Jews now seemed destined to remain apart.

It is from this position that Eliot's bombastic persona Theophrastus Such attacks what he sees as a revival of mediaeval anti-semitism in the essay 'The Modern Hep! Hep! Hep!' (1879). The essay argues that the Jews' pride in their origins should be seen not as 'cosmopolitan indifference' to nationality but as an ideal example of a people who remembered its past as 'a bond of obligation'.[61] It was only such a national consciousness that enabled nations to maintain free institutions and to resist foreign conquest: 'The pride which identifies us with a great historic body is a humanising, elevating habit of mind, inspiring sacrifices of individual comfort, gain, or other selfish ambition, for the sake of that ideal whole' (p.156). In this argument, Semmel notes, Eliot signalled a move away from her earlier commitment to a Comtian 'religion of humanity', towards the 'idea of Nationality' and the protection of 'distinctive national characteristics'.[62] The object of her satire here, however, is not only mediaeval inquisitors but liberal 'anti-Judaic advocates' who, having fought for the emancipation of the Jews, now charge that they 'hold the world's money-bag, that for them all national interests are resolved into the algebra of loans, that they have suffered an inward degradation stamping them as morally inferior' (pp.154, 155). The insistence by these 'liberal gentlemen' on absolute assimilation, Theophrastus concludes, is no more than 'a blinding superstition ... that a theory of human wellbeing can be constructed in disregard of the influences which have made us human' (p.165). The mystical note struck at the end of the essay once again underlines an intellectual kinship between the irrational intolerance of mediaeval Christianity and modern liberalism.

Despite its ironic scrutiny of English national attitudes, Eliot's essay and its discussion of anti-semitism is firmly located 'at this stage of *European* culture' (p.143, our emphasis). Indeed, *Daniel Deronda* has also recently been read as an intervention into the Jewish Question as it was being debated across Europe throughout the nineteenth century. These debates were articulated through two models of the nation: the civic model, based on democratic, humanistic principles, and the German-romantic model, based on a homogeneous culture. Eliot's novel, in Amanda Anderson's reading, likewise 'generates two distinct understandings of the project of Jewish nationalism, represented respectively by Deronda and Mordecai. Deronda's nationalism persistently moves toward the universalist civic model of nationality often associated with John Stuart Mill and built on the principle of democratic debate, while Mordecai's follows the collectivist-romantic model of a unified national will and a projected national destiny'.[63] Whereas Mordecai sees individual choice as the acceptance of an already fixed national destiny, Daniel, in contrast, engages in a dialogue with his past. While Mordecai speaks of mystical 'transmission', Daniel experiences a 'reflective return to his cultural heritage'.[64] Indeed, to his mother's question as to whether he will turn himself into a Jew 'just like your grandfather', Daniel responds: 'That is impossible. The effect of my education can never be done away with. The Christian sympathies in which my mind was reared can never die out of me' and later he tells Joseph Kaloymos: 'I shall call myself a Jew... But I will not say that I shall profess to believe exactly as my fathers have believed. Our fathers themselves changed the horizon of their belief and learned of other races.'[65] In the end, the competing aesthetic-cosmopolitan and racial-national constructions of Jewishness are resolved in the figure of Deronda who, as Anderson argues, actively 'forges an identity out of hybrid traditions'.[66]

This collection of essays suggests that literary and cultural texts are especially able to tease out the complex contradictions between the universalistic ideals and the racial-particularistic realities of the liberal nation-state in nineteenth-century Europe. In chapter 42 of *Daniel Deronda* George Eliot sets up a debate between these two versions of the nation when the prophetic Mordecai confronts Pash, a 'small, dark, vivacious, triple-baked Jew', with his vision of a redemptive Jewish nationalism as opposed to Pash's belief in liberal equality and citizenship:

> What is the citizenship of him who walks among a people he has no hearty kindred and fellowship with, and has lost the sense of

brotherhood with his own race? It is a charter of selfish ambition
and rivalry in low greed. He is an alien in spirit, whatever he may
be in form; he sucks the blood of mankind, he is not a man. Sharing
in no love, sharing in no subjection of the soul, he mocks at all.[67]

Those who supported Jewish 'emancipation' in the mid-nineteenth
century predicated their liberal embrace on the supposed rational
utilisation of 'Jewish wealth'. By the 1870s, as Jonathan Freedman has
shown, figurative Jews routinely embodied the contradictory desires
which governed capitalism itself, often in transnational bestsellers such as
Trilby (1894).[68] In Mordecai's terms, Jews were no longer bounded by the
logic of reason and could therefore represent everything that was
fearfully coveted by the capitalist market. Without a sense of racial
'brotherhood', cosmopolitan Jews were alien bloodsuckers who were
selfish and greedy, hence the need for a curative Jewish nationalism. Most
worrying of all, no one could detect these severe faults by observing the
outward 'form' of the Jews. It was according to the alternative logic of
'race' that Jews, beyond exteriority, were deemed to be outside the
purview of both narrative realism and the liberal nation-state.

Some critics have applauded Eliot's novel for 'step[ping] outside the
predominant configuration of Jewish identity in English discourse'.[69]
This may be true in relation to a traditional evangelical millenarianism,
which had hitherto argued that the restoration of the Jews in Palestine
would bring about the Second Coming of Christ. However, it is clear
that *Daniel Deronda*, with its structural comparison of good and bad
Jews, was deeply mired in the racism of liberal 'English discourse'. It is
precisely this critical debate that sustains our collection. Can we separate
out a philosophy of enlightenment from the Semitic racial discourse
which shadowed and underscored the belief in liberal tolerance? In
holding apart liberalism and anti-semitism, there is an implicit refusal to
acknowledge the possible continuities between the two. What this
collection proposes is that throughout nineteenth-century European
culture there was an uneasy exchange between liberalism and anti-
semitism. Rather than focusing on particular national discourses, we have
here begun to show the ways in which many European literary and
cultural texts engaged with this unforeseen and uncomfortable product of
the Enlightenment.

NOTES

1. Two important recent Anglo-American studies are David Brauner, *Post-War Jewish Fiction: Ambivalence, Self-Explanation and Transatlantic Connections* (New York and Basingstoke: Palgrave, 2001) and Jonathan Freedman, *The Temple of Culture: Assimilation and Anti-Semitism in Literary Anglo-America* (New York and Oxford: Oxford University Press, 2000).

2. Zygmunt Bauman, 'Allosemitism: Premodern, Modern, Postmodern' in *Modernity, Culture and 'the Jew'*, ed. by Bryan Cheyette and Laura Marcus (Stanford, CA: Stanford University Press; Cambridge: Polity Press, 1998), p.153.

3. David Feldman, 'Was Modernity Good for the Jews?' in *Modernity, Culture and 'the Jew'*, ed. by Bryan Cheyette and Laura Marcus (Stanford, CA: Stanford University Press; Cambridge: Polity Press, 1998), pp.171–87.

4. See also *Assimilation and Continuity: The Jews in Nineteenth-Century Europe*, ed. by Jonathan Frankel and Steven J. Zipperstein (Cambridge: Cambridge University Press, 1992) and *Toward Modernity: The European Jewish Model*, ed. by Jacob Katz (New Brunswick, NJ and Oxford: Transaction Books, 1987).

5. Feldman, 'Was Modernity Good for the Jews?' (see note 3), p.183. It has also been argued of Italy that 'the absence of mass politics smoothed emancipation, whereas the expansion of political participation exacerbated the relations of religious minorities with the majority society'. See Stephan Wendehorst, 'Emancipation as path to national integration' in *The Emancipation of Catholics, Jews and Protestants: Minorities and the Nation-State in Nineteenth-Century Europe,* ed. by Rainer Liedtke and Stephan Wendehorst (Manchester and New York: Manchester University Press, 1999), p.200.

6. For a summary of this debate see the roundable discussion between David Cesarani, David Feldman, Tony Kushner, Peter Mandler, Mark Mazower and Bernard Wasserstein, 'England, Liberalism and the Jews: An Anglo-Jewish *Historikerstreit*', *Jewish Quarterly* 44.3 (Autumn, 1997), 33–8.

7. Todd M. Endelman, 'The Social and Political Context of Conversion in Germany and England, 1870–1914', in *Jewish Apostasy in the Modern World*, ed. by Todd M. Endelman (New York and London: Holmes and Meier, 1987), p.102.

8. Ibid., pp.94, 95. Elsewhere, Endelman argues, in contrast, that the discomfort inflicted by anti-semitic popular culture in liberal states 'may have done more to encourage the flight from Jewishness than social exclusion and occupational discrimination'; Todd M. Endelman, 'Comparative Perspectives on Modern Anti-Semitism in the West' in *History and Hate: The Dimensions of Anti-Semitism* (Philadelphia: Jewish Publication Society, 1986), p.103.

9. See note 6.

10. Bill Williams, 'The Anti-Semitism of Tolerance: Middle-Class Manchester and the Jews 1870–1900', in *City, Class and Culture: Studies of Social Policy and Cultural Production in Victorian Manchester* (Manchester: Manchester University Press, 1985), pp.75, 78.

11. Ibid., pp.81, 89–90.

12. Frances Malino, 'French Jews', in *The Emancipation of Catholics, Jews and Protestants: Minorities and the Nation-State in Nineteenth-Century Europe* ed. by Rainer Liedtke and Stephan Wendehorst (Manchester and New York: Manchester University Press, 1999), pp.83–99.

13. Reinhard Rürup, 'German Liberalism and the Emancipation of the Jews', *Leo Baeck Institute Yearbook* 20 (1975), 61.

14. Reinhard Rürup, 'Jewish Emancipation in Britain and Germany', in *Two Nations: British and German Jews in Comparative Perspective*, ed. by Michael Brenner, Rainer Liedtke and David Rechter (London: Leo Baeck Institute; Tübingen: Mohr Siebeck, 1999), p.58.

15. Malino (see note 12), p.90.

16. Gadi Luzzato Voghera, 'Italian Jews', in *The Emancipation of Catholics, Jews and Protestants*, pp.169–87.

17. David Feldman, *Englishmen and Jews: Social Relations and Political Culture 1840–1914* (New Haven and London: Yale University Press, 1994), p.136.

18. See, for example, Bryan Cheyette, *Constructions of 'the Jew' in English Literature and Society: Racial Representations 1875–1945* (New York and Cambridge: Cambridge University Press, 1993) and James Shapiro, *Shakespeare and the Jews* (New York: Columbia University Press, 1996).
19. Cheyette, *Constructions of 'the Jew'* (see note 18), p.269.
20. Michael Ragussis, *Figures of Conversion: 'The Jewish Question' and English National Identity* (Durham, NC and London: Duke University Press, 1995).
21. Frank Felsenstein, *Anti-Semitic Stereotypes: A Paradigm of Otherness in English Popular Culture, 1660–1830* (Baltimore and London: Johns Hopkins University Press, 1995) and Andrea Freud Loewenstein, *Loathsome Jews and Engulfing Women: Metaphors of Projection in the Works of Wyndham Lewis, Charles Williams, and Graham Greene* (New York and London: New York University Press, 1993).
22. Till van Rahden, 'In Defence of Differences: A Comment on Tony Kushner', in *Two Nations: British and German Jews in Comparative Perspective*, ed. by Michael Brenner, Rainer Liedtke and David Rechter (London: Leo Baeck Institute; Tübingen: Mohr Siebeck, 1999), p.113.
23. Wendehorst, 'Emancipation as path to national integration' (see note 5), p.203.
24. David Cesarani, 'Jewish Emancipation: From Teleology to a Comparative Perspective: A Comment on Reinhard Rürup', in *Two Nations: British and German Jews in Comparative Perspective*, ed. by Michael Brenner, Rainer Liedtke and David Rechter (London: Leo Baeck Institute; Tübingen: Mohr Siebeck, 1999), p.66. For Bauman's discussion of ambivalence see 'Allosemitism: Premodern, Modern, Postmodern' (note 2), pp.143–4.
25. Quoted in Steven Aschheim, *Culture and Catastrophe: German and Jewish Confrontations with National Socialism and Other Crises* (New York and London: New York University Press, 1996), p.32.
26. Cynthia Scheinberg, *Women's Poetry and Religion in Victorian England: Jewish Identity and Christian Culture* (New York and Cambridge: Cambridge University Press, 2002), pp.55–8 for the influence of Heine on Arnold's thinking.
27. For this argument in more detail see Freedman, *Temple of Culture* (note 1), pp.47–50 and Bryan Cheyette, 'On Being a Jewish Critic', *Jewish Quarterly*, 50.1 (Spring 2003), 63–70.
28. For a comparative study of religious minorities in nineteenth-century Europe, see *The Emancipation of Catholics, Jews and Protestants: Minorities and the Nation-State in Nineteenth-Century Europe*, ed. by Rainer Liedtke and Stephan Wendehorst (Manchester and New York: Manchester University Press, 1999).
29. George Eliot, letter to John Sibree, 11 February 1848, in Gordon S. Haight (ed.), *The George Eliot Letters: Volume I, 1836–51* (Oxford: Oxford University Press, 1954), pp.246–7.
30. George Eliot, *Daniel Deronda* (London: Penguin, 1995), p.324.
31. Mark Howard Gelber, 'What is Literary Anti-Semitism?', *Jewish Social Studies*, 47 (Winter 1985), 1–20.
32. Scott's novel lay behind a number of American narratives of the birth of a nation out of opposite religious or ideological factions, or of people of different European descent, which also sought to maintain the whiteness of the nation. See Alide Cagidemetrio, 'A Plea for Fictional Histories and Old-Time 'Jewesses'', in *The Invention of Ethnicity*, ed. by Werner Sollors (New York and Oxford: Oxford University Press, 1989), pp.14–43.
33. Ragussis (see note 20), pp.126, 113, 116.
34. Aschheim (see note 25), p.32.
35. Ibid. For more on the relationship between Jews, *Bildung*, liberal thought and liberal politics, see George L. Mosse, *Confronting the Nation: Jewish and Western Nationalism* (Hanover, NH: Brandeis University Press, 1993), chs.9 and 10.
36. Quoted in Aschheim (see note 25), p.31
37. See, for example, Nancy Stepan, *The Idea of Race in Science: Great Britain, 1800–1960* (London: 1982), Sander L. Gilman, *The Jew's Body* (New York: Routledge, 1991).
38. Mitchell Hart, 'Picturing Jews: Iconography and Racial Science', *Studies in Contemporary*

Jewry 11 (1995), 159-75 (p.159). See also John Efron, *Defenders of the Race: Jewish Doctors and Race Science in Fin-de-Siècle Europe* (New Haven: Yale University Press, 1994).
39. Hart (see note 38), pp.160, 166.
40. Quoted in William Greenslade, 'Fitness and the Fin de Siecle', in *Fin de Siècle/Fin du Globe: Fears and Fantasies of the Late Nineteenth Century*, ed. by John Stokes (Basingstoke: Macmillan, 1992), p.44. For fictions of contamination in 1890s Britain see Alexandra Warwick, 'Vampires and the Empire: Fears and Fictions of the 1890s' in *Cultural Politics at the Fin de Siècle*, ed. by Sally Ledger and Scott McCracken (Cambridge: Cambridge University Press, 1995), pp.202-20.
41. Jan Goldstein, 'The Wandering Jew and the Problem of Psychiatric Anti-Semitism in Fin-de-Siècle France', *Journal of Contemporary History* 20 (1985), 521-52; Sander L. Gilman, *Freud, Race, and Gender* (Princeton: Princeton University Press, 1993), pp.93–113 and ibid., *The Jew's Body*.
42. Gilman, *The Jew's Body* (see note 37), pp.234-5.
43. Goldwin Smith, 'The Jewish Question', *The Nineteenth Century* 10 (1881), 494-515.
44. For a recent account of Siegfried Sassoon in these terms see Peter Lawson, 'Otherness and Affiliation: Anglo-Jewish Poetry from Isaac Rosenberg to Elaine Feinstein' (unpublished PhD thesis, University of Southampton, 2002), ch.3.
45. Daniel Pick, *Faces of Degeneration: A European Disorder, c.1848-1918* (Cambridge: Cambridge University Press, 1989), pp.222, 215.
46. Freedman, *Temple of Culture* (see note 1), discusses throughout the fraught relations between low, middlebrow and high culture.
47. Feldman, 'Was Modernity Good for the Jews?' (see note 3), p.179.
48. Ibid.
49. Bryan Cheyette (ed.), *Between 'Race' and Culture: Representations of 'the Jew' in English and American Literature* (Stanford, CA and London: Stanford University Press, 1996), pp.1–17.
50. Eve Kosofsky Sedgwick, *Epistemology of the Closet* (Berkeley: University of California Press, 1990), p.75.
51. Ibid., p.79.
52. See Carol Ockman, 'When is a Jewish Star Just a Star? Interpreting Images of Sarah Bernhardt', in *The Jew in the Text*, ed. by Linda Nochlin and Tamar Garb (London and New York: Thames and Hudson, 1995), pp.121–39; Rachel M. Brownstein, *Tragic Muse: Rachel of the Comédie Française* (Durham and London: Duke University Press, 1995). See also Sander L. Gilman, 'Salome, Syphilis, Sarah Bernhardt, and the Modern Jewess', in *Love + Marriage = Death and Other Essays on Representing Difference* (Stanford, CA: Stanford University Press, 1998), pp.65–90.
53. Quoted in Joseph H. Udelson, *Dreamer of the Ghetto: The Life and Work of Israel Zangwill* (Tuscaloosa and London: University of Alabama Press, 1990), p.145.
54. Zygmunt Bauman, *Modernity and Ambivalence* (Cambridge: Polity Press, 1991), for this argument.
55. Feldman, 'Was Modernity Good for the Jews?' (see note 3), p.183.
56. Quoted in Bernard Semmel, *George Eliot and the Politics of National Inheritance* (New York and Oxford: Oxford University Press, 1994), p.107.
57. Ragussis (see note 20), ch.6; Gauri Viswanathan, *Outside the Fold: Conversion, Modernity, and Belief* (Princeton, NJ: Princeton University Press, 1998), ch.1; Irene Tucker, *A Probable State: The Novel, the Contract, and the Jews* (Chicago: University of Chicago Press, 2000), ch.1, are recent critical works that read Eliot's text as challenging anti-semitism.
58. George Eliot, letter to Harriet Beecher Stowe, 29 October 1876, in Gordon S. Haight, *The George Eliot Letters Vol VI 1874–1877* (Oxford: Oxford University Press, 1956), pp.301–2.
59. Eliot, *Daniel Deronda* (see note 30), p.530.
60. Semmel (see note 56), p.127.
61. George Eliot, *Impressions of Theophrastus Such* (London: William Pickering, 1994), pp.155, 146.

62. Semmel (see note 56) p.132.
63. Amanda Anderson, 'George Eliot and the Jewish Question', *The Yale Journal of Criticism* 10.1 (1997), 41.
64. Ibid., pp.49, 51.
65. Eliot, *Daniel Deronda* (see note 30) pp.661, 725.
66. Anderson (see note 62), p.48 and Cheyette, *Constructions of 'the Jew' in English Literature and Society* (see note 18), ch.2 for a reading of *Daniel Deronda* in these terms.
67. Eliot, *Daniel Deronda* (see note 30), p.528.
68. Freedman, *Temple of Culture* (see note 1), ch.3 and Daniel Pick, *Svengali's Web* (London and New Haven: Yale University Press, 2000).
69. Ragussis (see note 20), p.290.

Towards a Comparative Jewish Literary History: National Literary Canons in Nineteenth-Century Germany and England

NILS ROEMER

The history of modern Judaism has often been described in terms of polarised concepts such as assimilation and reassertion, inclusion and exclusion. Within this perspective, European nationalist movements demanded that Jews assimilate as part of a tacit agreement over emancipation. Yet European nationalism helped to shape hybrid modern Jewish identities in England and Germany and informed the imagining of a new Jewish community across national boundaries. Lacking a common territory and language, modern Jews possessed nevertheless 'a myth of common descent, common historical memories [and] elements of shared culture', which Anthony Smith describes as key components in the nationalisation of an ethnic group.[1] Newspapers like the *Allgemeine Zeitung des Judenthums* in Leipzig (1837), the *Archives Israélites* in Paris (1840), the *Jewish Chronicle* in London (1841) and international Jewish organisations like the *Alliance Israélite Universelle* functioned in various ways in this refashioning of Jewish communities across borders. The newspapers informed the emerging new public sphere about Jews in the East and West, while the *Alliance* provided a sense of Jewish political representation.[2] Aside from the importance of modern mass communications and politics, the collection and creation of a national Jewish heritage and literary canon carried out by nineteenth-century Jewish scholars contributed to the imagining of a Jewish transnational community and, eventually, to the formation of modern Jewish cultures. In this respect, European nationalism compelled Jewish scholars to produce a national Jewish history and literature within the realm of world history and literature. To paraphrase Homi Bhabha, while nationalism attempted to produce identity, it effectively aided the demarcation of difference and the process of self-assertion.[3]

Beyond the postulated opposition between European nationalism and modern Jewry, the place of Jews within modern societies was not only determined by their role as in- and outsiders within respective nation-

states, but by their status as a social, religious and cultural group that
stretched beyond territorial boundaries.[4] It was precisely because of the
Jews' ambiguous status as a religious and transnational group that
Wissenschaft des Judentums [Science of Judaism] scholars were able to
dislodge nineteenth-century debates over Jewishness, Germanness,
Englishness, and German-Jewish and Anglo-Jewish literature from
particular national contexts as well as racial taxonomies.

Modern historians within the burgeoning field of scholarship on
nineteenth-century constructions of Jewish identities have drawn
attention to the centrality of racial discourses in the self-understanding of
modern Jews.[5] Aided by the growth of mass communications during the
latter half of the nineteenth century, anti-semitic positions were asserted
increasingly in public debates and shaped popular representations of Jews
in Victorian England and Wilhelmine Germany. Influenced by the
increasing importance of these studies, Michael Kramer has recently
argued that the scholars of *Wissenschaft* relied on racial definitions of
Jewish literature.[6] With its emphasis on the centrality of racial discourses
as an all-powerful *episteme*,[7] the modern Jewish literary canon is, in
Kramer's view, intimately linked to modern racism and illustrates
dynamics of influence, adaptation and assimilation.

Kramer, however, does not do justice to the complex interaction of
racial discourse and the internal Jewish dynamics of self-fashioning. In his
sweeping argument, he obfuscates the ways that racial definitions
remained a highly multivalent and evolving form of categorisation that
comprised cultural, national and biological elements.[8] Moreover, he
homogenises both anti-Jewish discourses and Jewish engagement with
these constructions of Jewish identities and forms of self-assertion. As this
article will argue, Jews and other German and English writers actively
employed, refashioned and reinvented these concepts in various ways and
did not simply adopt them.[9] Even though anti-semitism represented a
powerful cultural force in Germany and England, Jewish responses to
modern constructions of identity were not limited to anti-semitic
representations, nor did they follow a clearly charted path, but rather
encompassed multiple voices.[10]

Nineteenth-century literary studies in Europe were organised along
national lines and became embedded in the construction of distinct
national pasts.[11] With the increasing acceptance of literature as a field of
scholarly inquiry and instruction in university establishments, 'literature'
became an epithet of 'nation'. For Jewish participants, national discourse
exerted an exclusionary tendency and provided an important framework
for their formulation of the Jewish past and its literature. Confronted
with emerging European nationalism, scholars of *Wissenschaft* countered

the narrow confines of German nationalism by adopting a global national Jewish perspective in their writings. They defined Jewish literature not within respective national canons but rather within the annals of *Weltliteratur*. Their various contributions to the field of Jewish historical and literary studies were an active form of imagining and fostering a Jewish tradition, and an act of re-imagining the contours of European, German and English history and literature.

From the inception of modern Jewish historiography at the beginning of the nineteenth century in Berlin, Jewish scholars attempted to come to terms with the distinct features of Jewish history and literature. The leading figures of the *Verein für Kultur und Wissenschaft der Juden* [Society for the Culture and Science of the Jews] during the 1820s took Europe as their reference point, not Germany. Its president, Eduard Gans, asserted that it was incumbent upon the *Verein* to take up a European historical perspective. Gans, the *Wunderschüler* of Hegel, posited that history progresses according to a clearly charted path mapped out by a specific idea. Accordingly, it was the task of the historian to elucidate this idea and to delineate its progressive fulfilment.

In a subtle turn against Hegel, Gans postulated that to trace the historical place and nature of this idea, one would have to clarify 'what is the present Europe' and 'who are we Jews'.[12] In contrast to Hegel, Gans replaced the German Reich as the fourth empire along the lines of the prophecies contained in Daniel with Europe as an organic entity into which the 'spirit' was unfolding.[13] Insofar as members of the *Verein* adopted a European perspective, they effectively created a transnational frame of reference. From this vantage point, their constructions of modern Jewish history entailed, for example, a comprehensive survey of the process of emancipation within the European nations. They associated the advent of modernity with the politics of tolerance in the Netherlands, Frederick the Great, Moses Mendelssohn and the French Revolution. During the 1830s and 1840s, historians like Julius Fürst even contended that Jewish world citizens could not neglect the non-European history of the Jews.[14]

The European or world historical perspective was forged out of the Enlightenment heritage against the narrow confines of national Romantic discourse. Yet by circumventing the national setting of Jewish history with a global perspective, Jewish scholars created national histories of the Jews. If Isaac Jost, the first author of a comprehensive history of the Jews entitled *Geschichte der Israeliten* [History of the Israelites, 1820–29], distanced himself from the term 'nation', he nevertheless could not do without it.[15] Subsequently, from the 1850s to the 1870s, Heinrich Graetz wrote a national history of the Jews that did

not centre on German-Jewry; for example, he envisioned a unification of
Germany and France initiated by Heinrich Heine and Ludwig Börne.[16]
The world historical role of Jews and Judaism, which for Graetz would
pave the way to the messianic epoch, manifested itself not within the
framework of national histories but in Jewish history as a whole.[17]

It was within the framework of *Wissenschaft des Judentums* and
German scholarship that Jewish literary studies took shape. The
invention of the German literary canon was instrumental for the political
aspirations of the emergent German nationalist ideology. This literary
tradition culminated in the works of Gotthold Ephraim Lessing, Johann
Wolfgang Goethe and Friedrich Schiller. Each author could be seen as an
essential progression in the conception of a German literary tradition.
Whereas Lessing shaped German literature by utilising English models in
his turn against French tradition, Goethe drew his inspiration from
Rome and Schiller from Greece. German literature, therefore, appeared
as the successor of antiquity and the culmination of English and French
literature. This unity in the world of *belles lettres* legitimised and
promised Germany's political unification.[18]

At the inception of modern Jewish historiography, Leopold Zunz, a
member of the *Verein*, suggested in his programmatic essay of 1818
entitled *Etwas über die rabbinische Literatur* [On Rabbinic Literature]
replacing the designation 'Rabbinic literature' with 'new-Hebrew
literature' or 'Jewish literature'.[19] For Zunz, Jewish literature reflected
the history of the Jewish people. The literature of the nation was, Zunz
contended, the 'entrance to a comprehensive understanding of its cultural
development'.[20] Accordingly, the study of Jewish literature would be
intimately linked to conceptions of Jewish history, or, to use Heinrich
Graetz's formulation, Jewish literature 'formed the core of Jewish
history that the history of suffering wrapped in a bitter shell'.[21]

In a small article for the Brockhaus encyclopaedia, Zunz revised his
narrow understanding of Jewish literature, which came to connote works
from all areas of knowledge based in Hebrew language, but not restricted
to it.[22] After he had contested theological definitions of Jewish literature,
Zunz postulated in his 1845 *Zur Geschichte und Literatur* [On History and
Literature] that Jewish literature was an integral element of world
literature, that had its distinct forms and expression.[23] Inspired by the
ideal of a *Weltliteratur*, Zunz countered the confining national discourse
in Germany as well as the established hierarchy in the study of world
literature, which had, as Edward Said has pointed out, 'Europe and its
Latin Christian literatures at its center and top'.[24] Zunz took his cue not
from Goethe's notion of *Weltliteratur*, which embodied the classics and
European literature, but rather from Herder, whose enchantment with

the spirit of various peoples [*Volksgeist*] negated the notion of a cultural hierarchy.[25]

Reasserting the place of Jewish literature within the literatures of the world and formulating the homogeneous nature of a Jewish literary canon remained a central task on *Wissenschaft*'s scholarly agenda. Concurrent with Zunz, Moritz Steinschneider provided the first in-depth encyclopaedic survey of Jewish literature in 1850. Steinschneider contended that Jewish literature comprised everything Jews had ever written, regardless of the subject or language. Realising full well that this hardly provided a clear definition, he emphasised that Jewish literature, despite its resembling a conglomerate of various origins and forms, was an 'organism'. Steinschneider based the cohesive and organic nature of Jewish literature on the postulated unity of Jews and Judaism throughout time. This was not merely a defensive strategy, since Steinschneider was fully cognisant of the fact that definitions of *Judentum* maintained a certain ambiguity. Playing on the double meaning of *Judentum* in German, which denotes both the Jewish people and the religion, Steinschneider wrote that *Judentum* was as a 'religious community not sufficiently [explained], and with the term "nation" just barely described'.[26]

The governing perception of European history that had framed these early literary studies, however, rapidly changed with the publication of additional volumes of Graetz's *Geschichte der Juden* [History of the Jews]. If, from a historical point of view, Graetz continued to stress Jews' and Judaism's central role in the creation of the modern world, he nevertheless became critical of contemporary modern European culture.[27] Quoting extensively from Heinrich Heine's *Shakespeares Mädchen und Frauen* [Shakespeare's Girls and Women, 1839], Graetz turned the relationship between Judaism and Europe on its head:

> The rest of Europe too raises itself to the level of the Jews. I say raises itself – for even in the beginning the Jews bore within them the modern principles which only now are visibly unfolding among the nations of Europe.[28]

Graetz believed that Europe had to follow Judaism's lead and increasingly regarded Europe as a morally corrupt outgrowth of paganism.[29] In his *Briefwechsel einer englischen Dame über Judenthum und Semitismus* [Correspondence with an English Lady on Judaism and Semitism, 1883], he buttressed this contention by referring to statistics on the spread of syphilis, the increase in prostitution and the growing number of illegitimate children.[30] These examples, maintained Graetz, are the 'successes' of European culture, which is the outcome of unresolved vestiges of paganism in Greek culture and Christianity, manifesting itself in depravity and carnal lust.[31] Only ethical monotheism, which demands sexual chastity, could safeguard against this abyss.[32] In response to this portrayal, the English lady asked Graetz whether one could 'de-Europeanize us?'[33]

Graetz's repositioning of Jews and Judaism in opposition to Europe emphasised the irreducible religious quality that shaped Jewish life and culture. The increasingly religious rhetoric that defined the essence of Judaism also framed the new and more sweeping descriptions of Jewish literature. Two graduates from the Breslau Jewish Theological Seminary, Gustav Karpeles, the editor of the *Allgemeine Zeitung des Judentums*, and Marcus Brann, the editor of the prestigious scholarly journal, the *Monatsschrift für Geschichte und Wissenschaft des Judentums*, dominated this realm of research, in addition to the eminent Anglo-Jewish scholar and co-founder of the *Jewish Quarterly Review*, Israel Abrahams.

Karpeles considered all writings by Jews in any language, regardless of content and at least up until the modern era, as part of Jewish literature, which formed an important aspect of world literature.[34] Adopting this wide cultural definition helped him emphasise the non-theological nature of these works. Karpeles contended that Jewish literature would be ill-defined if one continued to call it rabbinical literature. Like Steinschneider, he characterised it as a religious-national literature.[35] Consequently, noted Karpeles, a 'systematic representation' of Jewish literature was fraught with difficulties in comparison to other national literatures. In order to overcome the existing ambiguity, Karpeles significantly narrowed his definition of Jewish literature when he added a content dimension to his description. He classified as Jewish literature only works by Jews in which 'Jewish views of the world and life [*Welt-und Lebenanschauung*], Jewish culture and art, Jewish thinking and feeling' are expressed.[36]

Whereas Zunz and Steinschneider had promoted an all-inclusive understanding of Jewish literature to contest a purely religious definition, Karpeles's reference to a Jewish *Weltanschauung* highlights the increasingly topical definitions of Jewish literature. Taking this notion a bit further, Marcus Brann, in his 1895 *Geschichte der Juden und ihrer Litteratur: Für Schule und Haus* [History of the Jews and their Literature: For School and Home], decided to include only those Jewish writers who furthered Jewish spirituality. According to Brann, all other Jewish authors who had contributed a great deal to general culture were not part of Jewish, but rather of other, national literatures.[37]

While in Karpeles's and Brann's works allusions to the specificity of

Jewish literature remained fairly vague, Israel Abrahams's study of Jewish literature from the destruction of the Second Temple to the death of Moses Mendelssohn provided him with the opportunity to account for 'the genius of the Hebrew people'.[38] He postulated the unity of Jewish literature as being shaped by an all-encompassing and formative ideal of righteousness along the lines of Matthew Arnold's influential *Literature and Dogma: An Essay Towards a Better Apprehension of the Bible* (1873).[39] This religious and essentialist dimension, Abrahams posited, 'gave more harmony to Jewish literature than is possessed by many literatures more distinctively national'.[40]

These increasing references to the religious quality of Jewish history and literature more clearly differentiated Jewish from European culture. At the same time, the re-evaluation of the Jews' place within European history also led to the growing importance of regional studies during the last decades of the nineteenth century. These more narrowly defined accounts combatted anti-semitic representations of Jewish internationalism with studies that described Jews' integration into and participation in their respective national societies. Rather than adopting Isaac Jost's and Heinrich Graetz's global conceptions of Jewish history, these Jewish historians sought to understand Jewish history within their respective national contexts. They attempted to locate Jewish history and literature within specific national contexts to ascertain its exceptional providential and religious character.

These two tendencies – the local and theological perspectives – are apparent in Moritz Lazarus's programmatic 1894 speech *Was heißt und zu welchem Ende studiert man jüdische Geschichte und Litteratur?* [What is and to what end do we study Jewish history and literature?]. Alluding to Schiller's lecture *Was heißt und zu welchem Ende studiert man Universalgeschichte?* [What is and to what end do we study universal history?] at Jena in 1789, Lazarus did not engage in a debate regarding the universal significance of the history of the Jews. For him, this history had ended with the destruction of Bethar, the last Jewish stronghold in the war against Rome, and thereafter, only Prussian, German or French history existed. He contended instead that of the history of the Jews, only a history of Judaism continued to manifest itself.[41] Grounded in a religious understanding of Jewish history, Lazarus detected the unity of Jewish literature in the special 'essence' [*Wesen*] or 'spirit' [*Geist*] of Judaism that had shaped these writings.[42]

Along similar lines, Anglo-Jewish scholars believed that Jewish history held a new elevated and providential status within world history.[43] These notions of the providential quality of Jewish history provided sufficient rhetorical grounding for the unprecedented interest in local histories of the Jews that resulted in the foundation of the German-Jewish Historical Commission in 1885 and the Jewish Historical Society of England in 1893.[44] The emergence of these societies' more narrowly defined research projects was a response to increasing nationalism in Germany and England. As concepts of 'Germanness' and 'Englishness' became more clearly defined, Jews felt compelled to renegotiate their relationship with their particular national environments.

Contrary to recent claims, it seems that specific Anglo- and German-Jewish cultural identities were rather a late construction.[45] While elements of these hybrid identities had already emerged out of the battle over emancipation and religious reform, the boundaries at least had remained in flux.[46] This is particularly the case in Germany, where concepts of 'Germanness' remained unstable and the unification in 1871 did not automatically forge a homogeneous notion of the German nation. Similarly, a German-Jewish identity remained tenuous and Germany's separation from Austria in 1866 failed to create an instantaneous Austrian-Jewish identity.[47]

Yet with the increasing importance of historical and literary studies and modern anti-semitism, Jews in England and Germany fashioned and promoted a new cultural identity that attempted to reconcile Jewishness with English and German traditions respectively in response to renewed challenges. In his well-known article in the *Preussische Jahrbücher* in 1879, Heinrich von Treitschke, the doyen of German historiography, endowed the anti-semitic movement in Germany with a great measure of respect when he exclaimed that 'the Jews are our misfortune'.[48] For Treitschke, Jews' repeated attempts to preserve a Jewish identity while simultaneously claiming the right to fully participate in German national life were sources of antagonism between Germans and Jews. Moreover, Treitschke was enraged by the increasing numbers of Eastern European Jewish immigrants in Germany.

After briefly elaborating on the notorious topic of the alleged influence Jews wielded over the German press, Treitschke turned to the works of Heinrich Graetz. Treitschke considered the Jewish historian's writings to be the most influential on Jewish history. Because of this, he attacked Graetz for his denunciation of German heroes and for his hatred of Christianity.[49] Treitschke also took issue with Graetz's portrayal of Shylock, whose image had been transformed by Heine in the nineteenth century from a despised and heartless figure to a loving father.[50] Graetz quoted from Heine and postulated that 'in fact no Jew was a Shylock, but a Christian was'.[51] In the ensuing public exchange that quickly became known as the *Berliner Antisemitismusstreit*, Graetz referred to a case from the sixteenth century in which a Christian, after winning a bet, demanded a portion of a Jew's flesh.[52] Graetz followed this up a few years later and devoted a separate study to the history of Shylock, in which he likewise relied on Heine.[53]

As part of these debates, Moritz Lazarus engaged in an elaboration on the nature of nations. For Lazarus, *Volk* was not an ethnic homogeneous entity but an intellectual and cultural construction based on a common language. Judaism, therefore, did not pose an obstacle to Jews' integration into German society any more than Kant's Scottish ancestry disqualified him as a German.[54] It is in the context of these debates that Jews in Germany more actively forged a tradition of German Jewry based on postulated similarities between Judaism and German culture. Whereas Graetz had quoted Heine's passage on the role of Jews in the modern world at full length, later historians only cited the first lines:

> Striking, indeed, is the deep affinity which prevails between these two ethical nations, Jews and Germans... Fundamentally, the two peoples are alike, – so much alike, that one might regard the Palestine of the past as an oriental Germany, just as one may regard the Germany of today as the home of the Holy Word, the mother-soil of prophecy, the citadel of pure spirituality.[55]

At the same time that a German-Jewish identity was being more vigorously promoted, Jews in England started to envision themselves more clearly as English Jews. In the early 1880s, following the recent challenges to Benjamin Disraeli's patriotism, Goldwin Smith, an Oxford-educated professor of English literature and constitutional history at Cornell University in the United States, published an article in *Nineteenth Century* that contained glaring misrepresentations of medieval Jewish history. Smith, who reviewed the German anti-semitic movement in his article, was, not unlike Treitschke, disturbed by the influx of Eastern European Jewish immigrants into European countries. Like Treitschke, Smith framed his critical view of contemporary Jewish life and culture within a larger survey of Jewish history in general and the Anglo-Jewish past in particular. In response, the *Jewish Chronicle* highlighted the need for historical studies to rebut these challenges.[56]

Consequently, an unprecedented interest in Jewish history manifested itself at the Anglo-Jewish Exhibition in 1886, in the publication of *Jewish Quarterly Review* and the foundation of the Jewish Historical Society of England in 1896. At a time when Anglo-Jewry was publicly commemorating the Resettlement Day of 1655 in 1894 and the 250th anniversary of the Whitehall Conference of 1656 in 1906, English Jews turned toward Anglo-Jewish history.[57] Whereas Heinrich Graetz, in closing his lecture at the Anglo-Jewish exhibition in 1886, marvelled at

the prospect of a Jewish academy that would engage in a critical study of
Jewish religion, philosophy and history, Anglo-Jews were much more
concerned with a more narrowly defined research agenda.[58] If the
founders of the Jewish Historical Society of England cited Graetz's
address as the Society's inspiration, they artfully veiled the fact that their
association operated in various ways in opposition to Graetz and the
German-Jewish community of scholars. Along these lines, Israel
Abrahams, the eminent Anglo-Jewish historian, rebuked Heinrich
Graetz's work as unscientific in his presidential address entitled 'The
Science of Judaism'. According to Abrahams, Graetz's work was not the
starting point of a school, but rather an end of one.[59] For the Society,
turning to the study of Anglo-Jewry represented taking 'possession of our
rightful inheritance', which non-Jewish authors and German-Jewish
scholars had previously dominated.[60]

English Jews began not only to study their past, but, as S. Levy, the
honorary Secretary of the Jewish Historical Society and member of the
Council of the Union of Jewish Literary Societies reminded his readers,
their new research was conducted by scholars 'on English soil to whom
England is their home'. Levy thus turned here against English historians
and Jewish historians from the Continent.[61] Moreover, the importance of
Englishness as an instrumental element in the construction of an Anglo-
Jewish past becomes apparent when, in a separate article, Abrahams
explained that historical truth was only attainable if scholars shared not
only 'our general Jewish sentiments' but also 'local patriotism'.[62]
Jewishness and Englishness were thus woven into the fabric of scholarly
inquiry and Jewish self-assertion. Notwithstanding these self-assertive
gestures, Joseph Jacobs, the historian and co-organiser of the Anglo-
Jewish exhibition, felt compelled to justify the study of Anglo-Jewish
history. Invoking the exceptional status of Jewish history, Jacobs
countered those who maintained that Anglo-Jewish history lacked
cohesiveness and displayed only intriguing events, persons and details.[63]

Whereas local studies of the Jewish past proved largely unproblematic
insofar as they were grounded in notions of a comprehensive and
unifying Jewish essence, the same did not hold true for literary studies.
Reverend Levy, who had elaborated on Anglo-Jewish history, challenged
the otherwise widely accepted consensus about the nature of Jewish
literature when he published an article in the *Jewish Quarterly Review*.
Levy's article, which was based on a lecture he delivered in 1903 at the
North London Jewish Literary and Social Union, created a considerable
stir.[64] Refuting Karpeles, he promoted a narrower understanding of
Jewish literature and limited it to works written in Hebrew, most likely
in an effort to sever these writings from Anglo-Jewish history. Promoting

a linguistic definition, Levy poignantly stated: 'No *Jewish* language, no *Jewish* literature.'[65]

In the subsequent volume of the *Jewish Quarterly Review*, the eminent Jewish-Hungarian scholar Wilhelm Bacher challenged Levy by pointing out various inconsistencies in his arguments. In addition to his criticism, Bacher restated Karpeles's position. Bacher asserted that Levy's basic mistake was his application of categories that were commonly used in the description of other national literatures. Bacher, along the lines of Steinschneider, maintained that Jewish literature was a case *sui generis*. For Bacher, Jewish literature was limited to works that expressed 'spiritual ambitions and the orientation of a believer in Judaism'.[66]

Despite this confident dismissal, Levy's challenge exerted a certain influence. Levy had not only defied a widely shared scholarly consensus, but had carried out this task in the *JQR* volume that contained a reprint of Steinschneider's pivotal lecture on Jewish literature during the Middle Ages.[67] To say the least, Karpeles was annoyed and took up Levy's article in a lengthy review of new publications on Jews and Judaism. The importance Karpeles attributed to these quarrels can be gleaned from the fact that his review started out with a rebuttal of Levy, even before he reported on the still ongoing *Bibel-Babel* controversy that centred on comparisons between Babylonian culture and the world of the Bible.[68]

The fact that Karpeles devoted a good deal of energy to this debate illustrates that Levy's article had disputed a hitherto unquestioned scholarly consensus. The *Jewish Encyclopaedia* (1901–06), for example, followed Levy's definition with slight alterations. When Israel Davidson composed the entry on literature, it comprised only works written by Jews in Hebrew and Aramaic. Works written by Jews but not on Jewish subjects were only treated under the name of the respective authors, while even Yiddish works were not described in the major entry but under a separate heading.[69]

Notwithstanding these attempts to formulate a new concept of Jewish literature, its study slowly moved away from grand narratives to explorations of its various forms. Modern Hebrew literature as well as Yiddish writing became an object of scholarly inspection, while at the same time Jewish scholars turned to German- and Anglo-Jewish writers.[70] Yet instead of writing about Anglo-Jewish or German-Jewish literature, these scholars delineated only the role of Jews and Judaism within the respective national literatures.

During 1903–04, Ludwig Geiger, editor of the Goethe yearbooks, delivered a series of lectures that appeared as *Die deutsche Literatur und die Juden* [German Literature and the Jews].[71] In this work, he explicitly

argued against anti-semitic literary historians like Adolf Bartels, who had
adopted a racial definition of Jewish literature, as well as against narrow
Jewish nationalist conceptions.[72] Geiger took issue with this and asserted
the international and cosmopolitan nature of German literature, writing:
'Whoever looks upon German literature and art will be forced to say that
a solely German art has almost never existed.'[73] Consequently, Geiger
viewed Jewish literature as essentially European literature.

Countering racial definitions, Geiger described Jewish active and
passive participation in German literature. He asserted that no Jewish
literature existed, but only Jews in German literature.[74] He detected
therefore a Jewish presence in the early modern defender of the Talmud,
Johannes Reuchlin, as well as in the works of Herder, Schiller and
Goethe. He elaborated also on the impact of Moses Mendelssohn,
Ludwig Börne, Moritz Veit, Gabriel Riesser, Berthold Auerbach and Karl
Emil Franzos on German literary culture. If Geiger intended to show
how the presence of Jews and Judaism influenced German literature, his
analysis of Goethe and Schiller in particular amounted to little more than
mentioning their personal contacts and references in their works on Jews
and Judaism.[75] Moreover, he had to contend with their rather disparaging
views of Jews and Judaism. Nevertheless, he described Schiller's influence
upon the Jews and Rahel Varnhagen portrayed as the 'messenger of
Goethe's evangelism in Berlin'.[76]

Despite the newly expressed emphasis on Anglo-Jewish history,
the investigation of Jews in English literature became mostly dominated
by Jewish scholars in America. Reading through the lens of the
American-Jewish experience, David Philipson, for example, in his
survey of Jewish representations in English literature, *The Jew in English
Fiction* (1899), noted the largely anti-semitic portrayals of Jews.[77] Harry
Levi, in his textbook *Jewish Characters in Fiction: English Literature*
(1903), similarly observed that the portrayal of Jews in English literature
remained a caricature and a 'perverted vision'.[78] Influenced by Heine and
Graetz, Philipson and Levi rallied against Shakespeare's Shylock, one of
the most pivotal characters in the arsenal of the anti-Jewish
imagination.[79]

Edward Nathan Calisch, a graduate of the Hebrew Union College in
Cincinnati, Ohio and Reform rabbi and scholar, continued this re-
evaluation of Shylock in his *The Jew in English Literature, as Author and
as Subject* (1909).[80] Reflecting on the contentious debates about the nature
of Jewish literature, Calisch argued in favour of a clear definition that
might be 'arbitrarily placed', but not without 'sound reasons'.[81] His
attempt at defining his subject matter led him to exclude 'the literary
production of the vast provinces and numerous dependencies of the

British Empire' in addition to American literature.[82] Calisch's subject matter was defined not linguistically, but rather culturally along the lines of an imagined homogeneous English literary canon. It entailed literature 'that had [been] put forth by the English people themselves'.[83]

To inscribe Jews and Judaism into the respective national textual traditions presupposed their distinctiveness in the same way that Heinrich Graetz and others had done. In order to elevate the influence of Jews and Judaism on German and English literature, these Jewish historians invoked a pre-existing notion of Jewishness that was not itself subject to scrutiny. Put differently, their performances of assimilation reasserted differences. Like Geiger, Calisch did not write a history of Anglo-Jewish literature, but rather chronicled the 'attitude of the British nation ... toward the Jews, and the unconscious influence Jews had upon its literature'.[84] Whereas writers such as Grace Aguilar, Israel Zangwill and Israel Abrahams were occluded in the English literary canon, Calisch detected their presence and a general Jewish presence in English literature.[85] To widen the impact of the Hebraic spirit upon English literature, Calisch described, in addition to poetry, fiction and drama, its influence also on historiography, travel and scientific literature.[86] Thus, while Calisch, not unlike Zunz, Steinschneider, Karpeles and Geiger, inscribed Jewish literature into English literature, he also reasserted Jewish uniqueness.

At the same time, inscribing Jewish works into the annals of German and English literature contributed to the formation of these respective literary canons themselves. Calisch agreed with several English, American and German scholars that English literature had derived its particular character from the Hebrew Bible.[87] Whereas German scholars often disparaged these influences, some English scholars accepted them and buttressed their arguments by relying heavily on the works of German-Jewish scholars.[88] Calisch based his work on these assumptions but extended them to post-biblical, notably Anglo-Jewish, writers. Israel Abrahams, whom Calisch quotes, asserted that 'there were no Jews round the table of King James I's compilers of the Authorised Version' but medieval exegetes like David Kimchi had nevertheless a profound influence upon the translation.[89] English national ideals, claimed Calisch, were 'so permeated with the Jewish spirit, that one sometimes hesitates to deny the Anglo-Israel claim that after all the English are the Lost Ten Tribes'.[90] Calisch's case in point is Milton's *Paradise Lost*, in which he detects 'Hebraic ideals' as well as the Jewish 'general optimism and hopefulness, the belief in the ultimate triumph of truth and justice'.[91] The antagonism between Jews and pagans that had informed German-Jewish scholarship is resolved when Calisch postulates 'the Hellenic and the

Hebraic spirit [sic] are not antipodes, they are supplementary to each other'.[92] He therefore also pointed out the prominent role Jewish scholars like Sidney Lee and Israel Gollancz had played in the field of Shakespearean scholarship. Ludwig Geiger had a similar role as the editor of the prestigious Goethe yearbook.[93] Thus, the fact that *Wissenschaft* scholars reconstructed established literary traditions from the margins failed to throw these traditions into disarray. Rather, they solidified their existence.[94]

The debate about the nature of Jewish literature throughout the nineteenth century reflects the increasing unravelling of Jewish culture and notions of an essence of Judaism. Confronted with an increasing number of literary texts in European languages that did not simply correspond to notions of a Jewish history of learning and suffering, historians put forward new definitions in an attempt to regain a cohesive body of text. They comprehended a distinct Jewish literature within the framework of pre-existing German and English literary canons. Insofar as these Jewish scholars fused particularism and universalism, global and local perspectives and religious and national elements in their descriptions, they created an ambiguity that could not be assimilated into the existing master narratives of nations or races.

Writing from the perspective of the present, Jewish historians constructed different literary canons in response to new historical contingencies. Despite such fundamental changes, however, the definitions of Jewish literature displayed continuity and change even beyond national boundaries. Nevertheless, the reformulation of the contours of Jewish literature was never completed but remained in flux, reflecting the dialectics of assimilation and self-assertion. Through their various contributions on the question of Jewish literature, Jewish historians created a canon that they themselves could not unanimously define, but which was established nevertheless within broader ongoing debates. Abrahams and Levy were not only members of the Anglo-Jewish Historical Society, but also belonged to the Union of Jewish Literary Societies that had been created in 1902. This umbrella organisation comprised numerous local branches itself and launched an unprecedented educational programme to refashion and strengthen modern Jewish identities.[95] These historical and literary associations organised public lectures, published lists of suggested lecture topics and created local Jewish libraries. Such activities had been modelled on the already existing German-Jewish Union of Associations of Jewish History and Literature that was formerly created under the leadership of Gustav Karpeles in 1892.[96] Unstable and in transition, the construction of Jewish literary canons functioned through these newly founded associations as an essential component in the invention of hyphenated and transnational Jewish cultures in England and Germany.

ACKNOWLEDGEMENTS

I would like to thank Professor Bryan Cheyette and Professor Tony Kushner, Dr Nadia Valman and my wife, Jennifer, for their comments on earlier drafts of this paper and their help in preparing this manuscript.

NOTES

1. Anthony D. Smith, 'The Myth of the "Modern Nation" and the Myths of Nations', *Ethnic and Racial Studies* 11 (1988), 1–26 (p.9).
2. Michael Graetz, *The Jews in Nineteenth-Century France: From the French Revolution to the Alliance Israelite Universelle* (Stanford, CA: Stanford University Press, 1996); Robert Liberles, 'Emancipation and the Structure of the Jewish Community in the Nineteenth Century', *Yearbook of the Leo Baeck Institute* 31 (1986), 51–67 and B. Mevorah, "Ikvoteha shel 'alilat Damesek be-hitpathuta shel ha-'itonut ha-yehudit be-shanim 1840–1846', [Hebrew] *Zion* 23–24 (1958), 46–65.
3. Homi Bhabha, 'Of Mimicry and Man: The Ambivalence of Colonial Discourse', *The Location of Culture* (London and New York: Routledge, 1994), pp.85–92 (p.86).
4. Gilles Deleuze and Felix Guattari, *Kafka: Toward a Minor Literature* (Minneapolis: Minnesota University Press, 1986), p.19 and Abdul JanMohamed and David Lloyd, 'Introduction: Toward a Theory of Minority Discourse: What is to be Done?', in *The Nature and Context of Minority Discourse*, ed. by Abdul JanMohamed and David Lloyd (Oxford: Oxford University Press, 1990), pp.1–16.
5. *The Jew in the Text: Modernity and the Construction of Identity*, ed. by Linda Nochlin and Tamar Garb (London: Thames & Hudson, 1995), pp.6, 10.
6. Michael P. Kramer, 'Race, Literary History, and the "Jewish" Question', *Prooftexts* 21. 3 (Fall 2001), 287–321. For other contributions to this timeless question see *What is Jewish Literature?*, ed. by Hana Wirth-Nesher (Philadelphia and Jerusalem: Jewish Publication Society, 1994) and Ruth R. Wisse, *The Jewish Canon: A Journey Through Language and Culture* (New York and London: Free Press, 2000).
7. On the concept of episteme see Michael Foucault, *The Archaeology of Knowledge and the Discourse on Language*, trans. by A.M. Sheridan Smith (New York: Pantheon Books, 1972), p.191.
8. Kenen Malik, *The Meaning of Race: Race, History and Culture in Western Society* (Basingstoke: Macmillian, 1996).
9. See also Bryan Cheyette, 'A Response from Bryan Cheyette [to Michael Kramer], *Prooftexts* 21.3 (Fall 2001), 322–24, and Bryan Cheyette, *Constructions of 'the Jew' in English Literature and Society: Racial Representations, 1875–1945* (Cambridge: Cambridge University Press, 1993), p.268.
10. Bryan Cheyette, 'From Apology to Revolt: Benjamin Farjeon, Amy Levy and the Post-Emancipation Anglo-Jewish Novel, 1880–1990', *Transactions of the Jewish Historical Society of England*, 24 (1982–86), 253–63; Nadia Valman, 'Semitism and Criticism: Victorian Anglo-Jewish Literary History', *Victorian Literature and Culture* 27.1 (1999), 235–48; Joachim Doron, 'Rassenbewußtsein und naturwissenschaftliches Denken im deutschen Zionismus während der wilhelminischen Aera', *Jahrbuch des Institutes für deutsche Geschichte* 9 (1980), 389–427 and John M. Efron, *Defenders of the Race: Jewish Doctors and Race Science in fin-de-siècle Europe* (New Haven: Yale University Press, 1994).
11. David Perkins, *Is Literary History Possible?* (Baltimore: Johns Hopkins University Press, 1992); Gerald Newman, *The Rise of English Nationalism: A Cultural History, 1740–1830*

(Basingstoke: Macmillan, 1997), pp.109–14, 123–7 and 240–44; Peter Uwe Hohendahl, *Building a National Literature: The Case of Germany 1830–1870* (Ithaca: Cornell University Press, 1989); Jürgen Fohrmann, *Das Projekt der Deutschen Literaturgeschichte: Entstehen und Scheitern einer nationalen Poesiegeschichtsschreibung zwischen Humanismus und Deutschen Kaiserreich* (Stuttgart: J.B. Metzler, 1988).

12. Salman Rubaschoff, 'Erstlinge der Entjudung: Drei Reden von Eduard Gans im Kulturverein', *Der jüdische Wille*, 1 (1918), 30–35, 108–21 and 193–203, (pp.110–11) and Roland Goetschel, 'Die Beziehung zu Europa im deutsch-jüdischen Denken', *Judaica* 51 (1995), 154–77.

13. Salman Rubaschoff, 'Erstlinge der Entjudung: Drei Reden von Eduard Gans im Kulturverein' and Georg Wilhelm F. Hegel, *Vorlesungen über die Philosophie der Geschichte*, ed. by Eva Moldenhauer and Karl Markus Michel (Frankfurt am Main: Suhrkamp, 1986), pp.133–41.

14. Michael Meyer, 'Where Does the Modern Period of Jewish History Begin?' *Judaism* 24 (1975), 329–38 and Moshe Zimmermann, 'Eintritt in die Bürgerlichkeit: Vom Selbstvergleich deutscher mit außereuropäischen Juden im Vormärz', in *Bürgertum im 19. Jahrhundert: Deutschland im europäischen Vergleich*, ed by Jürgen Kocka, 3 vols (Munich: Deutscher Taschenbuch Verlag, 1988), II, 372–91.

15. Isaak Jost, *Geschichte der Israeliten seit der Zeit der Maccabäer bis auf unsre Tage nach den Quellen bearbeitet*, 9 vols (Berlin, 1820–28), I, vii–viii; Isaak M. Jost, 'Beitrag zur jüdischen Geschichte und Bibliographie', *Wissenschaftliche Zeitschrift für jüdische Theologie* 1 (1835), 358–66 (p.358) and Isaak M. Jost, *Geschichte des Judenthums und seiner Secten*, 3 vols (Leipzig, 1857–1559), I, 1–10.

16. Heinrich Graetz, *Geschichte der Juden von den ältesten Zeiten bis auf die Gegenwart. Aus den Quellen neu bearbeitet*, 11 vols (Leipzig, 1853–1874), XI, 406–7.

17. Ibid., XI, 407.

18. Klaus L. Berghan, 'Von Weimar nach Versailles: Zur Entstehung Der Klassik-Legende im 19. Jahrhundert,' in *Die Klassik-Legende*, ed. by Reinhold Grimm and Jost Hermand (Frankfurt am Main: Athenaeum-Verlag, 1971), pp.50–78 and Peter Uwe Hohendahl, *Literarische Kultur im Zeitalter des Liberalismus, 1830–1870* (Munich: C.H. Beck, 1985).

19. Leopold Zunz, 'Etwas über rabbinische Literatur' (1818), in *Gesammelte Schriften*, 3 vols (Berlin, 1875–76), I, 1–31 (p.1).

20. Ibid., p.6.

21. Heinrich Graetz, *Geschichte der Juden vom Untergang des jüdischen Staates bis zum Abschluß des Talmuds* (Leipzig: O. Leiner, 1866), IV, 4.

22. Leopold Zunz, 'Juden und jüdische Literatur' (1845) and Leopold Zunz, 'Juden' and 'Judenthum', in *Gesammelte Schriften* I, 86–114, (pp.101, 110).

23. Leopold Zunz, *Zur Geschichte und Literatur* (Berlin, 1845), p.2.

24. Edward W. Said, *Culture and Imperialism* (New York: Random House, 1993), p.45.

25. Friedrich Gundolf, *Goethe* (Berlin: Bondi, 1930), p.681 and Isaiah Berlin, *Vico and Herder: Two Studies in the History of Ideas* (London: Hogarth Press, 1976), p.161.

26. Moritz Steinschneider, 'Jüdische Literatur', in *Allgemeine Encyklopädie der Wissenschaften und Künste*, ed. by J.S. Ersch and J.G. Gruber (Leipzig, 1850), XXVII, 357–471 (p.357).

27. Graetz, *Geschichte der Juden* (see note 21), I, 14 and XI, 385.

28. Ibid., XI, 401 and the English translation quoted here in *The Poetry and Prose of Heinrich Heine*, ed. by Frederic Ewen (New York: Citadel Press, 1948), p.678.

29. Jonathan M. Elukin, 'A New Essenism: Heinrich Graetz and Mysticism', *Journal of the History of Ideas* 59 (1998), 135–48 and Yaacov Shavit, *Athens in Jerusalem: Classical Antiquity and Hellenism in the Making of the Modern Secular Jew*, trans. by Chaya Naor and Niki Werner (London: Littmann Library of Jewish Civilization, 1997), pp.176–84.

30. Heinrich Graetz, 'The Correspondence of an English Lady on Judaism and Semitism', in *Heinrich Graetz: The Structure of Jewish History and Other Essays*, ed. by Ismar Schorsch (New York, Jewish Theological Seminary, 1975), pp.191–258 (pp.197–8).

31. Ibid., p.199.

32. Shavit (see note 29), p.178.

33. Graetz, 'Correspondence of an English Lady' (see note 30), p.213.
34. Gustav Karpeles, *Geschichte der jüdischen Literatur*, 2 vols (Berlin, 1886), I, iii, 1.
35. Ibid., I, 2, 9.
36. Ibid., I, 3. See also Meyer Kayserling, *Die jüdische Literatur von Moses Mendelssohn bis auf die Gegenwart* (Trier, 1896); Israel Abrahams, *Chapters on Jewish Literature* (Philadelphia: Jewish Publication Society, 1899) and Israel Abrahams, *A Short History of Jewish Literature from the Fall of the Temple (70 C. E.) to the Era of Emancipation (1786 C. E.)* (London: T. Fisher Unwin, 1906).
37. Marcus Brann, *Geschichte der Juden und ihrer Litteratur: Für Schule und Haus* (Breslau, 1895), p.449.
38. Abrahams, *Chapters on Jewish Literature* (see note 36), p.5. On Abrahams see Elliot Horowitz, 'Jewish Life of Israel Abrahams', in *The Jewish Past Revisited: Reflections on Modern Jewish Historians*, ed. by David N. Myers and David B. Ruderman (New Haven: Yale University Press, 1998), pp.143–62.
39. Matthew Arnold, *Literature and Dogma: An Essay Towards a Better Apprehension of the Bible* (London, 1873), pp.26, 36–7, 56.
40. Abrahams, *Short History of Jewish Literature* (see note 36), p.xi and idem, *Chapters on Jewish Literature* (see note 36), p.12.
41. Moritz Lazarus, *Was heißt und zu welchem Ende studiert man jüdische Geschichte und Litteratur? Ein Vortrag* (Leipzig, 1900), pp.9–20 and Hans Otto Horch, 'Was heißt und zu welchem Ende studiert man deutsch-jüdische Literaturgeschichte? Prolegomena zu einem Forschungsprojekt', *German Life and Letters* 49 (1996), 124–35.
42. Moritz Lazarus, *Jüdische Geschichte und Litteratur* (see note 41), p.29.
43. Joseph Jacobs, 'The Typical Character of Anglo-Jewish History', *TJHSE* 3 (1896–1898), 126–43 (p.143).
44. Nathan M. Kagnanoff, 'AJS at 90: Reflections on the History of the Oldest Ethnic Historical Society in America', *American Jewish History*, 71 (1982), 466–85; Robert Liberles, 'Postemancipation Historiography and the Jewish Historical Societies of America and England', in *Reshaping the Past: Jewish History and the Historians*, ed. by Jonathan Frankel (Oxford: Oxford University Press, 1994), pp.45–65 and Ira Robinson, 'The Invention of American Jewish History', *American Jewish History*, 81 (1994), 309–30.
45. Johannes Heil, 'Deutsch-jüdische Geschichte, ihre Grenzen, und die Grenzen ihrer Synthesen. Anmerkungen zur neueren Literatur', *Historische Zeitschrift*, 269 (1999), 653–80 and David Cesarani, 'British Jews', in *The Emancipation of Catholics, Jews and Protestants: Minorities and the Nation State in Nineteenth-Century Europe*, ed. by Rainer Liedtke and Stephan Wendehorst (Manchester and New York: Manchester University Press, 1999), pp.33–55.
46. David Sorkin, *The Transformation of German Jewry, 1780–1840* (New York and Oxford: Oxford University Press, 1987) and David Feldman, *Englishmen and Jews: Social Relations and Political Culture, 1840–1914* (New Haven and London: Yale University Press, 1994).
47. Steven Beller, 'Patriotism and the National Identity of Habsburg Jewry, 1860–1914', *Yearbook of the Leo Baeck Institute*, 41 (1996), 215–38.
48. *Der Berliner Antisemitismusstreit*, ed. by Walter Boehlich, 2nd edn. (Frankfurt an Main: Insel Verlag, 1965), p.13.
49. Ibid., p.11. I follow with only a slight modification to the translation in *The Jew in the Modern World: A Documentary History*, ed. by Paul Mendes-Flohr and Jehuda Reinharz (New York and Oxford: Oxford University Press, 1995), p.344.
50. Graetz, *Geschichte der Juden* (see note 21), XI, 400.
51. Ibid., XI: 197 and *Der Berliner Antisemitismusstreit* (see note 48), p.42.
52. Ibid., p.51.
53. Heinrich Graetz, 'Shylock in der Sage, im Drama und in der Geschichte', *Monatsschrift für Geschichte und Wissenschaft des Judenthums* 29 (1880), 337–54 and 385–403.
54. Moritz Lazarus, 'Was heißt national?', *Treu und Frei: Gesammlte Reden und Vorträge über Juden und Judenthum* (Leipzig, 1887), pp.53–113 (pp.71–2).
55. Heinrich Graetz, *Geschichte der Juden* (see note 21), XI: 401. Here I follow the English

translation in *Poetry and Prose of Heinrich Heine* (see note 28), p.678. See, for example, Adolf Kohut, *Geschichte der deutschen Juden: Ein Hausbuch für die jüdische Familie* (Berlin, 1898) pp.5–6 and P.F. Frankl, 'Ueber die Stellung der deutschen Juden innerhalb der gesammten Judenheit', *Monatsschrift für Geschichte und Wissenschaft des Judenthums*, 33 (1884), 1–22 (p.4).

56. Goldwin Smith, 'The Jewish Question', *Nineteenth Century* 10 (July–December 1881), 494–515; Hermann Adler, 'Recent Phases of Judaephobia', *Nineteenth Century*, 10 (July–December 1881), 813–829 and 'The History of the Jews in England', *Jewish Chronicle*, 21 Oct. 1881, p.3. See also Isaac Besht Bendavid 'Goldwin Smith and the Jews', *North American Review*, 153 (September 1891), 257–272 and Cesarani, 'British Jews' (see note 45), p.53.

57. 'The Whitehall Conference: Celebrations of the 250th Anniversary', *TJHSE*, 5 (1902–1905), 275–300; David Cesarani, 'Dual Heritages or Duel of Heritages? Englishness and Jewishness in the Heritage Industry', in *The Jewish Heritage in British History: Englishness and Jewishness*, ed. by Tony Kushner (London, Frank Cass, 1992), pp.29–41; and David Cesarani, 'Social Memory, History and British Jewish Identity', in *Modern Jewish Mythologies*, ed. by Glenda Abramson (Cincinnati: Hebrew Union College, 2000), pp.15–36.

58. Heinrich Graetz, 'Historical Parallels in Jewish History', in *The Structure of Jewish History and Other Essays* (see note 30) pp.259–74, esp. pp.273–4.

59. Israel Abrahams, 'The Science of Jewish History', *TJHSE* (1902–1905), 193–201 (p.195).

60. S. Levy, 'Anglo-Jewish Historiography', *TJHSE* 6 (1908–1910), 1–20 (p.14). See also 'Introductory', *Jewish Quarterly Review* 1 (1888), 1–3 (p.1).

61. Levy, 'Anglo-Jewish Historiography' (see note 60), pp.14–15.

62. Abrahams, 'The Science of Jewish History' (see note 59), p.198.

63. Joseph Jacobs, 'Typical Character of Anglo-Jewish History' (see note 43), pp.127–8 and Levy, 'Anglo-Jewish Historiography' (see note 60), p.3.

64. S. Levy, 'Is there a Jewish Literature?' *Jewish Quarterly Review* 15 (1903), 583–603.

65. Ibid., p.587.

66. W. Bacher, 'What is Jewish Literature?" *Jewish Quarterly Review* 16 (1904), 300–306. See also A. Wolf, 'What is Jewish Literature?' *Jewish Quarterly Review* 16 (1904), 307–22 and S. Levy, 'What is Jewish Literature?' *Jewish Quarterly Review* 16 (1904), 323–9.

67. Moritz Steinschneider, 'Allgemeine Einleitung in die jüdische Literatur des Mittelalters', *Jewish Quarterly Review*, 15 (1903), 302–29. Steinschneider originally gave this lecture between 1859 and 1897.

68. Gustav Karpeles, 'Literarische Jahresreview', *Jahrbuch für Jüdische Geschichte und Literatur* 8 (1905), 16–51.

69. Israel Davidson, 'Literature, Hebrew', *The Jewish Encyclopaedia: A Descriptive Record of the History, Religion, Literature and Customs of the Jewish People from the Earliest Times to the Present Day*, 12 vols (New York: Funk & Wagnalls, 1901–06), VII, 108–11.

70. See, for example, Max Gruenbaum, *Jüdischdeutsche Chrestomanie: Zugleich ein Beitrag zur Kunde der hebraischen Kultur* (Leipzig, 1882); Max Gruenbaum, 'Die jüdisch-deutsche Literatur', in *Geschichte der poetischen, kabbalistischen, historischen und neuzeitlichen Litteratur der Juden*, ed. by K. Winter and August Wünsche (Trier, 1896), pp.533–623; Leo Wiener, *The History of Yiddish Literature in the Nineteenth Century* (New York, 1899); M. Pines, *Historie de la littérature Judéo-Allemande* (Paris, 1910); Nahum Slouschz, *La Renaissance de la Littérature Hébraïque (1743–1885), Essai d'histoire littéraire* (Paris: Société novelle de libraire et d'édition, 1903) and Moses Debré, *Der Juden in der französischen Literatur von 1800 bis zur Gegenwart* (Phil. Diss. Würzburg, 1909).

71. Ludwig Geiger, 'Die Juden und die deutsche Literatur', *Zeitschrit für die Geschichte der Juden in Deutschland*, 1 (1887), 321–65 and Ludwig Geiger, *Die deutsche Literatur und die Juden* (Berlin: Georg Reimer, 1910).

72. Geiger, *Die deutsche Literatur* (see note 71), pp.5–7 and 11. See, for example, Eugen Duehring, *Die Judenfrage als Racen,- Sitten- und Culturfrage* (1881) and Adolf Bartels, *Judentum und deutsche Literatur: Vortrag gehalten am 29. Juni 1910 im Deutschvölkischen Studentenverband in Berlin* (Berlin, 1912).

73. Geiger, *Die deutsche Literatur* (see note 71), p.5.
74. Ibid., p.12. See also Andreas Kilcher, 'Was ist deutsch-jüdische Literatur: Eine historische Diskursanalyse', *Weimarer Beiträge*, 45 (1999), 485–513 (pp.494–7).
75. Geiger, *Die deutsche Literatur* (see note 71), pp.12, 81–101 and 125–60.
76. Ibid., pp.92 and 143–146.
77. David Philipson, *The Jew in English Fiction* (Cincinnati: Robert Clarke and Co., 1899), pp.12–14. See also Charles B. Mabon, 'The Jew in English Poetry and Drama,' *Jewish Quarterly Review* 11 (1899), 411–30 (p.411) and S. A. Hirsch, 'Some Literary Trifles', *Jewish Quarterly Review* 13 (1901), 595–619.
78. Harry Levi, *Jewish Characters in Fiction: English Literature* (Philadelphia: Jewish Chautauqua Society, 1903), pp.8–9.
79. Philipson (see note 77), pp.34–53 and Levi (see note 78), pp.21–9. In general see Linda Rozmovits, *Shakespeare and the Politics of Culture in Late Victorian England* (Baltimore: John Hopkins University Press, 1998).
80. Edward Calisch, *The Jew in English Literature, as Author and as Subject* (Richmond, VA: The Bell Book and Stationary Co. Publishers, 1909), pp.66–85.
81. Ibid., p.11.
82. Ibid., p.12.
83. Ibid.
84. Ibid., p.11.
85. The canonisation of English literary traditions rested on a subtle process of exclusion. See Franklin E. Court, *Institutionalizing English Literature: The Culture and Politics of Literary Study, 1750–1900* (Stanford, CA: Stanford University Press, 1992); Michael Ragussis, *Figures of Conversion: 'The Jewish Question' and English National Identity* (Durham, NC: Duke University Press, 1995) and Bryan Cheyette, *Constructions of 'the Jew' in English Literature and Society* (Cambridge: Cambridge University Press, 1993).
86. Calisch (see note 80), p.18.
87. Thomas G. Tucker, *The Foreign Debt of English Literature* (London, 1907), pp.253–7.
88. See Albert S. Cook, 'Old English Literature and Jewish Learning', *Modern Language Notes* 6: 3 (March 1891) 142–53, who cites whole passages from Heinrich Graetz's *History of the Jews*.
89. Israel Abrahams, *Jewish Life in the Middle Ages* (London, 1890), pp.xix and 16.
90. Calisch (see note 80), p.31.
91. Ibid., p.32.
92. Ibid., p.16.
93. Ibid., pp.182–4.
94. I differ here from Homi Bhabha's assessment. See his 'Representation and the Colonial Text: A Critical Exploration of Some Forms of Mimeticism', in *The Theory of Reading*, ed. by Frank Gloversmith (Brighton: Harvester Press, 1984), p.102.
95. 'Conference of Jewish Literary Societies', *Jewish Chronicle*, 4 July 1902, pp.12–17; *Suggestions for Lectures on Subjects of Jewish Interest* (London, 1902). For a list of local branches of Jewish literary societies in England see *Jewish Literary Annual* 1 (1907), 127–64. I hope to devote a separate study to a comparative exploration of German, French, English and American-Jewish historical and literary associations around the turn of the century.
96. Nils Roemer, 'The Historicizing of Judaism in 19th-Century Germany: Scholarly Discipline and Popular Historical Culture' (unpublished doctoral dissertation, Columbia University, 2000), pp.181–230 and Jacob Borut, 'Vereine für Jüdische Geschichte und Literatur at the End of the Nineteenth Century', *Yearbook of the Leo Baeck Institute*, 41 (1996), 89–114.

Africans, Indians, Arabs, and Scots: Jewish and Other Questions in the Age of Empire

MICHAEL GALCHINSKY

Increasingly in the new European order, it is difficult to think of the Jewish diaspora without also thinking of the other European diasporas created by labour migrations, globalisation and ethnic cleansing's refugee transfers. In Germany, Jews are constantly aware of the impact on their own political and social status of the changing status of Turks, Armenians, Roma, Sinti and Poles. In France, Jews keep a close eye on the success of North African Muslims vying for political and civil rights. In Britain, Jews position themselves ambivalently between the terra firma of the white Christian majority and the shaky territory of marginality shared by Pakistanis, Indians, Africans and Caribbeans. In attempting to understand the way in which a given European nation – or the European Union as a whole – treats its diverse diasporas, scholars hope to comprehend the extents and limits of the rights of the European subject in the post-Cold War era.

Much recent journalism notwithstanding, migrations, diasporas and even globalisation are not phenomena originating in the post-colonial, post-industrial or post-Cold War period:[1] population transfer, at least, was already a prominent feature of the post-Enlightenment, post-French Revolutionary periods of national consolidation and imperial expansion. Yet the approach scholars take to the Jewish Question today seems utterly different from the approach they have taken to the Jewish Question in the nineteenth century. Perhaps because of a perceived moral imperative in the wake of the Shoah to produce a teleological history, scholars have written about the nineteenth-century version of the Question as though it were the central (if not the single) concern of Europeans' discourse of marginality or as though the Shoah were the retrospective reference point through which to analyse the period.[2] But the idea of the Jewish Question's centrality would have quite staggered many nineteenth-century Europeans, even those engaged with 'semitic' representations of one kind or another. For Jews' status as citizens and subjects was not the only – and was not at all points the most significant – question around which non-Jewish Europeans organised their responses to the increasingly visible minorities in their midst.

Europeans frequently saw the Jewish Question as a subset of a larger set of questions about how Europe's Others might be brought into relation with the emerging nation-states and empires. This larger set of questions included debates about the social and political status of freed slaves, of immigrants from the colonies, of migrants from annexed domestic regions and of non-conforming religious groups. It included scientists' attempts to demarcate and prioritise all the imagined shades of colour they called races. By magnifying the significance of the Jewish Question relative to other questions of Otherness, recent scholarship has done unintended disservice to the study of images of European Jews: by neglecting to study how the discourse of 'semitism' functioned as a subset of the discourse of marginality, scholars have hindered our own fledgling efforts to understand how such discourses functioned in writers' attempts to construct national identities.[3] Ironically, by neglecting to compare semitism with other discourses of marginality, scholars have missed an opportunity to gain knowledge about semitism. For my contention is that national and marginal identities alike are both relational: their constructed meaning depends in large part on the definitions they gain through juxtaposition.

Taking nineteenth-century England as my test case, I propose to demonstrate the inalienability of discourses on Africans, Indians, and Arab Muslims from the Anglo-Jewish Question during the Revolutionary, Regency, and Victorian periods. I will discuss the interdependent relations between 'semitic' representations and, among other things, the debates over the abolition of the slave trade that occurred during the period of the French Revolution and Napoleonic wars and again during the debate over the Second Reform Bill, the debate over Indian Education in the 1830s, and the debates over the pseudoscientific hierarchy of races of the 1840s and 1850s. I will examine in some depth the writings of Burke, Carlyle and Macaulay, and in less depth the writings of Godwin, Scott, Disraeli, Arnold and Eliot, all of whom wrote comparatively about Jews and at least one other marginalised group. Whether they were liberal, radical, or conservative, these writers used semitic representations in their polemics and literary texts as part of a larger project: the project of disciplining the conceptual borders of the nation-state.

During the revolutionary years of the late-eighteenth century, English public figures began to meditate on the extent and limits of the rights to be held by Jews and other marginalised communities within British dominions. In a broader sense, they contemplated how the increasing numbers of aliens on British shores ought to influence the way they conceived of citizenship in the nation and empire. In this endeavour, the Jewish Question was not, to begin with, of very great importance, since Jews had only undertaken a steady trickle of immigration to Britain from the time of the Jew Bill in 1753 and still numbered fewer than 20,000 by the end of the Napoleonic wars.[4] So unimportant was the Jewish Question that no one had yet made a link between the issue of their rights and the rights of other minority groups. (We might contrast this with the contemporary situation in Germany, in which Lessing's *Nathan Der Weise* was already meditating in a comparative way on the citizenship of Jews and Muslims).[5]

While *Jews* were not yet on the English public agenda in a major way, the public *was* increasingly preoccupied by the treatment of *Africans*. Although the triangular trade in slaves, luxury goods and weapons was 200 years old, public scrutiny of the trade had been relatively quiet until the 1770s and 1780s. The African Company was a well-respected public-private partnership, and the West Indian plantation system at its high point had put as many as 100,000 newly captured African slaves a year to work. The protectionist mercantile economy driven by the slave system had worked efficiently from the African coasts without a perceived need to extend trade into, or gain knowledge of or control over the interior of Africa. But by the 1770s, in the wake of the Industrial Revolution, the mercantile system had begun to break down. Protectionism began to give way to free trade under pressure from manufacturers looking for unfettered access to new markets. Traders saw the interior of Africa as a potential gold mine of new markets. The movement of Europeans into the interior led to the demand that the heathen be civilised, and the missionary project picked up support.[6]

Thus, by the late-eighteenth century, the African Company was coming under increased public scrutiny, and the slave trade was becoming the object of increased public discourse. Abolitionism, never before a strong strain in British thought, now found its supporters, particularly amongst Whigs and evangelical Dissenters (and under Wilberforce the movement would achieve the trade's abolition in 1807). Even Tories who did not support abolition on moral grounds began to see the trade's usefulness wane as the old mercantilist economic system began to be supplanted by the new free trade economy.[7] A number of these Tories began to attempt to regulate the trade so as to ameliorate the brutal treatment of slaves.

A representative of this Tory position was the founder of political conservatism, Edmund Burke. Burke wrote a number of proposals and speeches on the treatment of Africans, especially his 'Sketch of a Negro Code' from 1780. He also wrote glancingly about Jewishness in his *Reflections on the Revolution in France* from 1790. A comparison of the Negro Code to his *Reflections* illuminates the differences in the ways African and Jews could be understood in this period.

Although Burke was among those who opposed abolition, he was not blind to the slaves' suffering: he himself referred to the trade as 'inhuman traffick'.[8] But as the Member of Parliament for Bristol, whose constituents included some of the nation's wealthiest slave traders, Burke believed he was not in a position to turn his moral revulsion into an abolitionist stance.[9] Moreover, although he was in favour in certain instances of the right to revolt against oppression – he famously supported the American colonists' right to rebel against the Crown – he positively denied that African slaves had the same right. In 1778, in the wake of Lord Dunsmore's attempt to incite a slave insurrection in Virginia and Maryland on behalf of the colonists, Burke denied what he called 'a crew of fierce, foreign barbarians and slaves' the right 'to judge which of their masters were in rebellion' on the ground of 'the utter impossibility of containing them and keeping them in order'.[10] He went on to claim that the slave barbarians desired only to make themselves 'masters of the houses, goods, wives and daughters of their murdered lords'.[11] Apparently for Burke the right to rebel against one's oppressors, even against an 'inhuman traffick', was not a fundamental human right, but a right dependent on one's level of civilisation.

Nevertheless, two years later Burke was still so bothered by the brutal treatment of slaves that he circulated his 'Sketch of a Negro Code' in which he proposed to regulate the trade. The Code's goals were twofold: 'to provide against the manifold Abuses to which a Trade of that nature is liable'; and to 'civiliz[e the Natives], and enabl[e] them to enrich themselves by means more desirable' than slave trading.[12] The proposed Code includes prohibitions on the sale of any person who can read, or of anyone over 35, or of pregnant women.[13] It prohibits forcing pregnant women to engage in fieldwork, prohibits 'unlawful communication' between European officers and women slaves, recognises slave marriages and prohibits splitting up families.[14] It establishes schools and ministers for slaves, and calls for planters to provide each slave with 'a good and substantial Hut'.[15] It limits to 13 the number of blows or stripes an overseer could mete out without the permission of a justice of the peace, and it directs that slaves 'are to be led by all due means into respect for our holy Religion'.[16] Clearly for Burke the slave trade's brutality was a stain on England's civility. While Burke did not support a barbarian's right to revolt against oppression, he believed that a civilised nation ought not to act in a barbaric fashion. He worked to make oppression itself a more civil, and civilising, undertaking.

What is perhaps most important for us about Burke's Negro Code is its level of detail. He understood the slave trade in all its dimensions and undertook to enact positive, concrete, enforceable laws to ameliorate it. We might profitably contrast his thick description of the trade in the Negro Code with his thin depiction of Jewishness in his *Reflections on the Revolution in France*.[17] In the *Reflections*, Burke enacts no Jewish Code to ameliorate Jewish suffering. He does not consider the oppressions endured by Jews, does not meditate on how Jews' historical suffering reflects on European civility. No Jews appear in the text. Rather, in the *Reflections*, Burke uses Jewishness as a metonymy, a rhetorical figure for Jacobinism, as we will see in more detail in a moment.[18] Here it suffices to see that the *figure* of Jewishness, rather than Jews themselves, merits Burke's close analysis. In contrast, in regard to Africans he expounds upon the details of the treatment and behaviour of slaves, not the rhetorical figure of slavishness.

Burke begins his meditation on the Jewishness of the French radicals rather innocently with his attack on Price. Before long Burke employs a metonymy to identify all English radicals with the building in which the radicals met. He calls them 'these gentlemen of the Old Jewry'.[19] He refers to their principles as 'the spurious revolution principles of the Old Jewry'.[20] What makes the revolution, figuratively speaking, Jewish? The revolution strikes Burke as a direct attack on both the Christian and aristocratic characters of the nation. What horrifies him is the possibility that newcomers, such as Jews and the new middle class, might gain power in a nation built on reason and individual merit. In a Christian and aristocratic nation, by contrast, the law of inheritance would prevent the diminution of Church and noble influence. As it is, in France, the nobility has been 'disgraced and degraded', and the next generation of nobles, Burke projects, 'will resemble the artificers and clowns, and money-jobbers, usurers, and Jews, who will be always their fellows, sometimes their masters'.[21] Apparently there can be no greater degradation than a descent into Jewishness.

To avoid a similar degradation of England's Christian aristocracy, Burke disclaims, as he says, 'all communion' with the British radicals.[22] His pun on the eucharist implies that he will not work with those Dissenters fuelling British revolutionary zeal, for in his view they are not entirely Christian (and maybe they are even a bit Jewish). He despises those who, as he says, 'convert' to the Enlightened ideals of Rousseau and Voltaire.[23] George Gordon, on the other hand, the famous British convert to Judaism, comes in for some of Burke's most acrid criticism, as if Burke feared Gordon's choice would become the British fate if the nation were to take a step down the road toward Enlightenment.[24] For Burke, Jacobinism is, figuratively speaking, a form of Jewishness.

Burke's use of abstraction – his rhetorical use of Jewishness as a figure for an ideology promulgated by French Deists and English Dissenters – would become a favourite method throughout the nineteenth century. At various times, Jewishness was abstracted and figuratively identified with every aspect of the nation from its legal system to its outbreaks of socialism to its stock exchange to its monarchy to its journalism. By 1869, in *Culture and Anarchy*, Matthew Arnold was able to express this abstraction of Jewishness in an extreme form without any sense of impropriety. He defined 'Hebraism' in general as a type of energy, specifically an 'energy driving at practice, this paramount sense of the obligation of duty, self-control, and work'.[25] Arnold sees Hebraism as one of two rival energies (the other being Hellenism) within the English national character. Which is to say, for Arnold, Hebraism has little to do with Jews. This move to abstraction is one of the hallmarks of nineteenth-century representations of Jews, and is here all the more visible in juxtaposition to the 'Negro Code'.

In Burke's discourses of Otherness, then, we see a radical disjunction. The oppression of Africans (of which many middle- and upper-class Englishmen had second- if not first-hand knowledge), is to be considered carefully and ultimately condoned, but Africans' suffering is to be ameliorated. Jews, on the other hand, are not yet large, well-organised, visible or oppressed enough as a group to merit detailed consideration. Their citizenship rights are not yet at issue. Burke's position on the relative differences in the treatment of Jews and Africans was not to stand, however. During the first two-thirds of the nineteenth century, as the Jewish population grew through natural increase and trickling immigration (to 20,000 persons by 1815, and 60,000 by 1850), as the Board of Deputies began to agitate for Jewish emancipation, and as the Anglo-Jewish subculture began to produce novels, polemics, histories and other texts in the public sphere, the quality of the comparisons between Africans and Jews would change considerably.

It was the fire-breathing essayist and social critic Thomas Carlyle who articulated a coherent basis by which Tories might approach England's relations with both its Jewish and African Others. A comparison of his anonymous 1853 pamphlet 'The Jew Our Lawgiver' with 'Shooting Niagara', his infamous 1867 essay on the question of the Second Reform Bill, will demonstrate a number of structural similarities (and some crucial differences) in his approach to Jews and Africans.[26] In the pamphlet on Jewish emancipation, Carlyle considers the topical question of whether Jews ought to be permitted to sit in Parliament. (Jews finally gained the right to sit without taking the odious Oath of Abjuration four years after Carlyle's essay was published in 1857). In the essay he ultimately rejects the right of Jewish subjects to stand for public office on several grounds. He revives the charges of deicide and dual loyalty and accuses Jews of attempting to undermine the Christian basis of the state. Worse (in his view), permitting Jews to sit in Parliament will be yet another step in the path to total enfranchisement of all British subjects, a horrific result of adhering too closely to what he calls 'infidel liberalism'. He believes the result of increasing the numbers of eligible participants in the national government would be unChristian chaos.

By 1867 when he contemplated the popular support for the Second Reform Bill that aimed to extend the franchise, he had resigned himself to the success of 'infidel liberalism'. Nonetheless he looked on liberalism as a social experiment that would inevitably take England on a national barrel ride down Niagara Falls to crushing oblivion. As he puts it at the start of the essay: 'Democracy to complete itself; to go the full length of its course, towards the Bottomless or into it, no power now extant to prevent it or even considerably retard it – till we have seen where it will lead us to, and whether there will then be any return possible, or none.'[27] As a last-ditch effort to avert the catastrophe of liberal Reform, he asks his readers to contemplate the outcome of the American Civil War and particularly what he calls 'the Settlement of the Nigger Question'.[28] How Americans have dealt with diversity in general and Africans in particular is, for him, a test of how far liberal Reform may fare in England. In his own mind he is quite sure how far Africans are suited to play a role in national governance. As he says, 'One always rather likes the Nigger; evidently a poor blockhead with good dispositions, with affections, attachments, – with a turn for Nigger melodies and the like: – he is the only Savage of all the colored races that doesn't die out on sight of the White Man.' But Carlyle insists that 'the Almighty Maker has appointed [the Nigger] to be a Servant'.[29] Given the existence of humans within the British dominions who are naturally – divinely – appointed to be servants, Carlyle finds it 'inexpressibly delirious' that the Public should desire democratic reforms. He describes reform as 'the calling in of new supplies of blockheadism, gullibility, bribability, amenability to beer and balderdash, by way of amending the woes we have had from our previous supplies of that bad article'.[30]

We see then that the existence of both Jews and Africans inspired Carlyle to examine the issue of democratic Reform and in both cases to place limits on the extension of the franchise. Unlike Burke he understands both groups as metonyms for liberalism, but also understands both (not just Africans) as problems in their own right that had to be resolved. We also see that for him these Others are not completely commensurate. Carlyle denies Jews the full rights of citizenship on the basis of their threat to the Christian character of the state; in contrast, he denies Africans citizenship on the basis of their congenital blockheadedness, or in other words their race, understood as a divine inheritance. He distinguishes between religious and racial Otherness, although his overweening resistance to liberalism informs his approach to both types of marginalisation.

The similarities in the treatment of otherness are still greater when the comparison is not between Jews and Africans, but between Jews and Indians – at least as long as Indians were considered only in regard to their religious difference. Perhaps because of the indelibility of race, religious and racial minorities seemed to have less in common than did two religious minorities. The figure who best illustrates this point is the Whig historian and MP Thomas Babington Macaulay, known both for his speech on the 'Civil Disabilities of the Jews' (1831) and for his 'Minute on Indian Education' (1835).[31] In these two speeches, Macaulay self-consciously laid out a liberal paradigm for how the British Empire ought to deal with religious differences at home and abroad.[32] Presented during the debate on the first of Robert Grant's Bills for Jewish Emancipation, Macaulay's speech on Jewish disabilities self-consciously placed the issue of Jews' emancipation in a series of comparative contexts. In the context of religious difference, he compares Jews to Hindus, Muslims, Parsees, Catholics and Huguenots.[33] Mimicking the voice of an MP resistant to including Jews in the polity, Macaulay says, 'But where are we to stop, if once you admit into the House of Commons people who deny the authority of the Gospels? Will you let in a Mussulman? Will you let in a Parsee? Will you let in a Hindoo who worships a lump of stone with seven heads?'[34] In his own voice he responds to the resisting 'honourable friend' as follows: 'I will answer my honourable friend's question by another. Where does he mean to stop? Is he ready to roast unbelievers at slow fires?'[35] A liberal nation ought not to be a brutal one, but rather should learn to tolerate religious differences. In fact, liberal nations have already learned this lesson with other groups, as he reminds the House when he asks, 'Why not try what effect would be produced on the Jews by that tolerant policy which has made the English Roman Catholic a good Englishman and the French Calvinist a good Frenchman?'[36]

Nor does Macaulay admit a distinction between an otherness based on religious belief and one based on divinely appointed race. He several times compares Jews to African slaves, saying in one instance, 'We treat [Jews] as slaves, and wonder that they do not regard us as brethren.'[37] This would seem to suggest that toleration might be applied to Africans as well. True, he maintains a distinction between the civilised and the savage, but he reminds his audience that 'in the infancy of civilisation, when our island was as savage as New Guinea, this contemned people [the Jews] had their fenced cities and cedar palaces, their splendid Temple, their fleets of merchant ships, their schools of sacred learning'.[38] That is, he shows how the opposition between civilisation and savagery might easily be reversed. It's the British who have the history of savagery – and in the fashion of good Whig history these savages have been able to develop and progress. As for the Jews, there is 'nothing in their national character which unfits them for the highest duties of civilisation'.[39] They, too, might participate in the Whig paradigm of progress and development. Although he does not make the argument, it is hard to see why the same might not be said of African slaves.

Thus the liberal politician articulates a standard of toleration for religious and racial others when it comes to the rights of citizenship in the nation. We should not imagine, however, that toleration means full participation in the nation. Although Macaulay says, 'Let us do justice to them', he does not suggest that *they* should or will have the same status as *us*. Doing justice does not mean dissolving the Christian power structure. Christianity will indeed triumph, but through toleration rather than bigotry, just as it has already 'triumphed over the superstitions of the most refined and of the most savage nations'.[40] Macaulay adopts the classical stance of English philo-semitism: we will convert Jews to Englishness (and Christianity) more effectively if instead of brutalising them we show them how tolerant we can be.[41]

It is remarkable to see how minutely this programme of Anglicisation and philo-semitic conversionism is transferred to the programme Macaulay set forth in his Minute on Indian Education four years later. As President of the Committee on Public Instruction in India, he is asked to comment on whether he thinks the Indian school curriculum should focus on traditional Arabic and Sanskrit texts or on English texts. In casting his vote for English, he employs the same rhetoric of tolerant Anglicisation that he had employed in the speech on Jewish civil disabilities. Just as he believed Jews would benefit by exposure to Christianity in a tolerant context, he believed that Indians would benefit by exposure to English history, philosophy, religion and literature in their schools. For Macaulay (who admits to having no fluency in any of the languages of India),[42] it is a given that 'the dialects commonly spoken among the natives contain neither literary nor scientific information'.[43] He is also certain that 'a single shelf of a good European library was worth the whole native literature of India and Arabia'.[44] Yet if these lines sound like nothing more than the arrogant self-justifications of a hegemon, we should consider that by 1835 the East India Company was beginning to be nationalised and to become an official arm of the British government. The Empire was beginning to be formalised. In the Company's employ were hundreds of thousands of Indian sepoys, whose chance of upward mobility would depend on their capacity to mimic their English higher-ups in learning, fashions and religion.[45] Macaulay's programme was designed to help these functionaries attain a measure of success within the imperial system. In both his 'Minute' and his speech on Jewish disabilities, Macaulay tried to ameliorate the marginalised group's suffering while ensuring the maintenance of English Christian power.

If there is a difference in Macaulay's programmes for Jews and Indians, it is that Jews (perhaps because of their small unthreatening population or their European acculturation) are not conceived to be as great a threat to the power structure as Indians. Macaulay even complains against the existence of a political glass ceiling for Jewish citizens, lamenting that 'The Jew may be a juryman, but not a judge... He may rule the money-market but he must not be a Privy Councillor.'[46] Indian schoolchildren, on the other hand, might learn all of Locke and Milton and Newton, but until Independence they would never rise above secondary administrators, and they were not meant to. The realisation on the part of Anglicised Indians that their glass ceiling was intended to be permanent helped fuel the Mutiny of 1857.[47]

But although English Christians considered Jews to have similarities both to racial and colonial others, the marginalised groups considered most similar to Jews during the first two-thirds of the nineteenth century wavered among Catholics, Irish, Scots or Arab Muslims. What is crucial to note is that between comparisons there are two kinds of shifts in meaning: the meaning of both Englishness and Jewishness alters depending on which group Jews are compared to. These comparisons thus demonstrate the non-existence of national and marginal 'characters' or 'essences'. Rather, national and marginal identities develop relationally.

Catholics and Jews both sought emancipation from civil disabilities beginning in the 1820s and 1830s. Indeed the passage of the Catholic Emancipation Act in 1829 directly inspired two Jews, Isaac and Frances Goldsmid, to petition Parliament for Jewish relief the following year.[48] A comparative study of the Emancipation Bills and the rhetoric surrounding them might yield important conclusions about the parameters of English national identity with regard to religion. In this comparison, Jewishness as a religious identity is paramount.

In the comparison between Jews and Scots or Irish, the diasporic aspect of Jewishness is brought to the fore. By 1794, when William Godwin wrote his revolutionary novel *Caleb Williams*, he was already linking Jewishness to England's oppression of its regional Other, the Irish. When Caleb Williams takes on a series of disguises to escape his oppressor, he ends up donning the clothing of both an Irishman and a Jew.[49] Like Joyce over a century later, Godwin correlates Irish and Jewish dispossession.[50] During the Regency period, Walter Scott made a similar comparison between Jews' diaspora and the Scots' lack of regional autonomy. In the *Waverley* novels, Walter Scott contemplates the past and future of Scottish regional identity in the wake of the 1707 Act of Union with England. That he ends the series with a Jewish historical romance in *Ivanhoe* would seem to imply a parallel between Scots and Jews, between regional and diasporic identity – a parallel based, perhaps, on both groups' dispossession of territory and sovereignty. Rebecca of *Ivanhoe* is essentially the Flora MacIvor of the Jews. When in *Waverley* Flora sings in her hidden bower of the Scots' former national glory and their current dispossession of territory and sovereignty, she becomes what the narrator calls the Scots' 'Celtic muse'.[51] Her song contains the essence of the Scottish 'national character'.[52] Scott borrows the idea of national essences or characters from Herder, the German philosopher of romantic nationalism. So, too, in *Ivanhoe*, Rebecca functions as the essence of the Jewish national character, long since separated from its former national glory.[53] Although Victorian Jewish writers like Grace Aguilar had their difficulties with Scott, Aguilar nonetheless absorbed his lesson of the parallel between regional and diasporic identity. She herself even wrote not only a Jewish historical romance patterned after *Ivanhoe* but also a Scottish historical romance, *The Days of Bruce* (1852).[54] In the comparison between Jews and a regional Other, the aspect of Jews' identity that emphasised their statelessness became paramount.

When comparing Jews and Arabs, what became paramount was the two groups' common history of wandering, their supposed oriental natures, and increasingly, the pseudoscientific 'evidence' of their shared racial inheritance. Early in the nineteenth century, Jews and Arab Muslims were both seen as romantic, nomadic, oriental peoples.[55] Cain, Byron's brooding wandering Jew, holds a place in Byron's world view equivalent to the Giaour, Byron's brooding wandering Muslim.[56] Like gypsies, both Jews and Muslims partook of the spirit of wandering (although the myth of the 'wandering Jew' did have its own separate history and significance). By the 1840s, the young Disraeli had absorbed Byron's romanticisation of Jewishness and turned it in a nationalistic and racist direction, both in his early historical romance *Alroy* and in the later novel *Tancred*. But in the latter he also claims that an Arab is 'but a Jew on horseback'.[57] Here he gives voice to an understanding of semitism as a racial inheritance shared by Jews and Arabs. George Eliot's *Daniel Deronda* most self-consciously invokes the nomadic and oriental when the author sends her hero wandering off to found a Jewish nation in the East.[58] She also accepts, at least in part, a racial explanation of semitic inheritance. Daniel Deronda does not need to convert once he has discovered the biological truth of his inherited Jewishness. This racial understanding perhaps explains the most perplexing feature of the text, Daniel's and Mirah's self-exile to the East. While in correspondence Eliot explained that she deliberately set out to use her final novel to raise the level of liberal toleration of Jews, the novel itself seems to suggest quite a different conclusion – namely, that Jews ought to leave England to set up their own nation-state rather than remaining as English citizens. In this, Eliot copied the ending of her friend Harriet Beecher Stowe's sentimental blockbuster, *Uncle Tom's Cabin*, which she much admired. There, the archetypal liberated blacks set out to found their own colony in Canada. Thus Eliot borrows a plot element to express a racial understanding of Jewishness – an excellent example of how representations of the Other could cross-fertilise one another. So in an unexpected way, a novel by a tolerant writer that set out to question the racial divisions of English society ends up reconfirming those divisions.

From this brief survey, we can see that the term 'Jewish' was available for a variety of readings due to Jews' category indeterminacy – their capacity to be understood in diasporic, religious, national, racial or ethnic terms. One important means of determining which category is being invoked at any given time is to ask which group the Jews were being compared to and for which ideological purposes. By using a comparative lens, we can inquire in a sophisticated way how Jews were used in the larger discursive endeavour of shaping the identity of the English nation and the British Empire. Better still, if we assume with Benedict Anderson that national identity itself is never a fixed quantity, but is rather a never-realised, ever-shifting set of imaginary blueprints, then perhaps we can ask how each instance of Jewishness functions to help a particular writer articulate a particular national blueprint at a particular moment.[59]

Yet even if this method succeeds in recontextualising semitic discourse, it will still be insufficient to account for the complex interplay of images of Jews in nineteenth-century England. For it is limited to the claim that what gives representations of Otherness their significance is only what they tell us about the anxieties of those among whom the Others lived. An approach using this kind of conceptual framework cannot generate a comprehensive knowledge of either nationalism or marginalised identities, including Jewish identity.

To fill in the picture new research might compare the ways in which Jews and other marginalised subjects of the British Empire responded in relation to the images of them produced by others. Against the images produced by English Christian writers scholars might juxtapose the products of marginalised subjectivity – for example, Olaudah Equiano's slave narrative from 1789, Hasan Shah's autobiographical novel of Indian life *The Dancing Girl* from 1790, Grace Aguilar's *History of the Jews of England* from 1847 – in order better to conceive of the imagined nation as a dialectical series of encounters between major and minor writers.[60] We might try to find out to what extent Jews identified their own Otherness with the regional, colonial, diasporic, racial or religious differences of the multiple aliens living in the British dominions; and to what extent Jews attempted to build bridges across these differences and to form intergroup alliances. Literary critics and historians might work on elucidating how Jews grappled with genres and ideas they inherited from mainstream culture or from other marginalised communities, and to what degree Jews were able to alter what they had assimilated in order to create new hybridised forms. Finally, by employing a relational methodology, scholars might continue the task of nudging the discussion of images of Jews in nineteenth-century Europe out of its splendid, teleological isolation and back into history.

NOTES

1. See for example Barbara Crossette, 'Europe Stares at a Future Built by Immigrants', *New York Times*, 2 Jan 2000, sec. 4, p.1.
2. For a critique of modern Jewish history's teleological orientation, see Michael Andre Bernstein, *Foregone Conclusions: Against Apocalyptic History* (Berkeley: University of California Press, 1994). For an instance, see Peter T. Park, 'Thomas Carlyle and the Jews', *Journal of European Studies* 20 (1990), 1–21.
3. For the idea that representations of Jews are tools in producing national identity, see Michael Ragussis, *Figures of Conversions: 'The Jewish Question' and English National Identity* (Durham: Duke University Press, 1995). For a similar argument vis-à-vis Scots and Irish, see Katie Trumpener, *Bardic Nationalism: The Romantic Novel and the British Empire* (Princeton, NJ: Princeton University Press, 1997).
4. See V.D. Lipman, *Social History of the Jews in England, 1850–1950* (London: Watts, 1954).
5. See Gotthold Ephraim Lessing, *Nathan the Wise*, trans. by Bayard Quincy Morgan (New York: Continuum, 1988).
6. See Woodruff D. Smith, *European Imperialism in the Nineteenth and Twentieth Centuries* (Chicago: Nelson-Hall, 1982), pp.34–7.
7. Ibid., ch. 2.
8. See Edmund Burke, *The Writings and Speeches of Edmund Burke*, vol. 3, ed. by W.M. Elofson and John A. Woods (Oxford: Clarendon Press, 1996), p.340.
9. Ibid., p.563.

10. Ibid., p.359.
11. Ibid.
12. Ibid., p.565.
13. Ibid., p.568.
14. Ibid., pp.571–8.
15. Ibid., pp.576, 579.
16. Ibid., pp.580, 567.
17. For the anthropological distinction between thick and thin description, see Clifford Geertz, *Interpretation of Cultures* (New York: Basic Books, 2000), Introduction.
18. My argument about Burke's *Reflections* draws on Ragussis (see note 3), pp.119–25.
19. Edmund Burke, *Reflections on the Revolution in France*, ed. by Thomas H.D. Mahoney (New York: The Liberal Arts Press, 1955), p.18.
20. Ibid., p.19.
21. Ibid., p.55.
22. Ibid., p.96.
23. Ibid., p.97.
24. Ibid., p.95.
25. Matthew Arnold, *Culture and Anarchy*, ed. by Dover Wilson (Cambridge: Cambridge University Press, 1971), p.129.
26. See Thomas Carlyle, 'The Jew Our Lawgiver' (London: Thomas Bosworth, 1853) and 'Shooting Niagara: And After?' (London: Chapman & Hall, 1867).
27. Carlyle, 'Shooting Niagara' (see note 26), p.1.
28. Ibid., p.5.
29. Ibid.
30. Ibid., pp.10–11.
31. See Thomas Babington Macaulay, 'Civil Disabilities of the Jews', *Edinburgh Review* 52 (Jan 1831): 40–60; and 'Minute on Indian Education' in *Macaulay: Prose and Poetry* ed. by G.M. Young (Cambridge, MA: Harvard University Press, 1967).
32. For an excellent cross-reading of the two speeches, see Gauri Viswanathan, *Outside the Fold: Conversion, Modernity, and Belief* (Princeton, NJ: Princeton University Press, 1998), pp.5–8.
33. Macaulay, 'Civil Disabilities' (see note 31), pp.44, 50, 55–6.
34. Ibid., p.44.
35. Ibid.
36. Ibid., p.56.
37. Ibid., p.57.
38. Ibid., p.58.
39. Ibid.
40. Ibid., p.59.
41. On English philo-semitism, see David Katz, *Philo-Semitism and the Readmission of the Jews to England, 1603–1655* (Oxford: Clarendon Press, 1982); Todd Endelman, *Radical Assimilation in English Jewish History 1656–1945* (Bloomington: Indiana University Press, 1990); and Michael Galchinsky, *The Origin of the Modern Jewish Woman Writer: Romance and Reform in Victorian England* (Detroit: Wayne State University Press, 1996).
42. Macaulay, 'Minute' (see note 31), p.722.
43. Ibid., p.721.
44. Ibid., p.722.
45. See Homi Bhabha, 'Of Mimicry and Men: The Ambivalence of Colonial Discourse', *October*, 28: 125–33.
46. Macaulay, 'Civil Disabilities' (see note 31), p.47.
47. See Patrick Brantlinger, *Rule of Darkness*, (Ithaca, NY: Cornell University Press, 1988), ch. 7.
48. On the Emancipation debates see David Feldman, *Englishmen and Jews : Social Relations and Political Culture, 1840–1914* (New Haven and London: Yale University Press, 1994).
49. William Godwin, *Caleb Williams* (New York: W.W. Norton, 1977), pp.240, 264.

60

60 JEWISH CULTURE AND HISTORY

60 JEWISH CULTURE AND HISTORY

60 JEWISH CULTURE AND HISTORY

50. See Bryan Cheyette, *Constructions of 'the Jew' in English Literature and Society: Racial Representations, 1875–1945* (Cambridge: Cambridge University Press, 1993).
51. Walter Scott, *Waverley* (New York: Oxford University Press, 1986), p.106.
52. See Trumpener (note 3), ch. 3.
53. See Walter Scott, *Ivanhoe* (New York: NAL Penguin, 1983), esp. ch. 29.
54. See Grace Aguilar, *The Days of Bruce* (New York: D. Appleton & Company, 1903).
55. Edward Said, *Orientalism* (New York: Vintage Books, 1979), p.102.
56. See George Gordon, Lord Byron, *Byron*, ed. by Jerome J. McGann (New York: Oxford University Press, 1986), pp.207–46, 881–938.
57. Cited in Said (note 55), p.102.
58. George Eliot, *Daniel Deronda* (New York: Oxford University Press, 1984).
59. Benedict Anderson, *Imagined Communities: Reflections on the Origin and Spread of Nationalism*, rev. edn. (New York: Verso, 1991), Introduction.
60. See Olaudah Equiano, *Equiano's Travels*, ed. by Paul Edwards (Portsmouth, NH: Heinemann, 1967); Hasan Shah, *The Dancing Girl*, trans. by Qurratulain Hyder (New York: New Directions Books, 1993); Grace Aguilar, 'History of the Jews in England' *Chambers' Miscellany* 18 (Edinburgh, 1847): 1–32.

The Homeless Nation:
The Exclusion of Jews in and from
Early Nineteenth-Century
German Historical Fiction

JEFFERSON S. CHASE

The significance of Jewish figures in German literature is inseparable from the significance of Jews and Jewishness for modern society as a whole. 'Die Stellung der Juden ist allezeit der Barometerstand der Humanität' [The status of the Jew is at all times the barometer of humanity], wrote the German-Jewish author Berthold Auerbach in 1840, arguing that a society was only as progressive as the treatment it accorded its Jewish population.[1] One can refine this point. Modernity, as theorists from E.J. Hobsbawm to Anthony Giddens have claimed, erased local, traditional boundaries and required the invention of new, super-regional, national identities.[2] The nineteenth-century Swabian or Silesian found him- or herself in a position not unlike that of German Jews: forced to balance the desire for tradition and continuity with the need to integrate into a larger society by adopting new language, customs and behaviour. At the same time, the status of Jews in society, which had been determined locally by tradition and the needs and wishes of individual sovereigns, became an issue to be resolved on a national level. Jews were thus far more than the collective object upon which a code of morality or 'civilisation' was practised. They were a crux of both a political and a cultural transformation from traditional-local to modern-national society. To define Jews and Jewishness was to define Germans and what was typically German.

This connection helps explain the proliferation of Jewish figures in German literature in the period after Napoleon up to the failed popular-national revolution of 1848. Whereas Goethe and Schiller ignored, perhaps avoided, the topic of Jewishness, the leading writers between 1815 and 1848, Jewish and Gentile, were continually writing Jewish figures into their works. This essay surveys these literary representations, focusing on arguably the period's most important genre, historical fiction. The questions I address include the following: How did Jewish figures help construct narratives of greater German identity? Were these narratives coherent, or did they merely highlight the tensions and conflicts within the idea of a larger German community? What place did Jews have in the imagined native society? And how did treatments of Jewishness by Jewish authors compare with those of their Gentile counterparts? Furthermore, with particular reference to Walter Scott's *Ivanhoe*,[3] I will open up a comparative perspective on German historical fiction, identifying aspects of German particularity and suggesting a preliminary thesis as to its social and political origins.

In this regard, we must remember that Germany first came into existence as a political entity in 1871. Before that, there was a confederation of thirty-nine sovereign states, connected only by piecemeal political and economic arrangements and subject to the competing ambitions of Prussia and Austria. As recent historians have shown, the *kleindeutsch* [lesser German] nation that we know as Germany was merely one possible outcome among many, and German feelings of identity with this state were an *ex post facto* invention of historians, concerned with legitimising Bismarck's empire.[4] In the period under discussion, however, 'Germany' was without boundaries. It was an idea, an ideal, sometimes little more than a vague feeling of solidarity towards others capable of reading, writing or speaking something like the standard German idiom, which was itself being codified and revised at the time. More so than England or France, Germany had to be invented via literature in order to exist at all. The fictional representations of Jews that were an essential part of that invention partook equally of both the particularity and contingency of the German political situation.

As a start, it is helpful to categorise German literary treatments of Jewishness according to three *milieux*: Biblical, historical and contemporary. In addition, Jews also appear in apocryphal, mythological form, chiefly in the figure of the Wandering Jew, the shoemaker Ahasverus who refused Christ comfort during the march to Calvary and was sentenced by God to roam forever over the face of the earth.[5] This figure cuts across *milieux* and is invoked throughout pre-1848 German literature.[6] It is not possible here to give equal weight to all types of literature, and I will concentrate on historical fiction as being the most germane to the invention of identity. It is, however, important to keep the wider literary landscape in mind, if only in sketchy form.

Treatments of Biblical history are of comparatively little relevance to the topic at hand. Most writers at the time followed Goethe and Schiller in distinguishing between Biblical/historical and secular/contemporary Jewishness. Whereas the Hebrew religion and culture as depicted in the Bible were acknowledged as precursors to Christianity, nineteenth-century Judaism and Jewish culture were dismissed as a set of vestigial practices corrupted over time. Authors treating Biblical material thus tended not to address issues of secular Jewishness. This is the case with the German dramatist Friedrich Hebbel's 1840 tragedy, *Judith*, which uses the Old Testament tale as a forum for a philosophical investigation into despotism, transgression and the will to power, without raising contemporary issues of identity.[7] The Viennese humorist Johann Nestroy would exploit the disjunction to great comic effect in his 1849 travesty, *Judith and Holofernes*,[8] by transposing the dialogue of the Hebrew characters into the stereotypical dialect, or *Mauscheln*,[9] that was commonly used to represent Yiddish. Nestroy's success in wringing laughter from this situation underscores the distance between literary treatments of Hebrew history and Jewish presence in nineteenth-century society.

In contrast, recognisably Jewish characters appeared with some regularity in the contemporary social-critical novels, or *Zeitromane*, of the period. Favourite stock figures included the unsuccessfully assimilated *arriviste*, the grubby door-to-door peddler/thief and the dishonest moneylender. Negative as these figures often were, however, they did not usually reflect a fundamental anti-semitism among the authors concerned. Critical depictions of Jews most often occurred on the margins of the *Zeitroman*, in the context of a satiric attack on society as a whole. The funniest work of this genre was in fact the 1827 novella, *The Baths of Lucca*, by Heinrich Heine, an assimilated poet and prose writer of Jewish background.[10] *The Baths of Lucca* depicts a trio of Jewish figures – a non-assimilated ghetto Jew, his half-acculturated businessman-master and the poet himself – on a journey of edification or *Bildungsreise* through Italy. Although Heine avails himself of a host of Jewish stereotypes, from big noses to bad German to restricted cultural horizons, the novella is a forceful assertion of Jewish membership in the mainstream. The ghetto Jew Hirsch Hyacinth proves a sharp, if rustic commentator on others' foibles, with a voice not unlike Sancho Panza or Huck Finn. The *arriviste* butt of most of the jokes, Christian Gumpel, turns out to be a typical representative of the manic aspirations among the mercantile classes towards Goethean *Bildung*. And the first-person narrator emerges as the master of the situation, his quick wit and cultural fluency constantly trumping the hapless pretensions of his interlocutors, Jewish and Gentile. *The Baths of Lucca* thus provides an example of an author using familiar stereotypes to undermine the sense of innate Jewish particularity and inferiority.

Anti-semitic *Zeitromane* would become more prominent in German literature after 1848. In the years between the Congress of Vienna and the

ultimately unproductive Frankfurt Assembly, the importance of
historical fiction greatly overshadowed that of contemporary novels. The
reasons are multiple. Because of the political fragmentation of German-
speaking Europe, the romantic-essentialist aspects within German
nationalism came to compete with its liberal-constitutionalist elements.
The romantic-nationalist emphasis on grounding new identities upon
imagined continuities with the past programmed an intense interest in
history. At the same time, the oppressive censorship of the printed word
in the Germanic Confederation, Prussia and Austria encouraged many
politically-minded authors to address present concerns via the
'ideological screen' of the past.[11] Finally, though not exhaustively, there
was the influence of Sir Walter Scott's *Ivanhoe*, the period's biggest
bestseller. *Ivanhoe* was successful in part because it addressed a theme
close to the heart of many German readers, the formation of a national
identity via the reconciliation of hostile groups. Yet this popularity also
developed a momentum of its own, as ambitious young authors sought
to emulate Scott's success by modelling their works on his tale of Saxon-
Norman conflict, with its two central Jewish characters: the cowardly
merchant Isaac of York and his beautiful and noble daughter, Rebecca.
The result was a rather strange situation. Although the Jews' role in
'German' history had been at best intermittent, restricted to certain local
courts and specific socio-economic functions, German historical novels
were full of Jewish figures, most of which bore more than a passing
resemblance to either Isaac or Rebecca.[12]

As in Scott's novel, the Jewish figures in the works discussed here are
all treated with humanity and are all ultimately excluded from the native
community. These two contradictory impulses, however, receive
different ideological weighting in the German works from that in
Ivanhoe. For this reason, it is insufficient merely to identify the adoption
of stock figures or stereotypes from source to successor. We must also
consider the function of such figures in the basic plot of the work and in
the conclusions about Jewishness likely to be drawn as a result. In order
to do this, I call upon Emile Benveniste's distinction between *discours* (the
'official' ideological stance communicated by the author's direct
statements) and *histoire* (the actual upshot of the narrative communicated
in large measure via plot).[13] What one finds throughout historical fiction
concerned with Jewishness is a discrepancy between an authorial *discours*
of tolerance and a practical *histoire* of exclusion. This disjunction,
however, is far more extreme in German historical fiction than in the
works of Scott.

The first figure I would like to examine is that of the Beautiful
Jewess,[14] in the guise of Rahel from Franz Grillparzer's 'historical

tragedy', *The Jewess of Toledo*, partly written in 1839, completed in 1851, but first published in 1872.[15] The play is set in Spain in 1195 and relates the story of the unhappy relationship between the daughter of the rich merchant/moneylender Isaac bin Esra and King Alfonso the Eighth of Castille. Ignoring the official prohibition on Jews' entering royal grounds, Rahel lingers in the castle garden, where she hopes to be noticed by Alfonso. An encounter ensues in which she falls into, or perhaps simulates, hysterical paralysis and attracts his sympathetic interest. Installed in the royal residence for her own protection against the Jew-hating mob, she quickly becomes the king's mistress. The relationship prompts conflict, from both Alfonso's jealous wife Eleonore and from his court, who fear that the monarch's infatuation with the beautiful Jewess will distract him from imminent military campaigns against the Moors. Alfonso vacillates and dissatisfaction grows, until a bloodthirsty cabal storms the palace and murders Rahel. The king recognises his own guilt in pursuing the scandalous love affair and condemns the anti-Jewish prejudices of others that ultimately led to the drastic step of murdering a young woman. By way of penance, he decrees that all involved should go the battlefront, where God will decide if they are to pay with their own lives.

Like Scott, Grillparzer treats the Beautiful Jewess as both a source of dangerous instability and a sympathetic victim. King Alfonso initially appears an enlightened despot, protecting an innocent, whose only transgression was childish vanity. 'Was sie verunziert, es ist unser Werk,' Alfonso reflects in sympathy with the Jewish plight, 'Wir lähmen sie und grollen, wenn sie hinken.' [It is our work that disfigures them. We lame them and complain if they limp.][16] Such statements contextualise Rahel's vain excesses as a reaction to her social exclusion and cast the hostility of the mob and the party around Queen Eleonore in an unfavourable light. At the same time, Rahel's own behaviour tempts her eventual fate. She refuses to leave the castle for the safety of the ghetto, she dresses herself in royal vestments and playacts an imaginary dialogue between Alfonso and herself as queen, and she insists that she and Alfonso swap portraits of one another. These are all dangerous and ultimately ambiguous actions, for either Rahel has succumbed to her overheated imagination, or she is casting a magic spell upon the hapless Alfonso who, in contrast to the historical figure, is a mere youth without much experience with women. Before long, the king himself begins to suspect that he has been hexed: 'Man spricht von magisch unerlaubten Künsten, die dieses Volk mit derlei Zeichen übt, und etwas wie von Zauber, kommt mich an.' [One speaks of the forbidden dark arts that this people conjures up with such magic symbols, and something like a spell has indeed come upon

me.][17] Whatever one's interpretation of the Rahel figure, the upshot of
the text remains that her beauty represents an uncanny, erotic force that
disrupts the social order and leads the sovereign away from his duty to
his people. With that, the tragic end of the play becomes inevitable.

The parallels with Scott are numerous, the deviations therefore all the
more instructive. Both Isaacs are cowardly and money-hungry. Both
Rebecca and Rahel possess an enchanting beauty that derives from the
ancient origins of the Jewish people and gives them an exotic-erotic
power beyond that of native women. For Scott, however, the Beautiful
Jewess is a noble figure, who voluntarily renounces her love for the
Gentile hero so that he might fulfil his role in the native community.
Grillparzer presents an unredeemed version of the figure. In fact, he splits
Rebecca's attributes between Rahel and a sister, Esther, who warns at the
beginning of the drama against Rahel's encroaching upon the native
family and state. In the final lines of the play, Esther even suggests that
typically Jewish character flaws contributed to her sister's bloody demise.
The Jewess of Toledo thus ends in unresolved tension. Grillparzer takes
over Scott's rueful tone in his own sombre concluding scene, and yet,
despite all the *meae culpae* from the native figures, the eradication of the
Beautiful Jewess has led to what is, from the chauvinistic native
perspective, the right outcome. The King rededicates himself to his
people, and the natives all set off to defend their homeland, their *Heimat*,
against the heathen Moors. Although Grillparzer suggests at various
points that the negative image of the beautiful Jewess may be just a
psychological projection of those around her, the restoration of social
stability at the end of the play justifies such projections with concerns for
public welfare.

A text that adopted Scott's combination of the Beautiful Jewess with
the Noble Jewess was Karl Spindler's best-selling 1827 novel, *The Jew*.[18]
The central story line in this complexly plotted, three-volume work
revolves around the relationship of the Jewess Esther Ben-David and the
Gentile protagonist Dagobert Frosch. Although initially Esther appears
as vain and as frivolous as Grillparzer's Rahel, her character development
conforms more closely to the Scottian model. Much of the action consists
of the hero Dagobert rescuing the Ben-David family from threatening
situations, à la *Ivanhoe*, and in the end Esther, like Rebecca, voluntarily
renounces her claims upon the protagonist so that he can marry a Gentile
and start a family. Esther's development reflects a general authorial
strategy of using negative stereotypes to introduce characters who later
emerge as sympathetic, thereby undermining anti-semitic readers'
presuppositions and expectations. Esther's father, Ben-David Jochai, is
initially seen purchasing a Christian orphan from a dissolute nobleman.

This evokes the inflammatory blood libel that Jews used the blood of ritualistically slaughtered Christian children in the Pesach ritual.[19] Later on, it turns out that Ben-David wishes to sell the child to a recently bereaved Christian family, an act that ultimately re-unites the child with his real parents. Spindler further undermines the blood libel with a critical depiction of the kangaroo court that tries Ben-David and his father for the crime of ritual murder. The Ben-David clan, for all the faults of its individual members, emerges as the victim of Gentile intolerance and exclusion and requites the kindness of Dagobert Frosch with similar acts of goodwill.

In these respects, *The Jew* reaffirms the Enlightenment *discours* that informs *Ivanhoe*. As in Scott's novel, however, authorial pronouncements and sympathetic character depictions do not always square with the upshot of the plot. In *The Jew* as in *Ivanhoe*, Jewish presence in Gentile society is a sign of disorder. Although not depicted as the root cause of the problem, the Ben-David family is conjoined to a situation of social and familial chaos. The first volume of the novel, which sets the major plot lines in motion, takes place against the backdrop of the 1411 Papal Council in Costance. Spindler anachronistically casts this event as a conflict of nationality, describing Costance as a tower of Babel where the foreign predominates over the German, and of confession, with the Czech reformer Jan Hus standing in for Martin Luther. In the following two volumes of the novel, Spindler transfers the action to the familial sphere of the dysfunctional Frosch clan in Frankfurt. There, in contrast to the events of 1411, conflict can be satisfactorily resolved. As in *Ivanhoe*, the rescue of the Jewish victims, followed by their voluntary self-exclusion from the native community, is inseparable from the establishment of a stable native society. The connection is neither causal nor logical, but symbolic. The upshot of the plot thus undermines the considerable impetus towards tolerance, just as the philosemitic authorial pronouncements and characterisations undermine vulgar anti-Jewish stereotypes.

Since the same tension is operative in *Ivanhoe*, its presence in *The Jew* can hardly be seen as an instance of German particularity. In the differences between the two texts, however, we can identify a more radical impetus towards separation in Spindler than in Scott. Deviating from his model, Spindler introduces a Jewish highwayman, the murderous Zodick, who serves as the main villain. Significantly, Zodick first becomes a figure of absolute evil, when his fellow thieves force him to convert to Christianity. This ceremony has the effect, in Spindler's interior-monologue depiction, of freeing the villain from his last remaining moral constraints, his connection to Mosaic law. It is Zodick who, having sworn revenge on the Ben-David family, denounces Ben-David Jochai and causes the ritual murder trial that occupies most of the second volume. It is also Zodick who, in the third volume, conspires to let foreign troops into Frankfurt to sack the city and who attempts to turn Dagobert Frosch's wedding into a bloodbath. These developments suggest that Jewish conversion presents a danger to the native community. Spindler reinforces this message by introducing the figure of Esther's estranged brother, a Jewish convert to Christianity, who shows up telling horror stories about his experience and convinces her to renounce her claims on Dagobert. Spindler's elaboration on the *Ivanhoe* plot thus alters the fundamental message concerning Jewish exclusion from native society. Scott treats the separation of Jew and Gentile as an unfortunate by-product of the historical moment and as an example of European barbarism, which must be overcome in the future.[20] Spindler invokes the supposed divine fate of the Jewish people, who are condemned to a condition of homelessness, *Heimatlosigkeit*, and have little alternative but to wander until they die out. The nobility of the Beautiful Jewess resides not just in her renunciation of the hero, but in her embracing of this Jewish collective destiny. In the final pages of the novel Esther declares that she will bear no children, and the family moves on, ostensibly to Innsbruck, but actually to oblivion.

We encounter similar themes in a more tightly plotted and more historically specific context in Wilhelm Hauff's *The Jew Süß*, which was also published in 1827.[21] The novella retells the history of Josef Süss-Oppenheimer, minister without portfolio and general factotum under the eighteenth-century Duke Karl Alexander of Württemberg. In Hauff's fiction, Süß is a power- and money-hungry despot, who drives the local peasantry into ruin with ever-increasing taxes, dissolves the parliamentary Württembergian diet and plots to invite Catholic troops from neighbouring Würzburg to occupy the territory. In a sub-plot, he also tries, via extortion, to marry his beautiful sister Lea to the respected young Gentile Gustav Lanbek, the hero of the story. Just in the nick of time, Süß's plot is discovered and Karl Alexander dies, leaving Süß without royal protection. Süß is hanged to death in an iron cage suspended above the Stuttgart marketplace, and Lea drowns herself in the Neckar River.

Süß conforms to the stereotype of the Court Jew, the treacherous careerist who integrates himself into the highest echelons of Gentile society.[22] In Süß, the external and linguistic marks of Jewish difference have receded to the very margins, for instance in the 'cruel lines' around the character's mouth. The ability to pass makes him, from the perspective of the novella, more dangerous to the welfare of the native community than a caftan-wearing, pseudo-dialect speaking Ben-David or Zodick. Significantly, whereas Ben-David greets with dismay the prospect of Esther's marrying Dagobert, Süß actively plots the intermarriage of his sister with the Gentile hero as a means of increasing his power. Hauff's negative portrayal of Süß is offset by his positive depiction of Lea and by the narrator's occasional remarks concerning the role of anti-Jewish prejudice in making Süß the sole scapegoat of the Catholic plot. The noble Jewess Lea, whose beauty is also associated with bewitching, emerges as a tragic figure. She renounces her claims on the hero, acknowledges her brother's guilt and, after her pleas for clemency go unheeded, disposes of her own life. Strikingly, it is Gustav Lanbek himself who prosecutes Süß in the trial that leads to his execution. Lanbek fulfils this role out of a feeling of duty to the community, but the necessity of refusing Lea's pleas for mercy and the culpability that involves him in her suicide rob him of his *joie de vivre*. He remains unmarried and lives in the restored native community as an admired but somewhat isolated figure.

In *The Jew Süß*, the links between the symbolic resolution of conflict via Jewish figures and the pre-1848 political situation become clearly visible. The novella can be read as an allegory for the German experience under Napoleonic hegemony, in which many of the individual sovereigns initially allied themselves with the occupying forces, and French governmental institutions were established to administer the affected territories. One of the Napoleonic reforms forced upon the occupied territories was the legal emancipation of German Jews, a measure that was largely revoked after 1815 and was only generally re-established with the creation of the German nation-state in 1871. Yet, despite the text's tighter historical reference, the connection between social stability and Jewish exclusion remains symbolic – a fact that Hauff, astonishingly, acknowledges at various junctures. The narrator freely admits that others, namely Gentiles, were involved in the Catholic plot, thus implying that Süß was a scapegoat, but he also argues that the injustice was necessary so that the native community might recover from the trauma of political and confessional conflict. Accordingly, Hauff's text presents Süß as the only villain: none of the other conspirators nor even the Duke himself appear in the novella. The narrative decision is justified, on the level of *histoire*, by Hauff's conception of the Jews collectively as a people condemned to homelessness and strife with their native 'hosts'. Despite his sympathy for and attraction to Lea, Gustav Lanbek has to shudder at 'dem Fluch, der einen heimatlosen Menschenstamm bis ins tausendste Glied verfolgte und jeden mit ins Verderben zu ziehen schien, der sich auch den Edelsten unter ihnen auf die natürlichste Weise näherte' [the curse that followed a homeless tribe throughout the generations and seemed to drag its every member into ruination, the curse that afflicted even that tribe's most noble individuals].[23] The execution of Süß therefore eradicates a real, if uncanny threat posed to the native community by Jews *per se*. In the eyes of the historical novelist, the German people, in their struggle to found a new native community, need to be protected against the nation of Ahasverus, the people whose fate it was to wander the earth, forever homeless.

German historical fiction of this period is not unique, or even particular, in its use of stereotypes to depict Jewish figures. What is particular about the works I have discussed is the intensity of the impetus towards Jewish exclusion from the native community. To use the vocabulary of collective psychology, hopes for national integration become cathected with images of Jewishness. The arbitrariness of the perceived conflict between Jews and natives, which is depicted as unfortunate in *Ivanhoe*, is replaced by a somewhat ruefully tinged belief in the historical necessity of German–Jewish separation. To borrow a phrase from Hauff, moments of interaction between Jews and Gentiles reveal 'den Finger Gottes' [the hand of God] in human history,[24] pointing the German people in an exclusionary direction. This tendency expresses the acute difficulties faced by the nationalistically-minded German author in the face of nineteenth-century political realities. The need to find symbolic scapegoats to enact native solidarity *ex negativo* was all the greater because positive symbols of it were so manifestly lacking. This need gives German historical fiction from 1815 to 1848 its particular, exclusionary slant.

The particularity of German historical fiction becomes doubly apparent when we consider the largely failed attempts of authors of Jewish extraction to write in the genre during the period. One important work in this category is Heinrich Heine's novella *The Rabbi of Bacherach*, which was begun in 1824, never finished, and published as a fragment in 1840.[25] Heine's *Rabbi* shares a couple of major aspects with Spindler's *The Jew*. Set in the thirteenth century, the novella begins with a scene in which Jews are framed for ritual murder, and features similar depictions of *milieu*, from an account of a Pesach festival to an extensive description of the Frankfurt ghetto. In contrast to the three works by Gentile authors, however, Heine's narrative does not revolve around the relationship of a Beautiful Jewess and a Gentile hero. Instead, all the main figures are Jewish, so that the emphasis lies squarely upon the oppression of the minority, not on native social instability.

Heine was the most gifted writer of his generation, Gentile or Jewish, yet was unequal to the task of completing this work. The precise difficulties remain the subject of great debate and have in part to do with the vicissitudes of Heine's career.[26] However, even within the roughly two-and-a-half chapters Heine did manage to finish, tensions emerge that suggest his authorial discomfort with the genre in which he was trying to write. The beginning of the novella introduces a pair of characters – the eponymous Rabbi (the noble Abraham) and his beautiful wife Sara – that are familiar from the stock repertoire of the historical novel. Yet before the end of the chapter, Heine already slips into other modes of narrative. Forced to flee Bacharach to avoid the blood libel, Abraham and Sara are depicted floating down the Rhine on a raft, where Sara's internal thoughts about the tragic history of the Jewish people merge with the narrator's decidedly Romantic description of the landscape. 'Es war auch,' writes Heine, 'als murmelte der Rhein die Melodien der Agade...' [It was also as though the Rhine were humming the melodies of the Haggadah].[27] Another more acute disjunction occurs in the second chapter, as the protagonists enter the Frankfurt ghetto. There, the sense of being in the thirteenth century fades as Heine embarks on a description of the bustling ghetto typical of late eighteenth- and early nineteenth-century prose,[28] and he introduces a series of comic ghetto figures similar to Hirsch Hyacinth from the *Zeitroman The Baths of Lucca*. The journey depicted is thus one of both space and time, which aims to link the Jews of the medieval period, an era of cultural renaissance, with their counterparts in contemporary Germany. Yet without recourse to the established plot structure of Gentile-Jewish romance, which would have led him to recapitulate the exclusionary tropes of the historical novel, Heine was at a loss to extend his narrative. The result, as many critics have pointed out, was a number of breaches of narrative logic, making the novella seem artificial and implausible.[29] Although Heine did not definitively give up work on *The Rabbi of Bacherach* until 1840, he seems to have decided, consciously or not, that his aims could be better achieved in the genres of humorous lyric poetry, satiric travelogues and witty journalistic *reportage* than via the historical novel.

The period's other major German writer of Jewish extraction, Berthold Auerbach, also tried his hand at historical fiction, completing two novels, *Spinoza* (1837)[30] and *Poet and Merchant* (1840). Both are fictional biographies dealing with Jewish figures caught between their traditional origins and mainstream Gentile society, the subject of *Poet and Merchant* being Moses Ephraim Kuh, a minor late eighteenth-century poet. Auerbach's strategy for resisting the pull of exclusionary tropes was to focus intensively on the intellectual development of his protagonists. His historical novels forgo picturesque depictions of their respective eras and feature none of the standard scenes of derring-do and political intrigue. Instead, they depict intellectuals discussing various philosophical, social and cultural issues, in particular questions of Jewish identity and the possibilities for assimilation. The implications of these debates are then registered in the developing self-consciousness of the respective protagonists. Spinoza is able to transcend the limited horizons of his orthodox, fundamentalist Jewish background in his pursuit of strict rationalism and universal human truth. Kuh, in contrast, ultimately succumbs to *Judenschmerz*, the pain of being a Jew in a Gentile world: he descends into insanity and dies without completing anything beyond fragments and epigrams. Auerbach thus depicts two outcomes, one successful and one not, to the dilemma of having to reconcile majority and minority identity. It is revealing that the Spinoza novel ends with Ahasverus appearing to the philosopher in a dream, thanking him for freeing him from his fate of eternal homelessness – a symbolic representation of the aspirations Auerbach had for his fiction. By focusing on his Jewish characters' universally human search for cultural belonging, he sought to attract the sympathy of his Gentile audience and counter the generic demands of historical fiction, which marginalised Jews as the cursed descendants of Ahasverus.

Auerbach's novels represent an interesting experiment and a transitional step in German literature's progression from historical novels to Realism. They were not, however, particularly successful in either an artistic or commercial sense, and Auerbach, like Heine, soon redirected his efforts. In contrast to Heine's pursuit of urbane humour, Auerbach oriented his imagination on the German concept of *Heimat* – geographical and cultural roots – and the feelings of being-at-home they entailed. He more or less invented the *Heimatroman* genre, which depicted the social and economic hardships of nineteenth-century rural life within the plot structure of the fairytale. Auerbach's multi-volumed *Black Forest Village Stories* were among the bestselling works of their time, although ironically they also served as the model for what was to become a deeply reactionary and chauvinistic genre.[31] In these works, Jewish figures continued to appear and were depicted positively, but only at the very margins. The protagonists, whose problems were directly addressed and usually solved by the narrative, were exclusively Gentile.

Heine and Auerbach both wrote, first and foremost, as members of the German-language mainstream. Their sense of identity with their Jewish backgrounds, while present, was intermittent, largely secular and comparable in intensity to the feelings of regional identity among Gentile authors. Their 'local identity' was, however, problematic in a way that was not true for their Swabian or Silesian counterparts, and the difficulties they encountered were not restricted to their hostile public pigeonholing as 'Jews' but also included the generic constraints that influenced the literature of their time. Historical fiction provided Gentile authors with a forum for working through and resolving, at least symbolically, their own conflict-ridden feelings about larger German identity. The exclusion of Jewish figures at the end of the typical Gentile work of historical fiction helped give the illusion of a traditional, local native past being transferred seamlessly to the modern, national present. The genre proved resistant, however, to non-Gentile authors' efforts to redirect its focus, to establish links between the Jewish past and integration into the modern German mainstream. Writers like Heine and Auerbach therefore had little success with historical fiction and turned to other alternatives, humour and *Heimat*.

NOTES

1. Berthold Auerbach, *Dichter und Kaufmann*, in *Gesammelte Schriften*, vols. XII–XII, (Stuttgart: Cotta, 1864), here XIII: 38.
2. See Eric Hobsbawm, 'Inventing Tradition', in *The Invention of Tradition,,* ed. by Eric Hobsbawm and Terence Ranger (Cambridge: Canto, 1983), pp.1–14; and Anthony Giddens, 'The Nature of Modernity', in *The Giddens Reader,,* ed. by Philip Cassell (Basingstoke: Macmillan, 1993), pp.284–316. These are, of course, just two of the many theoretical works one could cite on this topic.
3. The edition used is: Walter Scott, *Ivanhoe*, ed. by Ian Duncan (Oxford: Oxford University Press, 1996).
4. See in particular John Breuilly, *The Formation of the First German Nation-State 1800–1871* (Basingstoke: Macmillan, 1996).
5. On the Wandering Jew legend in general, see *The Wandering Jew: Essays in the Interpretation of a Christian Legend*, ed. by Galit Hasan-Rokem and Alan Dundes (Bloomington, IN: Indiana University Press, 1986).
6. There is no comprehensive treatment of the Wandering Jew in European or even German literature. For a discussion of the figure across various genres, see Mona Körte, *Die Uneinholbarkeit des Verfolgten: Der Ewige Jude in der literarischen Phantastik* (Frankfurt and New York: Campus, 2000), esp. pp.69–132. An overview of the period in question can be found in *Ahasvers Spur: Dichtungen und Dokumente vom 'Ewigen Juden'*, ed. by Mona Körte and Robert Stockhammer (Leipzig: Reclam, 1995).
7. Friedrich Hebbel, *Sämtliche Werke: Historisch-kritische Ausgabe*. Vol. I,, ed. by Richard Maria Werner (Berlin: Behr, 1904), 1–82.
8. Johann Nestroy, *Stücke: Historisch-kritische Ausgabe*. Vol. 26/II,, ed. by John R. P. McKenzie (Vienna: Deuticke, 1998), 85–149.
9. See Matthias Richter, *Die Sprache jüdischer Figuren in der deutschen Literatur (1750–1933): Studien zu Form und Funktion* (Göttingen: Wallstein, 1995), esp. pp.97–113, 122–32.
10. See Heinrich Heine, *Die Bäder von Lucca*, in: *Sämtliche Schriften*, ed. by Klaus Briegleb (Berlin: Ullstein, 1981), pp.390–470. An extensive interpretation of the novella is contained in my *Inciting Laughter: The Development of 'Jewish Humor' in 19th Century German Culture* (Berlin and New York: Walther de Gruyter, 1999), pp.157–73.
11. See Harry E. Shaw, *Forms of Historical Fiction: Sir Walter Scott and his Successors* (Ithaca, NY: Cornell University Press, 1983), pp.51–149.
12. Criticism on German historical fiction has by and large failed to address to topic of Jewishness. For general characterisations of the genre, see: Hans Dieter Huber, *Historische Romane in der ersten Hälfte des 19. Jahrhunderts* (Munich: Wilhelm Fink, 1978); Hugo

Aust, *Der historische Roman* (Stuttgart: Metzler, 1994); and Brent O. Petersen, 'German Nationalism after Napoleon: Caste and Regional Identities in Historical Fiction 1815–1830', *German Quarterly* 68 (1995), 287–303.

13. See Lionel Gossman, *Between History and Literature* (Cambridge, MA: Harvard University Press, 1990), pp.242–3.
14. See Florian Krobb, *Die schöne Jüdin: Jüdische Frauengestalten in der deutschsprachigen Erzählliteratur vom 17. Jahrhundert bis zum ersten Weltkrieg.* (Tübingen: Niemeyer, 1993), esp. pp.1–13, 123–31.
15. Franz Grillparzer, 'Die Jüdin von Toledo', in *Sämtliche Werke*, vol. II, ed. by Peter Frank und Karl Pörnbacher (Munich: Carl Hanser, 1960–5), 449–518. The long delay between the play's completion and its first publication and performance was probably the result of scruples concerning its controversial erotic subject matter.
16. Ibid., 468.
17. Ibid. 477.
18. Karl Spindler, *Der Jude: Deutsches Sittengemälde aus der ersten Hälfte des fünfzehnten Jahrhunderts.* 3 vols (Stuttgart: Franckh, 1827).
19. There are no monographs specifically devoted to the blood libel as a literary motif. For historical accounts of its evolution and influence in nineteenth-century culture, see: Jonathan Frankel, *The Damascus Affair: 'Ritual Murder', Politics and the Jews in 1840* (Cambridge: Cambridge University Press, 1997); Rainer Erb and Werner Bergmann, *Die Nachtseite der Judenemanzipation: Der Widerstand gegen die Integration der Juden in Deutschland 1780–1860* (Berlin: Metropol, 1989), esp. pp.241–50; and Stefan Rohrbacher, *Gewalt im Biedermeier: Antijüdische Ausschreitungen in Vormärz und Revolution (1812–1848/9)* (Frankfurt am Main and New York: Campus, 1993), esp. pp.62–93.
20. Compare Scott (see note 3), pp.499–501, with Spindler (see note 18), III: 361.
21. Wilhelm Hauff, *Jud Süß*, in *Sämtliche Werke*, 3 vols,, ed. by Sybille von Steinsdorff (Munich: Winkler, 19700, II: 476–538. An extensive interpretation of Hauff's novella can be found in my 'The Wandering Court Jew and The Hand of God: Wilhelm Hauff's *Jud Süß* as Historical Fiction', *The Modern Language Review* (93) 1998: 724–40. As in that essay, I will use the spelling variant in German to differentiate between Süß the literary figure and Süss-Oppenheimer the historical person.
22. There are no monographs on the Court Jew as a literary figure, but a good general description is contained in Barbara Gerber, *Jud Süß, Aufstieg und Fall im frühen 18. Jahrhundert: Ein Beitrag zur historischen Antisemitismus- und Rezeptionsforschung* (Hamburg: Hans Christians, 1990), esp. pp.51–146.
23. Hauff (see note 21), 517.
24. Ibid., 521.
25. Heine, *Der Rabbi von Bacherach* in *Sämtliche Schriften*, ed. by Klaus Briegleb (Berlin: Ullstein, 1981), [vol.???]: 459–502.
26. Compare Briegleb in Heine, *Sämtliche Schriften* (see note 25), II: 827–41 with Manfred Windfuhr in Heinrich Heine, *historisch-kritische Gesamtausgabe der Werke* (Hamburg: Hoffmann und Campe, 1994), V: 500–612.
27. Heine, *Sämtliche Schriften* (see note 25), I: 473.
28. See *Geschichten aus dem Ghetto*, ed. by Jost Hermand (Frankfurt am Main: Athenäum, 1987), esp. the editor's introduction, pp.7–21.
29. See, for instance, Jeffrey Sammons, 'Heine's "Rabbi von Bacherach": The Unresolved Tensions', *German Quarterly*, 37 (1964): 26–38.
30. Berthold Auerbach, *Spinoza*, in *Gesammelte Schriften*, vols. XI–XII (Stuttgart: Cotta, 1864).
31. See Peter Zimmermann, *Der Bauernroman: Antifeudalismus-Konservatismus-Faschismus* (Stuttgart: Metzler, 1975).

Distinctiveness and Change:
The Depiction of Jews in Theodor Fontane
and Other Bourgeois Realist Authors

FLORIAN KROBB

Two labels have been used in German literary criticism to describe the second half of the nineteenth century as an epoch of literary history: 'Poetic Realism' [*Poetischer Realismus*] and 'Bourgeois Realism' [*Bürgerlicher Realismus*]. The former term is generally meant to indicate that no depiction of extra-literary reality in this period is self-contained/self-sufficient, that it is always intended to serve a higher, poetic purpose, and that consequently there exists a tension between any material substance ('reality') and its literary representation ('Realism').[1] The latter term draws attention to the fact that the main concern of this literary movement – arising from the personal backgrounds of its main authors and reflected in the social status of most of their works' characters – is indeed the bourgeoisie, from the *petit bourgeoisie* to the *haute bourgeoisie*, with a particular emphasis on the professional or industrial middle classes. The fringes of these social strata also come into view – impoverished artisans at the lower end for example, and particularly the social group that framed the social aspirations of the middle classes, the aristocracy, and other strands of nobility like the service nobility (military and administrative) or the Prussian landed gentry, the *Junkers*. But this kind of bourgeois literature is not only defined by its social context; the world view expressed in this literature, the debates on the individual and the collective, autonomy and responsibility, self-reliance and mutuality reflect middle-class concerns and perspectives as well.

The period that saw the transformation of society from a feudal, hierarchical and corporate structure to a potentially egalitarian and democratic, open and merit-based organism also witnessed the transformation of the Jewish community in German-speaking central Europe from a marginalised fringe group largely confined to an existence outside the mainstream of society (commonly referred to as 'the ghetto') to a minority group within the middle class which rapidly became the dominant political, social and cultural force. This process has been described as the 'embourgeoisement' of the German Jews; their forms of socialisation and association, their chosen professions and living standards, their educational preferences and political persuasions all provide indicators for their convergence with non-Jewish middle-class society.[2]

The emergence of a German-Jewish literature, in which the concerns of acculturated middle-class Jews since the 1830s were negotiated, is a reflection of this transition.[3] At the same time, the portrayal of Jewish characters in the works of non-Jewish authors of Bourgeois Realism is, first and foremost, an acknowledgement of the very presence of Jewish people in the German middle-class universe, the world depicted in their writings. Secondly, it is an attempt to define the Jews' position therein. Many of the conflicts and tensions that form the content of these narratives arise out of the discrepancies between the position in society Jews aspired to and indeed occupied in reality, and the position the Christian authors assigned them to. A further dimension in the portrayal of Jews transpires when the literary figures in question are not merely conceived as representations of reality but become symbols or even icons for complex social and cultural developments like a perceived decline in public morality, the commercialisation of inter-personal relationships, or various other (often 'scientific') aspects of (often undesired) 'progress'.

Amongst the first attempts to translate into literary practice programmatic ideas that pertained to the daily life of the middle classes is Gustav Freytag's novel *Soll und Haben* [Debit and Credit], 1855. It is no coincidence that this literary manifesto of Bourgeois Realism contains one of the most controversial Jewish figures of nineteenth-century German literature. *Soll und Haben*, together with Wilhelm Raabe's novel *Der Hungerpastor* (1862) – a novel that uses the same structural device of contrasting a Christian and a Jewish biography – are often seen as the most striking examples of literary anti semitism of their era. Racist ideologues found in them a wealth of propagandist material; for more recent critics they provide an object of moral indignation and an example of the mechanisms of stigmatisation.[4] Both responses fail to do justice to the two novels, and even though much research has been undertaken to explain and contextualise such contentious portrayals of Jews,[5] they continue to be quoted, and condemned, as prime examples of nineteenth-century stereotyping and stigmatising.[6] Certainly, the antagonists of these novels, Veitel Itzig and Moses Freudenstein alias Theophile Stein, are portrayed as dangerous to their Christian rivals, and their means of self-advancement as contradictory to such middle-class values as decency, honesty and uprightness. Certainly, they comply with and reinforce stereotypes of the 'ugly', ambitious, sexually aggressive Jew. Certainly, the texts allowed anti-semites of the day and of the first half of the twentieth century to find their own views confirmed in them, and only very careful analysis of both novels can counter such readings. However, there are wider contexts that have to be considered if we want to appreciate these two novels as documents of the public discourse of their time.

First of all, both novels document Jewish attempts to move from the fringes of society into its very centre. In this respect the literary figures are reflections of real social trends. If Jews were increasingly becoming part of the middle classes, if they participated in the professions, in trade and industry, they were being judged by the standards and values that the middle classes set for themselves. *Soll und Haben* and *Der Hungerpastor* demonstrate how Bourgeois Realist authors negotiate such standards and values; and the fact that they identify the shortcomings in this respect with *homines novi*, new ascendants to middle-class society, does not automatically exclude such new arrivals from the bourgeois consensus, but extends the standards and values to them, i.e. sets them as universal. Interestingly, many minor Jewish characters in both novels show the potential of becoming 'useful' members of bourgeois society if they do not follow in the footsteps of the antagonists who are found guilty of anti-social behaviour and selfish means of self-advancement. Both novels subject bourgeois society to public scrutiny by using the image of the Jew as a mirror; both novels debate the terms of bourgeois society by rejecting the admissibility of certain types of 'Jewish' behaviour into their folds, but by no means excluding Jews altogether.

On the contrary. The second half of the nineteenth century was the period in German literary history with more Jewish characters in works by non-Jewish authors than any other epoch. This in itself is testimony to the importance attributed to the Jewish element of the population in general, and of the middle classes in particular, by the authors of the time. The portrayals of Jewish characters are so varied and rich that no simple tendency or even dominant trend (e.g. anti- or philo-semitic) can be identified. Jewish characters can be found in the works of Freytag and Raabe (and by no means only the notorious works discussed above), in the works of Theodor Fontane and many other, lesser-known writers of the time. They occur in historical novels (Felix Dahn's *Ein Kampf um Rom* [A Fight for Rome] of 1876 was a huge bestseller), in *Bildungsromanen* (*Soll und Haben* and *Der Hungerpastor* are in fact examples of this genre that reflects middle-class ideology like no other), in contemporary and social novels, in fiction set in urban as well as in rural environments.

This illustrates two things: (1) It suggests that the construction of a bourgeois self-image involved Jews as 'new arrivals' who could, in literary representation, act as mirrors or foils for the concerns of non-Jews whose preoccupations, fears and aspirations were projected onto Jews and, as if in an experimental set-up, were negotiated through the image of Jews. (2) As pointed out above, it highlights furthermore that Jews were now acknowledged participants in bourgeois society. The literary texts can therefore help to identify where the negotiations about their place in society were located, how they were perceived, and which aspects of the relationship between minority and majority were problematic.

A study of representations of Jews in literary texts of this period can serve the very straightforward purpose of discerning the Jews' position and perception in society: in which professions, economic circumstances, family set-ups were they shown, with which political convictions are they associated, how assimilated or distinct were they perceived to be at this time? In this respect, the question of stereotyping is of course an important one, but the attempt to identify anti-semitic tendencies in the portrayal of Jews must also include investigating the reasons and purposes behind this phenomenon. The literary strategies involved in creating an effect that might appear misguided from today's vantage point must be understood in their own historical context, a context that can broadly be considered as the entire public debate on middle-class identity and the position of Jews within its framework. The literary debate on such issues follows its own conventions, uses its own devices (images, genres) and creates as well as reacts to its own intrinsic expectations. Such determinants also need to be taken into consideration. Not moral judgement, but historically adequate understanding should be the modern approach to historical depictions of Jews.

The œuvre of Theodor Fontane (1819–98) offers particularly rewarding material for this kind of investigation. While the image of the Jews and the author's attitude towards them has been the subject of much critical attention in the case of one of the outstanding representatives of mature German Realism, Wilhelm Raabe,[7] his contemporary Theodor Fontane has, until very recently, not been the subject of scholarly scrutiny with respect to his portrayal of Jews. In spite of the opinion – as one of the most knowledgeable Fontane scholars recently put it – that 'eine solche Arbeit ... mindestens ebensoviel Erkenntniswert [hat] wie noch so interessante Werkinterpretationen im Dutzend' [one such study could contribute to our knowledge as much as interesting interpretations of Fontane's work in their dozens],[8] the prevalent position of commentators is one of relative helplessness: ambiguity and ambivalence are the most common verdicts on the attitudes towards Jews of the author, who, paradoxically, was labelled a 'Philosemitic Antisemite'.[9] A survey of Fontane's letters could indeed lead to the conclusion that he harboured anti-semitic feelings against individuals in his acquaintance and against the entire group. In Fontane's anniversary year 1998, his alleged anti-semitism became the subject of much heated debate,[10] but the result remained largely inconclusive because it pursued the question of whether or not Fontane was an anti-semite, and not how his ambivalent stance illuminates and reflects the situation of his time.

Fontane's personal outbursts of an anti-semitic nature are not easily reconciled with the urbanity and enlightened social analysis that characterise his works. His works, after all, were what Fontane put into the public domain whereas his letters were indeed private; his works contain a view of reality that was not tempered by anger, disappointment or caprice. In this regard even the latest and most comprehensive study of Fontane and the Jews falls short in that it reiterates the view that 'latent anti-Semitism' is to be found in his thinking, but fails to address those aspects of his work that reflect not only personal opinion but general attitudes and characteristic views and images of Jews in society at the time.[11] It also fails to take account of the textuality of the depictions of Jews in Fontane's works, the fact that the author never depicted Jews solely in order to depict Jews, but that he always had additional aims in mind. It is the very accidental, or even peripheral, status of Jewish characters in Fontane's works that gives them their special value as unmediated, almost coincidental reflections of a collective societal discourse. Norbert Mecklenburg has summed this up in an apt formulation: Fontane's works, he writes, contain the social polyphony of his time, in a way that they actually sound polyphonous. In his works the discourses of his time are cited and 'exhibited'.[12] He allows readers glimpses at attitudes, views and images that capture dissonant standpoints, but it is the very multitude of voices that conveys something of the essence of the time that it reflects.

'Eigentlich alles schon wie Harem': The Outsider's Perspective

In Fontane's novels, the most vibrant, colourful and poignant portrayals of characters are provided in the conversations of other characters. However, by being part of direct speech, such information loses the authoritative weight that a narrator's voice (even an omniscient one) would have lent to the description. Every statement or judgement is dependent on its perspective, and more is revealed about the speaker than about the person discussed. An investigation into Fontane's Jewish characters, one could consequently claim, would hence reveal more about the commentators on Jewish issues and Jewish people in society than about the Jews themselves. This in itself is valuable since the interplay between Jewish and non-Jewish people contained the possibility of conflict and friction. In Fontane's novel *Die Poggenpuhls* (1896) the demise of a Prussian officer's family is narrated. When Leo von Poggenpuhl, the young officer stationed in an Eastern Prussian garrison, comments on life in this place, he does not give a reliable description of the person he refers to as epitomising the atmosphere in this town; he rather allows insights into his own preoccupations and narrow-mindedness:

> Greulich. Wenn nicht das bißchen Jeu wäre und die paar Judenmädchen... Oder die paar Christenmädchen; bloß die Jüdinnen sind hübscher. ...Schöne schwarze Person, Taille so, und Augen..., ich sage dir, Augen, die reinen Mandelaugen und eigentlich alles schon wie Harem.[13]

> [Horrible. If it wasn't for a bit of gambling and a few Jewish girls; or Christian girls, only the Jewish ones are prettier... Beautiful black-haired person, what a waist line, and eyes, I assure you, eyes, pure almonds, and really everything almost like a harem.]

The speaker here is evidently caught up in his own prejudices, in this instance visibly a clichéd image of the 'oriental', odalisque 'beautiful Jewess'.[14] The observation has nothing to do with any real encounter with small-town, Eastern, or more traditional Jewish women whose acquaintance would have been new for the young Berliner. The message of this passage is obviously not that any Jewess would have conformed to this stereotype, but rather that an inexperienced junior officer boasts about imaginary adventures by means of such juicy innuendoes. What this quotation illustrates holds true for most other instances of Jews in Fontane's works: their primary purpose is to characterise the people who make them. Their perspectives and the situations in which encounters take place (in this example, the Eastern garrison) contain the substantive information on the perception of Jews in society. It is, however, most revealing that the author seems to need 'others', third parties that is, as a foil or mirror against which the attitudes and viewpoints of his characters can be 'exhibited'. As regards the portrayal of Jews, the bottom line is that the reader is invited to share a non-Jewish perspective on the Jews, but that this perspective is at the same time exposed as biased, not generally valid or objective. The reader is hence encouraged to question the foundations and assumptions on which these perspectives are based. The conversations in Fontane's novels have been called 'rituals of demarcation' and negotiations of the terms of normality and apartheid, of similarity and distinctiveness.[15] Demarcation, the reconfirmation of difference, is one of the purposes of Fontane's portrayals of Jews, but one that is reciprocal in that it concerns Jews and non-Jews alike.

'Rebecca oder Rahel oder Sarah ...': Distinctiveness

The issue of identity is predominant in Fontane's works. The question whether those Jews with whom the gentile protagonists are confronted are recognisable as Jews, whether they have concealed their identity or why their Jewish identity is not immediately obvious becomes a topic of many a conversation amongst Jews and gentiles alike. The drafts and plans for *Storch von Adebar* illustrate Fontane's desire to make his central Jewish character immediately identifiable as a Jewess if that suited him:

> Rebecca oder Rahel oder Sarah ist eine reizende kleine Person, heiter, liebenswürdig, aber prononciert jüdisch in ihrem Profil, vor allem auch in Haltung und Bewegung der Arme.[16]

> [Rebecca or Rahel or Sarah is a delightful little person, jolly, pleasant, but strikingly Jewish in her profile, particularly in her comportment and the movements of her arms.]

In the end, Fontane chose the name Rebecca Gerson von Bleichröder for this character. This way, her Jewishness is indicated not only in her biblical first name, but also through her family name which is a clear and direct allusion to Bismarck's banker and allows an immediate location of the figure in a distinctly identifiable social context, that of Berlin's financial *haute bourgeoisie*.[17]

In a case where the immediate identification seemed undesirable for the development of the plot, i.e. where the Jewish identity of a given figure needed to come as a surprise, or needed to become the subject of speculation, Fontane exploits this to good effect: In *Unwiederbringlich* (1891) it is the encounter and identification with the Danish *Hoffräulein* (lady-in-waiting) Ebba von Rosenberg that leads to Count Holk's estrangement from his wife and his traditional reclusive and narrow lifestyle. The partly Jewish ancestry of Ebba von Rosenberg is revealed suddenly in a genealogical discussion that says more about the naïveté of Count Holk than about the descendant of the Swedish Court Jew herself. As one possible explanation of her name Holk offers the following:

> Gewiß, mein gnädigstes Fräulein, ich meine Rosenberg. Genealogisches zählt nämlich zu meinen kleinen Liebhabereien, und die zweite Frau meines Großonkels war eine Rosenberg; so bin ich

denn in ihre Geschlechtssagen einigermaßen eingeweiht. Alle
Rosenbergs, wenigstens alle die, die sich Rosenberg-Gruszczynski
nennen ... stammen von einem Bruder des Erzbischofs Adalbert
von Prag, der, an der sogenannten Bernsteinküste, von der Kanzel
herabgerissen und von den heidnischen Preußen erschlagen wurde
(NFA, V, 87).

[Certainly, my dearest lady, I mean Rosenberg. Genealogy counts
amongst my little hobbies, and the second wife of my grand uncle
was a Rosenberg, and I am quite familiar with the lore of this
dynasty. All Rosenbergs – at least those called Rosenberg-
Gruszczynski ... are descendants of a brother of the Archbishop
Adalbert of Prague who, on the so-called amber coast, was dragged
from the pulpit and slaughtered by pagan Prussians.]

To which proposition she replies:

'Zu meinem Bedauern auch das nicht. ...Ich bin nämlich eine
Rosenberg-Meyer   oder   richtiger   eine   Meyer-Rosenberg,
Enkeltochter des in der schwedischen Geschichte wohlbekannten
Meyer-Rosenberg, Lieblings- und Leibjuden König Gustavs III.'
    Holk schrak ein wenig zusammen; das Fräulein aber fuhr in
einem affektiert ruhigen Tone fort: 'Enkeltochter Meyer-
Rosenbergs, den König Gustav später unter dem Namen eines
Baron Rosenberg nobilitierte, Baron Rosenberg von Filehne,
welchem preußisch-polnischen Ort wir entstammen' (NFA, V, 87).

['Regrettably not that, either. As a matter of fact, I am a Rosenberg-
Meyer, or, more precisely, Meyer-Rosenberg, granddaughter of the
favourite Court Jew of King Gustav III, the Meyer-Rosenberg who
is so well-known in Swedish history.'
    Holk was a bit startled, but the lady continued in an ostensibly
calm tone: 'Granddaughter of Meyer-Rosenberg who was later
ennobled by King Gustav and given the name of Baron Rosenberg
of Filehne from which Prussian-Polish place I come.']

This episode illustrates not only that assumptions about identities derived
from names can be dangerous, since, in this case, the name in question
could be, with equal justification, traced back to a Christian martyr and
a Swedish Court Jew; it also shows how this bombshell is used more for
the characterisation of the figures involved than to provide substantial
information on historical or social facts pertaining to the situation or
perception of Jews in society: the narrative focus here is firmly on the
reaction of the characters – Holk's 'schrak ein wenig zusammen' [gave a

start] and Ebba's 'affektiert ruhige[r] Ton' [artificially calm tone of voice] – which are both apt epithets for their personalities and the roles they play in the story. At the same time, the reference to Court Jews as precursors of the middle-class Jewish community of Fontane's own times evokes the whole development of Jewish embourgeoisement, i.e. the historical development that brought persons like Ebba von Rosenberg into a similar social sphere to Holk's own in the first place. The interchangeability or arbitrariness of the derivations of the false and the correct explanations of the name is further highlighted by the fact that Ebba is able to add a genealogical anecdote of her own which matches Holk's in terms of the significance of their respective backgrounds:

> Und nun lassen Sie mich ... noch in Kürze hinzusetzen, daß es mit diesem Nobilitierungsakte allerdings eilte, denn drei Tage später wurde der ritterliche und für unser Haus so unvergeßliche König von Leutnant Anckarström erschossen. Ein ebenso balladenhafter Hergang wie der ermordete Bischof (NFA, V, 87).

> [Let me briefly add that the patent of nobilitation indeed came just in time, for three days later the knightly and, in our family, unforgettable king was shot by Lieutenant Anckarström. Quite as balladesque a plot as that of the murdered bishop.]

The fact that the histories of both names – the ancient noble name Holk recalls, and the relatively new one of the Jewish family – are almost interchangeable in terms of their anecdotal value, indicates a certain levelling of formerly clear-cut distinctions – the exclusivity of genealogies and family histories of old and noble dynasties – and must hence be understood as a sign of the changing times where the identifications and signifiers of old are no longer valid. This dimension of the character Ebba von Rosenberg (whether she, as a lady-in-waiting at a Christian court, was actually baptised or not, is never revealed in the novel) is foreshadowed by another Jewish character, a veterinary surgeon. In *Unwiederbringlich* the withholding and sudden revelation of Ebba's Jewish background is a central element in the development of the plot: it underlines the 'otherness' that had made her so alluring to Holk in the first place, and hence forms a milestone in the story of his dangerous attraction to her.

A second example: The novel *L'Adultera* (1882) is essentially the story of an adulterous affair between the wife of one newly-baptised financier and another. In the introduction of a guest to the van der Straaten household it is one single letter (and the pronunciation of a family name) around which the ironic discourse on the Jewish or non-Jewish identity of this character focuses. The speaker here is the Christian wife of the newly-baptised financier van der Straaten, who herself has, in their household, the function of diverting attention from the Jewish descent of the householder. Van der Straaten, the narrator insists, had for quite some time now enjoyed the privilege 'die Honneurs seines Hauses nicht durch eine Judith, sondern durch eine Melanie machen lassen zu können' [to have as a hostess not somebody called Judith but somebody called Melanie] (NFA, IV, 8). Their discussion of the expected house guest (who later becomes Melanie's lover) goes as follows:

> 'Ebenezer Rubehn', wiederholte Melanie langsam und jede Silbe betonend. 'Ich bekenne dir offen, daß mir etwas Christlich-Germanisches lieber gewesen wäre. Viel lieber. Als ob wir an deinem Ezechiel nicht schon gerade genug hätten! Und nun Ebenezer. Ebenezer Rubehn! Ich bitte dich, was soll dieser Accent grave, dieser Ton auf der letzten Silbe? Suspekt, im höchsten Grade suspekt!'
> 'Du mußt wissen, er schreibt sich mit einem h.'
> 'Mit einem h! Du wirst doch nicht verlangen, daß ich dies h für echt und ursprünglich nehmen soll? Einschiebsel. Versuchte Leugnung des Tatsächlichen, absichtliche Verschleierung, hinter der ich nichtsdestoweniger alle zwölf Söhne Jakobs stehen sehe' (NFA, IV, 18).

> ['Ebenezer Rubehn', Melanie repeated slowly, emphasising every syllable. 'I confess openly that I would have preferred something Christian and Germanic. Much preferred. As if we had not enough with your Ezechiel. I ask you, what is the purpose of this accent, this stress on the last syllable. Suspicious in the highest degree.'
> 'You need to know, he spells his name with an h.'
> 'With an h! I hope you don't think that I accept this h as genuine. An insertion, an attempt at negating the facts, deliberate camouflage behind which I still recognise all twelve of Jacob's sons.']

With the designation as 'suspect', Fontane re-uses an epithet that had been used in the introduction of van der Straaten himself, whose 'etwas suspekte[r]' name Ezechiel had long been changed to Ezel (NFA, IV, 9). The name change not only conceals the Jewish identity, it also possesses a mythological, Wagnerian edge, as if copied straight out of the *Nibelungenlied* (where Ezel is the name under which Attila the Hun features) – a narrative strategy that Thomas Mann was later to use in his novella *Wälsungenblut* where the assimilatory aspirations of the well-to-do Jewish parents are reflected in their naming their children Siegmund and Sieglind. In reality the change to allegedly un-Jewish names, intended to conceal identification as Jewish and to emphasise allegiance to the German nation, is shown as backfiring, as the artificial name draws attention to, and thus subverts, the original purpose of its adoption.

Fontane thus 'exhibits' the desire of assimilated Jewish families to keep their Jewish identity as unobtrusive as possible, to subsume it into a non-identifiable bourgeois identity, and their sensitivity towards anything that could be a reminder of a traditional Jewish existence that did not seem desirable or acceptable any more. Fontane thus exposes an assimilationist psychological or mental state, and probably ridicules it by means of this heated discussion about one single letter.

Apart from revealing names there are other significant features like, in the case of the female Jewish protagonist in the projected story *Storch von Adebar*, the movement of Rebecca von Bleichröder's limbs. She is described as 'prononciert jüdisch in ihrem Profil, vor allem auch in Haltung und Bewegung der Arme. Sie wußte das auch und scherzte darüber' [Jewish in quite an obvious way, as regarded her profile, her comportment and the movement of her limbs. She was actually quite aware of this and joked about it].[18] The heightened self-awareness and self-irony links her with Ebba von Rosenberg and contrasts both Jewesses to the two males with whom they come into contact, Graf Holk in *Unwiederbringlich* and Adebar in the fragment that bears his name as title. Both of them flirt with the more liberal, frivolous and self-deprecating outlook on life that the two young ladies represent, and both of them fail in their attempts at leaving behind the old-fashioned mode of thinking that they are caught in. The description and self-presentation of the two Jewesses also contrasts starkly with the image evoked in statements like that of Leo von Poggenpuhl. True identity is hence a matter of perception, Fontane suggests, and Jewish signifiers, names, genealogies and 'typical' behaviour can conceal just as much as they can reveal. Fontane's description of Jewish figures thus highlights the human desire for clear identifications and neat categories, but it also indicates just how misleading such signals can be.

Another feature of Jewish distinctiveness is their language. In *Der Stechlin* (1898) – the story of an old Prussian *Junker* and his family – the protagonist's Jewish banker Baruch Hirschfeld speaks German with a hint of 'jargon', the inverted syntax so characteristic of *Judendeutsch*. This treatment of the language of a character differs in no way from that of other, non-Jewish characters who are all marked by idiosyncrasies in their speech, ranging from the broad dialect of peasants, to brisk and dashing military parlance, to the educated or pseudo-educated lingo of other, gentile characters. Baruch Hirschfeld falls into this 'jargon' only in conversation with his own son Isidor in an exchange on the latter's political ambitions:

> Isidor ... Ich hab dich gesehn, als du hast charmiert mit dem Mariechen von nebenan und hast ihr aufgebunden das Schürzenband, und sie hat dir gegeben einen Klaps. Du hast gebuhlt um das christliche Mädchen. Und du buhlst jetzt, wo die Wahl kommt, um die öffentliche Meinung. Und das mit dem Mädchen, das hab ich dir verziehen. Aber die öffentliche Meinung verzeih ich dir nicht (NFA, VI, 151).

> [Isidor, I have watched your flirting with Marie next door. I have watched you untying her apron laces and she gave you a smack. You have courted the Christian girl. And now that the election is coming, you are courting public opinion. I have forgiven your advances to the girl, but the advances to public opinion I am unable to forgive.]

In this passage the old Jew voices a conservative opinion, one that is sceptical of populist political movements like Socialism. He remains true to his convictions and to his traditional position as a kind of Court Jew to old Dubslav von Stechlin who himself is a traditionalist dinosaur and considers old Baruch as his close friend.[19] This episode illustrates that it is not the Jews as a racially or otherwise defined group but a type of modern, progressive Jew that can be used to symbolise social, political and cultural change. This change is viewed mainly sceptically since it is perceived as muddying the water and undermining old hierarchies, thereby rendering inherited distinctions and demarcations meaningless. The unquestioned boundaries between old *Junker* and old Jew keeps their relationship a friendly and mutually beneficial one; their world seems in order as long as an old-style tolerance continues to acknowledge difference, and language is one tool that Fontane uses to underline this unconscious and hence unpretentious sense of distinctiveness. The new generation threatens to overthrow such neat distinctions, and with it the safety of time-honoured ways of cohabitation.

'Fortschrittlich, aber reell': Change

Jews are frequently associated by the non-Jewish characters in Fontane's works with an incomprehensible, and generally rejected, form of 'progress'. Or is it that this form of progress manifests itself in ways that are perceived to be inappropriate, since they originate from Jews – social parvenus? The veterinary doctor in *Unwiederbringlich* is a case in point.

The episode in which he features (insignificant for the development of the plot) seems to foreshadow Holk's encounter with Ebba in Copenhagen. Unlike Isidor Hirschfeld in *Der Stechlin*, his field of innovation is not politics but applied science. Heralded as 'Wunder von Tierarzt', 'tierärztlicher Pfiffikus und Mann der Aufklärung' [Miracle of a vet, veterinary know-it-all and man of enlightenment], his methods are said to be purely rational and work without 'alles Geheimnisvolle oder gar Wunderbare' [anything secretive or miraculous] (NFA, V, 13, 14). He thus becomes a representative of the scientific age, the secularised world whose approach is no longer marked by awe for the inexplicable. Again, the man himself does not appear in the novel at all, he is only spoken of. The Holks' decision not to receive him in their castle reveals more about the prejudices and insecurities of the castle's inhabitants than about the veterinarian himself; and most revealing is the fact that his reported stylistic *faux pas* of comparing the cleanliness of feeding troughs to that of baptismal fonts provokes his ostracisation. Understood as 'orientalischer Vergleich, den man ihm zugute halten muß' [an oriental simile that one should not hold against him], this supposed violation of good manners is ascribed to the Jewish origin of the veterinarian (NFA, V, 14). The revelation of the identity of the person in question is delayed so that the revelation of his Jewishness, like a punch-line, suggests a conclusive explanation to his behaviour and activates the prejudices of the readers as well (who else but a Jew would commit such a verbal desecration? is the suggestive conjecture implied). He is also identified by a 'revealing' name ['Er heißt nämlich Lissauer'] (NFA, V, 14). Moreover, we have here the equation of the secularised, demystified, scientific world view (which does not even respect the sacred symbols of religion) with the 'Jewish mind'. The family doctor Dr. Moscheles in *Der Stechlin* is a similar case. He is introduced with the rather cryptic but still evocative words 'neue Schule, moderner Mensch' [new school, modern person] which links his scientific outlook and methodology inexorably to his Jewish origin (NFA, VIII, 298).

Such passages seem to foreshadow the widespread anti-semitic stance of accusing Jews of over-intellectualism and of a deconstructive, subversive intelligence as well as a lack of genuine, productive or positive engagement. But again: the narratives are not concerned with the desirability of hygiene in animal husbandry or the advent of new treatment methods in human medicine; they are not concerned with the personalities or the professionalism of the Jewish scientists in question. Views like the ones quoted only reveal that bigotry and prejudice manifested themselves *vis à vis* scientific progress and projected change as well as *vis à vis* a previously confined social group. In the case of Lissauer and Moscheles Jewish intelligence and scientific innovation are linked, and this is no coincidence. The strategy seems to reflect contemporary ways of thinking in that intellectualism, scientific progress, Jewishness and blasphemy are identified as sides of the same coin, hallmarks of change and the perceived deterioration of old certainties, the old order. Fontane does not identify with this simplistic world view, he merely acknowledges its existence and exposes it in turn as a sign of his times.

Progress does not automatically mean deterioration. This kind of judgement can never be a universal one anyway; it is always bound to a particular point of view. Other views than these occur in Fontane's works. After science and politics, the Jews in *Mathilde Möhring* (written 1891, first published 1907) represent another social area in which Jews could be equated with 'progress': the economy. In a letter to her mother the protagonist Mathilde Möhring, herself a pragmatist who had masterminded her husband's rise to the position of provincial governor, comments on the reliability of a local Jewish businessman in looking after her late husband's affairs:

> Silberstein, Firma Silberstein & Ehrenthal, wird auch alles besorgen, es sind sehr reelle Leute, fortschrittlich, aber reell
> (NFA, VI, 300)

> [Silberstein of the company Silberstein & Ehrenthal will take care of everything; they are honourable people, progressive but honourable.].

If it were Jews alone who represented this realm of unwanted 'progress' (which is not the case – in *Der Stechlin* there are other figures much more caricatured than either Hirschfeld Junior or Moscheles; in *Unwiederbringlich* Ebba is by no means the only representative of the liberal atmosphere at the Danish court) or if, on the other hand, Jews were attributed this one role, to represent rapid and ill-conceived change (which is not the case, since they are also cited as examples of the old ways of thinking), then Fontane's literary treatment of the Jews could, with some justification, be labelled as anti-semitic. However, the analysis must lead to quite a different conclusion. With the help of Jewish figures, Fontane's works reveal the insecurity and helplessness of certain social groups in a time of transition and change. Fontane's representation of Jews is a device to 'exhibit' such insecurities and anxieties at a time when new and incomprehensible departures were becoming visible within the bourgeois universe. It is true that the feelings of insecurity – the gap opened by the crumbling of traditional ways of life and traditional certainties – were preyed upon by anti-semites; however, insecurity and puzzlement themselves are not intrinsically anti-semitic. The fact that such identifications could be made so easily, that encounters, discourses and conflicts could enter so freely into Fontane's narratives in itself suggests that the intention of the narratives was not to re-marginalise Jews or even to suggest their removal from society altogether (as is the case with Wilhelm von Polenz' novel *Der Büttnerbauer* [1895], a book Fontane knew and liked).[20] In spite of problems and tensions, misconceptions and misunderstandings, in Fontane's works the consensus of bourgeois society that embraced Jews and gentiles alike still holds.

'Kommen Sie, Cohn': Consensus

In Theodor Fontane's great late novel *Der Stechlin* it is an old, principled but prejudiced *Stiftsdame*, Adelheid von Stechlin, who, in a letter warning her nephew against a marriage outside the gentry of his home county, treats the Jews like any other social group she mistrusts:

> Da sind zum Beispiel die rheinischen jungen Damen, also die von Köln und Aachen; nun ja, die mögen ganz gut sein, aber sie sind katholisch, und wenn sie nicht katholisch sind, dann sind sie was andres, wo der Vater erst geadelt wurde. Neben den rheinischen haben wir dann die westfälischen. Über die ließe sich reden. Aber Schlesien. Die schlesischen Herrschaften ... sind alle so gut wie polnisch und leben von Jeu ... . Und dann sind da noch weiterhin die preußischen, das heißt die ostpreußischen, wo schon alles aufhört (NFA, VIII, 148).

> [There are, for example, the young ladies from the Rhine provinces, that means those from Cologne and Aachen; well, they may be all right, but they are Catholic, and when they are not Catholic then they are something else where their father was only recently ennobled. And besides those from the Rhineland we have those from Westphalia. We could talk about these. But Silesia. The Silesian magnates are all as good as Polish and live from gambling. Furthermore there are also the Prussians, or rather the East Prussians, that's where the world ends.]

The recently ennobled members of an unspecified denomination in the Prussian *Rheinprovinzen* must be read as an allusion to Jewish industrialists and bankers, an allusion that was presumably understood by Fontane's contemporaries. It seems that here, in the perspective of the Protestant noble spinster, the Jewish minority is seen as nothing special, that the Jewish *haute bourgeoisie* is considered as on a par with Catholic (Rhinelandish, Silesian or Eastern Prussian) aristocracy in the suitability stakes for the marriage prospects of her *Junker* nephew.

In another social sphere, an Eastern provincial town, a similarly
natural, unquestioned sense of the Jews as belonging to the community –
here the small-town notables – is expressed. In *Mathilde Möhring* the
company of Silberstein & Ehrenthal belongs to the institutions of the
small Prussian town, and the daughter of the house chairs a charity for
children 'aller Konfessionen' [of all confessions] together with the wives
of the mayor and the county governor (*Landrat*) (NFA, VI, 291). Later
the funeral of the mayor is attended by 'viel Adel aus der Nähe und die
ganze Bürgerschaft einschließlich der dritten Konfession' [much nobility
from the surrounds and the whole citizenry including the third
confession] (NFA, VI, 299). The 'third confession', it seems, is treated as
one group amongst others which have a place in the social order that is
neither questioned nor frowned upon.

These quotations seem to suggest an entirely unproblematic, even
harmonious relationship between Jews and non-Jews. However, two
observations modify this interpretation of these episodes. Firstly, it is
striking that in the excerpts quoted Fontane avoids identifying the group
in question by the name that was understood then and is still understood
now: Jews. In that respect he departs from his practice of clear, if
sometimes delayed, identification discussed above. To give hints and not
reveal everything in a straightforward way creates a sense of complicity
between narrator and reader; shared though secret knowledge signals
superiority *vis à vis* the third party. The ambivalence between the apparent
normality of a Jewish presence in the social spheres in question and the fact
that they are spoken of, and that something quite unmentionable
surrounds them, signals once more that the question of the portrayal of
Jews in this period defies simple answers. Secondly, none of the quoted
references are presented with any authorial authority. In the *Stechlin*
passage it is clear that the prejudices of a narrow-minded character are
reflected; Jewish 'equality' arises *ex negativo*. In *Mathilde Möhring* the
inclusive character of the community is a function of Mathilde's political
strategy of orchestrating the advancement of herself and her husband from
upstarts and blow-ins from Berlin to small-town mayor and mayoress with
'relaxed pragmatism'.[21] (This career and its methods in masterminding
their advancement are in themselves signs of the new times, of a changing
order.) Mathilde cannot afford to alienate any of the influential groups in
the small community that has appointed her husband chief administrative
officer. The positive image of the Jews in this novel is hence a result of this
non-dogmatic, liberal, but ultimately unprincipled and self-serving spirit.
Again, the passages merely 'exhibit' typical views and attitudes.

Present only in such rather insignificant episodes, conversations or
mere allusions, without any substantial influence on the development of

the plot, the Jewish characters in *Der Stechlin* have been labelled as 'all quite unnecessary, supernumerary'.[22] However, their function within the text does not lie in their contribution to the progress of the story (which, in the case of *Der Stechlin*, is only rudimentary anyway). It contributes to the characterisation of a whole wealth of orientations and persuasions which, in their reference to Jews, resemble one another quite strikingly and hence serve to underline the relativism of perceived notions. On the opposing end of the spectrum of outlooks and convictions from Tante Adelheid is Count Barby, a liberal diplomat who tells the following anecdote:

> Ich verkehre da viel in einem großen Bankierhause, drin alles nicht bloß voll Glanz, sondern auch voll Orden und Uniformen war. Fast zu viel davon. Aber mit einem Male traf ich in einer Ecke, ganz einsam und doch beinahe vergnüglich, einen merkwürdigen Urgreis ... , und als ich mich später bei einem Tischnachbar erkundigte, 'wer denn das sei', da hieß es: 'Ach, das ist ja Onkel Manasse.' Solche Manasses gibt es überall, und sie können unter Umständen auch 'Tante Adelheid' heißen (NFA, VIII, 266).

> [There is a large banker's house that I frequent quite a lot; everything is splendid in it, full of medals and uniforms. Almost too full. But once I met in a corner, completely alone but nonetheless quite content, a strange old man. When I later asked my neighbour at the dinner-table who he was I was told: 'Oh, that's Uncle Manasse'. Such Manasses exist everywhere, and sometimes they are even called 'Aunt Adelheid'.]

The passage is intended to show not only how limited and relative any judgement inevitably is; it also illustrates how closely related Jewish and Christian experiences actually are – insofar as they are all subject to the realities of human existence like the passage of time.

Ennobled Jewish industrialists from the Prussian Rhine provinces, Jewish bankers from Vienna with an ancient uncle Manasse sitting in a corner, Jewish country doctors, and traders in the provincial town who act as 'Court Jews' to the landed gentry: these few references to Jews in Fontane's *Stechlin* alone cover virtually the entire social and geographical universe of middle-class German Jewry at the time. They represent social reality in the second half of the nineteenth century as perceived by the bourgeois, middle-class writer (Eastern or orthodox Jews are auspiciously absent from his social horizon), and they reveal the utmost psychological and diagnostical perceptiveness *vis-a-vis* the social reality of his time and the various sub-groups of his own particular social sphere.

Fontane places his Jewish figures in characteristic contexts and locations: the Eastern fringes of the Prussian lands (*Poggenpuhls*, *Mathilde Möhring*), the liberal ambience of the Danish court in Copenhagen (*Unwiederbringlich*), or the circles of the *haute* (i.e. financial) *bourgeoisie* and *petit* nobility in the metropolis Berlin (*Poggenpuhls*, *L'Adultera*). Probably apart from *Unwiederbringlich*, where the descendant of a Court Jew is introduced in a rather unusual configuration, these were locations and social contexts that were visible and accessible for the middle-class Prussian writer; even the Jews on the Eastern fringes of the Prussian lands are bourgeois in terms of their professions, life style and political ambitions. Traditional, orthodox *Ostjuden*, Jewish lower classes (like the developing urban proletariat, itself largely fed by migrants from the East) never enter the picture.

In all cases, without exception as far as I can see, the narrative purpose of the inclusion of Jewish figures or allusions to Jewish themes is the characterisation of those gentile characters in relation to whom the Jews are shown; which means that Fontane's primary narrative interest was not the Jews themselves but those who encounter Jews, who are confronted with and challenged, puzzled, sometimes even derailed by the Jewish presence in German society at the time.

Fontane's famous poem in which he voices his disappointment that the Jews rather than the old Prussian élite led the congratulations for his 75th birthday, epitomises the discussion so far: Jews can be and must be identified as such, by their name in literary representation, by their appearance (physiognomy) in personal encounters. Here the names signal distinctiveness and function as devices of recognition and hence demarcation. However, such neat categorisation is undermined straight away with the reference to 'older' (i.e. biblical) nobility. Jews are also seen as forces of change; they are a new élite. The tenor of the poem is thus that Fontane presents himself as an author who has tried in his literature to stem the tide of history, but, remaining unrecognised for this effort, then resigns himself to acknowledging the forces of change rather than going without recognition at all.

An meinem Fünfundsiebzigsten	[On the Occasion of my 75th Birthday
Hundert Briefe sind angekommen,	A hundred letters have arrived
Ich war vor Freude wie benommen,	And I was drunken with joy,
Nur etwas verwundert über die Namen	However, a bit puzzled by the names
Und über die Plätze, woher sie kamen.	And places where they stemmed from.]

After listing some well-known Prussian names, and bemoaning the absence of these – all of whom, as he sourly states, he had written about – from the circle of gratulators, he continues:

Aber die zum Jubeltag da kamen
Das waren doch sehr sehr andere Namen,
Auch 'sans peur et reproche',
    ohne Furcht und Tadel,
Aber fast schon von prähistorischem Adel:
Die auf 'berg' und auf 'heim' sind
    gar nicht zu fassen,
Sie stürmen ein in ganzen Massen,
Meyers kommen in Bataillonen,
Auch Pollacks, und die noch östlicher
    wohnen;
Abram, Isack, Israel,
Alle Patriarchen sind zur Stell',
Stellen mich freundlich an ihre Spitze,
Was sollen mir da noch die Itzenplitze!
Jedem bin ich was gewesen,
Alle haben sie mich gelesen,
Alle kannten mich lange schon,
Und das ist die Hauptsache ...
    'kommen Sie, Cohn'.[23]

[Those who attended the celebrations
Had quite different names,
They, too, indicate
    fearlessness and bravery
But their nobility is almost prehistoric.
Those names ending in 'berg'
    and 'heim' are too many to grasp,
They come in huge numbers,
Batallions of Meyers
And Pollacks from Easternmost parts

Abraham, Isaac and Israel,
All the Patriarchs have assembled,
    Call me their leader.
I can do without the Itzenplitzes
when these people honour me so much,
They have all read me,
And knew me for a long time
And that, after all, is what's important.
    'Come along, Mr Cohn'.]

In this list, the Jewish names are not more stigmatised than the Prussian names listed in the stanza before, they are simply identifying names. Identification even becomes a topic of reflection, when Fontane indicates that names ending in '-berg' and '-heim' are not unequivocally identifiable as Jewish (a true observation, but also the implication that such names might be Jewish, as many Jewish families had adopted names relating to their places of origin, like Wertheim, Oppenheim etc., and that ennobled Jewish families often added '-berg' or '-stein' to their names, like Wertheimstein). That identification became stigma is a traumatic fact of German history, but it is not causally linked to such representations of Jews in literature such as Fontane's.

Pragmatism and recognition of social and political realities rather than insistence on outdated principles mark this poem. It is a confirmation, a celebration even, of Jewish presence in German bourgeois society. In turn, members of the Jewish middle class, in their desire to demonstrate their successful integration into non-Jewish society, utilised German literature as reference points. Their admiration for Goethe and Schiller was meant to demonstrate their identification with the ideals of self-development in freedom and responsibility. They related to Freytag's *Soll und Haben* as an exemplar of bourgeois ethics of punctuality, efficiency, honesty and reliability. And they read Fontane to learn the skills of refined social intercourse and witty conversation.[24]

Jews remain 'others'; but they are conceived as others of the closest possible proximity, far more part of the bourgeois world than workers or peasants who, in the works of Freytag, Raabe and Fontane, appear at the social horizon but, in the case of industrial workers, have not yet been recognised as a distinctive social group, let alone a social force. Jews are a distinct social group, they are recognised as such when they are ridiculed, criticised, branded or labelled. The relationship between Jews and non-Jews is not always easy, but they are acknowledged and depicted, and their presence is part of the reality the literature of this period programmatically intended to depict.

NOTES

1. Among the flood of secondary literature that discusses such issues only a few introductory works can be mentioned here: Hugo Aust, *Literatur des Realismus* (Stuttgart: Metzler, 1981); *Theorie des bürgerlichen Realismus*, ed. by Gerhard Plumpe (Stuttgart: Reclam, 1985); *Bürgerlicher Realismus und Gründerzeit 1848-1890*, ed. by Edward MacInnes and Gerhard Plumpe (Munich: Hanser, 1996).
2. See David Sorkin, *The Transformation of German Jewry, 1780-1840* (New York and Oxford: Oxford University Press, 1987); Jacob Toury, 'Der Eintritt der Juden ins deutsche Bürgertum' in *Das Judentum in der deutschen Umwelt 1800-1850. Studien zur Frühgeschichte der Emanzipation*, ed. by Hans Liebeschütz und Arnold Paucker (Tübingen: Mohr, 1977), pp.139-242.
3. See Florian Krobb, *Selbstdarstellungen - Untersuchungen zur deutsch-jüdischen Erzählliteratur im neunzehnten Jahrhundert* (Würzburg: Königshausen & Neumann, 2000).
4. Martin Gubser, *Literarischer Antisemitismus. Untersuchungen zu Gustav Freytag und anderen bürgerlichen Schriftstellern des 19. Jahrhunderts* (Göttingen: Wallstein, 1998).
5. See Hans Otto Horch, 'Judenbilder in der realistischen Erzählliteratur: Jüdische Figuren bei Gustav Freytag, Fritz Reuter, Berthold Auerbach und Wilhelm Raabe', in *Juden und Judentum in der Literatur*, ed. by Herbert A Strauss and Christhard Hoffmann (Munich: dtv 1985), pp.140-71. Wilhelm Raabe's portrayal of Jews and particularly his *Hungerpastor* have attracted a lot of critical attention, e.g. Marketa Goetz-Stankiewicz, 'Die böse Maske Moses Freudensteins. Gedanken zum Hungerpastor' in *Jahrbuch der Raabe-Gesellschaft* (1969), 7-32; Dieter Arendt, '"Nun auf die Juden!" Figurationen des Judentums im Werk Wilhelm Raabes' in *Tribüne. Zeitschrift zum Verständnis des Judentums* 19 (1980), 108-40; Jeffrey L. Sammons, 'Wilhelm Raabe and his Reputation Among Jews and Anti-Semites' in *Identity and Ethos. A Festschrift for Sol Liptzin on the Occasion of his 85th Birthday* (New York, Bern, Frankfurt/Main: Lang, 1986), pp.169-91.
6. See Ritchie Robertson, 'The Representation of Jews in British and German Literature: A Comparison', in *Two Nations. British and German Jews in Comparative Perspective*, ed. by Michael Brenner, Rainer Liedtke and David Rechter (Tübingen: Mohr Siebeck, 1999), pp.411-41, (pp.424ff).
7. See note 5.
8. Peter Goldammer, 'Nietzsche-Kult - Antisemitismus - und eine späte Rezension des Romans *Vor dem Sturm*: Zu Fontanes Briefen an Friedrich Paulsen' in *Fontane-Blätter* 56 (1993), 48-62 (p.56).
9. Ernst Simon called his contribution on the subject 'Fontanes jüdische Ambivalenz' in Ernst Simon, *Entscheidung zum Judentum. Essays und Vorträge* (Frankfurt/Main: Suhrkamp, 1980), pp.266-82. In a recent biography the author uses the expression 'Widersprüchlichkeit' [ambivalence, contradictoriness]: Wolfgang Hädecke, *Theodor Fontane. Biographie* (Munich: Hanser, 1998), p.350. But it was Wolfgang Paulsen who coined the notion of the philosemitic anti-semite: Wolfgang Paulsen, 'Theodor Fontane: The Philosemitic Antisemite', in *Leo Baeck Institute Year Book* 26 (1981), 303-22. The

latest contribution in this vein is the Fontane chapter in Hannah Burdekin, *The Ambivalent Author: Five German Writers and their Jewish Characters, 1848-1914* (Oxford: Lang, 2002).

10. A report and press review on these public debates is given in *Fachdienst Germanistik* 16/12 (1998), 5–14. At the main conference devoted to Fontane in the anniversary year 1998, four presentations deals with the topic of Fontane's relationship to the Jews: see the contributions by Wolfgang Benz, Hans Otto Horch, Henry H.H. Remek and Bernd Belzer in *Theodor Fontane: Am Ende des Jehrhunderts*, ed. by Hanna Delf von Wolzogen (Würzburg: Königshausen & Neumann, 2000), vol. I.

11. Michael Fleischer, *'Kommen Sie, Cohn':' Fontane und die Judenfrage* (Helmstedt: Fleischer, 1998), p.247; see Hans Otto Horch's review of this book in *Fontane Blätter* 67 (1999), 135–41. See also the following contributions to the debate: Michael Schmidt, '"Wie ein roter Faden". Fontanes Antisemitismus und die Literaturwissenschaft' in *Jahrbuch für Antisemitismusforschung* 8 (1999), 350–69; Peter Schumann, 'Theodor Fontane und die Juden', in *Geschichte in Wissenschaft und Unterricht* 49 (1998), 530–43.

12. Norbert Mecklenburg, 'Einsichten und Blindheiten: Fragmente einer nichtkanonischen Fontane-Lektüre' in *Text & Kritik Sonderband Theodor Fontane* (Munich: text & kritik, 1989), pp.148–62 (pp.152ff).

13. Theodor Fontane, *Werke: Nymphenburger Ausgabe*, vol. IV (Munich: Nymphenburger, 1954), p.30. Further references to this edition will be abbreviated as *NFA*. All translations into English are by Florian Krobb.

14. See Florian Krobb, *Die schöne Jüdin. Jüdische Frauengestalten in der deutschsprachigen Erzählliteratur* (Tübingen: Niemeyer, 1993), pp.173ff.

15. Gerhard Neumann, 'Das Ritual der Mahlzeit und die Realistische Literatur. Ein Beitrag zu Fontanes Romankunst' in *Das schwierige 19. Jahrhundert. Fachtagung aus Anlass des 65. Geburtstags von Eda Sagarra*, ed. by Jürgen Barkhoff, Gilbert Carr and Roger Paulin. (Tübingen: Niemeyer, 2000), pp.301–17.

16. *Theodor Fontane: Sämtliche Werke*, vol. XXIV: *Fragmente und frühe Erzählungen*, ed. by Rainer Bachmann and Peter Bramböck (Munich: Hanser, 1975), p.256.

17. Cf. Fritz Stern, *Gold und Eisen. Bismarck und sein Bankier Bleichröder* (Frankfurt am Main and Berlin: Fischer, 1978).

18. Fontane, *Sämtliche Werke*, vol. XXIV (see note 16), p.256.

19. Dubslav as a prototypical representative of the old feudal era when Jews were known only as ghetto inhabitants or Court Jews is discussed by Magnus Schlette, 'Fontanes Adelstypologie im Stechlin. Eine Untersuchung ihres sozialgeschichtlichen Gehalts' in *Literatur für Leser* 22 (1999), 127–43.

20. See the list of Fontane's reading provided in Hugo Aust, *Theodor Fontane – Ein Studienbuch* (Tübingen and Basel: Francke, 1998), p.38.

21. Expression used by Aust (see note 20), p.189.

22. Paulsen, 'The Philosemitic Antisemite' (see note 9), p.320.

23. NFA, XX, 409f.

24. See Marion Kaplan, *The Making of the Jewish Middle Class: Women, Family, and Identity in Imperial Germany* (New York and Oxford: Oxford University Press, 1991), pp.57f.

Building the Body of the Nation: Lombroso's *L'antisemitismo* and Fin-de-Siècle Italy

DAVID FORGACS

A cold wind is blowing across Europe, Cesare Lombroso wrote in 1893: 'A freezing blast, of savage hatred, sweeps among even the most civil peoples of Europe, giving rise to scenes that would hardly have been thought possible in the Middle Ages; it is the blast of anti-semitism, which took its name and gained headway in Germany, but which under other less scientific names had raged in earlier epochs and lay dormant among the lower strata of the European peoples.'[1] Lombroso, then 58, was internationally known for his work in forensic medicine and criminal anthropology, and in particular for his theory (already the subject of controversy at the time in the scientific community) that criminals were born with certain atavistic physical characteristics, throwbacks to an earlier stage of evolution, which predisposed them to crime. Anatomically they resembled, in his words, savages and apes and they possessed 'the ferocious instincts of primitive humanity and the inferior animals'.[2] Invited by the *Neue Freie Presse* in Vienna and the *Revue des Revues* in Paris to write about anti-semitism, he set out in *L'antisemitismo e le scienze moderne* (published in Turin in 1894 and in Leipzig in a German translation later the same year) to confute the claims of self-styled 'scientific' anti-semites that the Jews too were a degenerate sub-class of humans.

This pamphlet belongs to the period between on the one hand the rise of political anti-semitism in Germany and the Russian pogroms of the early 1880s and on the other the Dreyfus affair of the later 1890s (Dreyfus was first arrested in 1894 but the public controversy over his case erupted only at the end of 1897). Lombroso's immediate reference points were contemporary anti-semitic texts such as Edmond Picard's *Synthèse de l'antisemitisme* (Brussels, 1892). Picard was a jurist who argued that the primary cause of anti-semitism was racial antipathy. He considered as secondary such motives as religious hatred and envy by non-Jews of wealthy western Jews. 'La cause, la vraie cause, est dans l'antipathie de race, et dans le danger, confusément perçu, de la domination d'une race sur une autre.'³ The threat posed by Jewish wealth, for Picard, was separate from the social threat of an excessive concentration of capital. Again it was a matter of racial difference: 'C'est quand l'argent est aux mains d'une race étrangère et, qu'elle le veuille ou ne le veuille pas, foncièrement antagoniste, que le péril devient urgent et justifie les cris d'alarme.'⁴

Lombroso also refers to Renan's *Mélanges d'histoire et de voyages* (Paris, 1878), which, though less vehemently anti-semitic, helped propagate the notion of racial inferiority. Renan had claimed that the 'Semitic peoples lack the mental variety and breadth which are the conditions of perfectibility', that is to say they were less evolved and less capable of evolution than other peoples. In his opening lecture at the Collège de France in 1862 for the course in Hebrew, Chaldaic and Syriac, Renan had reviewed the contribution made by the Semitic peoples to civilisation, only to conclude that their innovations in politics, art, science and philosophy were either negligible or had been absorbed and surpassed by the Greeks. The fields in which he conceded they had made a major contribution were religion and moral and social ideas.⁵

Lombroso himself gave four reasons for the epidemic of anti-semitism at this particular moment: 'the work of governments and sects' in Bismarckian Germany and Tsarist Russia (pp.22–3); the rise of economic protectionism and defensive nationalisms, which led peoples 'to exclude one another and to confine themselves within their own borders'; the 'religious sentiment', in other words, a recrudescence of Christian anti-semitism; and the rise of socialist movements, with their attack on private property, financial oligarchies and plutocracy, associated in their propaganda with the Jews (pp.25–6).

As for the basic causes of popular anti-Jewish feeling, Lombroso dismissed claims such as Picard's that these lay in racial difference, since all European countries contained 'a mosaic of very varied races' ('un mosaico di razze variatissime', p.10), or in religious difference, since other religious groups, such as Buddhists and Muslims, did not arouse the same degree of antipathy as the Jews (ibid.). He argued that anti-Jewish attitudes derived, rather, from a self-satisfied feeling of superiority of non-Jews over Jews – perhaps a memory of ancient domination of freemen over slaves, a feeling which had recently been stoked by the rise of nationalism – and from what he termed the 'stratification of memory', in other words the transmission of the memory of earlier persecutions of Jews, from ancient Rome through the Christian middle ages (p.11). Like other forms of intolerance and prejudice giving rise to persecution, therefore, popular anti-semitism worked first by marking out a particular social group as inferior and then by transmitting and reinforcing this prejudice down the generations.

Lombroso's rebuttal of the 'scientific' anti-semites' claims about a degenerate Jewish type consisted essentially of the argument, elaborated in the middle part of his pamphlet, that there was no single Jewish race. Jews, rather, were a mixture of many races, including 'Aryans' and 'Indians', and they tended to have similar physical characteristics to other peoples living in the same regions. This argument can be found in some other nineteenth-century writers on race, such as Figuier, although others, like Gobineau, maintained that the Jewish racial type remained 'much the same' wherever Jews settled and for however long.[6] Lombroso for his part pointed out that among European Jews there was a great variety of colours of hair and eyes, of head sizes and shapes. In northern Europe, he claimed, as many as 29 per cent of Jews had fair hair; in England 'the Jew presents that very fine, blond straight hair, that raised forehead and those blue eyes that belong to the true Briton' (p.43).[7] He saw this hybridism or racial mixing as good because, like the grafting of plants, it tended to produce evolutionary improvements. In a series of appendices he provided tables of anthropometric statistics (body measurements) to substantiate these claims. He compared a sample of a hundred Jews in Turin with an equivalent number of Christians by height, by size and shape of head, and by colour of hair and eyes and found roughly the same distribution of physical characteristics in both groups.

Before getting on to this central section of the pamphlet, however, Lombroso had argued something else: that anti-semitism was not just the result of arbitrary prejudice by non-Jews, but was motivated in part by the actions of Jews themselves, that 'the character of the persecuted themselves [the Jews] also certainly contributed to the persecution' ('Certo contribuì pure alla persecuzione il carattere degli stessi perseguitati', p.13). He gave five examples of this: First, the Jews' prolonged practice of commerce had given them a habit of craftiness and the tendency to lie ('quell'abito della furberia e anche della menzogna', p.13). Second, their in-breeding had produced geniuses but also neurotics, megalomaniacs and obsessively ambitious types ('ambiziosi', p.13). Third, there was their 'strange conservation of the old customs' ('strana conservazione dei vecchi costumi').

> This conservatism was reinforced by religious conservatism, not only in the great theistic traditions but also in rituals that are out of tune with the present ... for example, the savage practice of circumcision which, as Spencer demonstrated, is a true symbolic

rudiment [sic: *rudimento*; probably an error for *rudere*: remnant] of human sacrifices, or the stupid rites of Passover matzoh which, because of their difference from those practised by peoples among whom the Jews live, naturally arouse ridicule and repugnance which grow according to the exaggerated importance attached to them by the orthodox.[8]

Fourth, there was their weakness of character ('scarso...carattere'). Jews were more obstinate than others; they masked this obstinacy as ductility and flexibility and this gave rise also to 'moral inferiority' (p.16). They had lost their ancient collective courage; they now had an 'almost instinctive timidity' and feared death: hence, says Lombroso, the low suicide rate among Jews (p.17). Fifth, and finally, there was their petulance and impatience, their propensity to lord it over others (p.19).

Lombroso's pamphlet, as one can see, uses a discursive technique in which both Jews and anti-semites are presented as others, as 'them'. At no point does its author declare an identity as a Jew himself. However, Lombroso's Jewish origins were common knowledge at the time. In *The Jewish Encyclopedia* of 1904 there are entries for six Lombrosos or Lumbrosos, described as a Sephardic family with branches in Tunis, Marseilles and Italy, including a long entry for Cesare. Born in Verona in 1835, he was descended from Levis on both his father's and mother's sides. On the side of his father, Aronne Lombroso, his family 'for many generations had been rich in rabbis and Hebraists. His maternal ancestors were chiefly manufacturers and bankers who had long been established at Chieri, Piedmont.'[9] One of the cousins of his mother, Zefora Levi, was David Levi, a former member of Mazzini's Young Italy movement who had become elected to the new parliament of united Italy. According to the life of Lombroso written posthumously by his daughter Gina, it was David Levi who taught the young Cesare to read, write and appreciate poetry as well as instilling in him 'the intense love of liberty, source of all progress'.[10] Levi was the author of the dramatic poem, *Il profeta* (1866), about the historical struggle of the Jews since early times. The second edition, published in the early 1880s, included an additional scene of the Prophet entering Rome in 1870 at the moment of its annexation to the Italian kingdom, when the principles of the rule of law and freedom of conscience are proclaimed. Levi also wrote a book *Il semitismo nella civiltà dei popoli* (1884), which Lombroso refers to in *L'antisemitismo* as a 'bellissima operetta' and in which Levi attributes the recent emergence of anti-semitism to the militarism and repressive anti-liberalism of Bismarckian Germany, as well as to the spread there of poverty, emigration and a 'menacing socialism'. He then sees it moving by propagation among the masses beyond Germany's borders to its neighbouring states: Poland, Russia, Hungary.[11]

Lombroso had studied medicine at Pavia, gaining his degree in 1858, just before Unification. He then served until 1864 as a volunteer doctor in the new national army and in 1862 he was involved in the Italian state's military campaign against brigandage in Calabria. 'Brigand' was the term most commonly used to designate those who formed outlaw bands in southern Italy in opposition to the authority of the new Italian state, which in the 1860s fielded more troops to repress this internal opposition than had been deployed against the Austrian and Bourbon armies in all the battles of the Risorgimento. In the same year Lombroso conducted anthropometric research (using the new method of craniometrics, an extension of phrenology into the statistical measurement and comparison of skulls and brain capacities) on 3,000 soldiers conscripted from different regions of Italy in order to investigate the ethnic diversity of the Italian people. He subsequently dated the origin of his theory of atavism to 1870. In January 1871 he reported to the Lombard Institute of Sciences on the skull of the 'brigand' Villella which, he claimed, contained a 'median occipital fossa' not normally found in humans but present in the lower primates (lemurs, specifically) and some rodents. Shortly before his death in 1909, he recalled this discovery as follows:

> This was not merely an idea, but a revelation. At the sight of that skull, I seemed to see all of a sudden, lighted up as a vast plain under a flaming sky, the problem of the nature of the criminal – an atavistic being who reproduces in his person the ferocious instincts of primitive humanity and the inferior animals.[12]

According to Giuliano Pancaldi, who has studied the diffusion of Darwinian and Spencerian ideas in Italy, the theory of atavism which Lombroso constructed out of the case of the Villella skull and others was derived not from Darwin but from pre-Darwinian comparative anatomy and from phrenology, with its deductions of brain size and shape from the form of the skull and its location of certain attitudes and dispositions in particular parts of the brain, as well as from the hypotheses of the Italian evolutionary biologist Giovanni Canestrini. The idea of a radical atavism, by which characteristics of a lower primate may appear in a human after thousands of years of evolution, had been advanced by Canestrini but it was not supported by the English evolutionists. Darwin held that a reversion in hereditary characteristics was only possible at most a few generations back in the same species. Huxley maintained that there was 'structural break' in the evolutionary chain between the lower and higher primates (the apes), such that a reversion in humans to characteristics of a lower simian such as the lemur, as claimed by Lombroso, would have been impossible.[13]

Alongside Pancaldi's reconstruction of the scientific context of Lombrosian forensic medicine is Daniel Pick's useful contextualisation of Lombroso's work in post-unification Italy and in contemporary Italian and French social science. Pick has argued that positivism was attractive to the young Lombroso both because of the weakness of the tradition of physical science in Italy and because it represented a powerful alternative to the classical theory of crime, which in Italy derived from Cesare Beccaria, as well as to Catholic social theory.[14] Both these theories held to a notion of free will and individual responsibility for crime. Even though Beccaria's treatise, published in 1764, had developed an explicitly secular approach to crime, distinguishing it from sin, and even though it contained some elements of a social theory of crime, such as its passing reference to the greater incidence of theft among the propertyless and the unfairness of fines as a means of punishing them, its juridical model was based on a principle of laws and punishments equal for all.[15] Beccaria conceived of punishments as deterrents against individuals who might be disposed to commit crimes and thereby break the social contract. In this respect his approach remained essentially congruent with the Catholic notion of sin and virtue as the result of individual dispositions. It also treated criminals in utilitarian terms as being, like other citizens, basically rational actors who would be dissuaded from crime if they could see clearly that the pain of being punished would outweigh the pleasure that might be derived from the crime. This whole utilitarian and contractualist approach was radically overturned by the positivists' emphasis on the variable social and economic determinants of crime and the influences of climate and heredity on human behaviour.

The context in which Lombroso worked was one of a new nation in formation, and he shared in a much wider enterprise, common to the liberal elites of united Italy in the post-unification period, of making an inventory of the country's social and physical conditions, developing knowledge of its problems by means of first-hand observation and measurement, and proposing what they considered to be enlightened, progressive solutions. The period between 1870 and 1905 saw pioneering social inquiries and investigations into conditions in Sicily, Lombardy, Basilicata and elsewhere, including the descriptions of the *mafia* (in Sicily) and *camorra* (Naples) as problems 'of the South', as well as a plethora of writings by journalists and novelists on social conditions and the social question.[16]

In his early work, Lombroso combined environmental and hereditarian explanations of ethnic diversity, crime and social disorder. It was only with his turn to the theory of atavism that the former were effectively displaced by the latter. As Pick has argued, his early publications on the South of Italy were striking, within the intellectual context of the time, 'for their emphasis on environmental determination and for the radical, social remedies they proposed for poverty': a breaking up of the large estates, redistribution of land to the peasants, drainage, irrigation, improved diet, health care and hygiene and better schooling. Even in the late 1870s his discussion of the problems of the mafia and camorra attributes the existence of these criminal organisations not to the bodies of individual criminals but to historical traditions (the repressive Bourbon governments of southern Italy had fostered a culture of rule through force and coercion which the camorra had then imitated), to environmental factors such as climate (which 'breeds' indolence) and to features of the collective mentality such as a religious outlook based on fear.[17] During the 1880s, however, Lombroso became increasingly obsessed, as Pick puts it, with 'the image of the material body in its history across generations and the patterns of its ethnic differentiation across the society', to the extent that the emphasis on inherited physical characteristics came to squeeze out that on environment.[18] His studies of 'political crimes', including anarchism, and of the female offender (written with Guglielmo Ferrero), which attribute deviant behaviour overwhelmingly to inherited physical characteristics, belong to the same period as his pamphlet on anti-semitism.[19] After the turn of the century, however, the persistent hostility voiced by his critics to his theory of the born criminal persuaded him to moderate his claims and he ultimately reduced to about 30 per cent of all crimes the proportion which might be attributed solely to the genetic make-up of the criminal.

There are several probable reasons for Lombroso's decision not to declare a Jewish identity in his text on anti-semitism, and they tend to overlap and converge. From a tactical point of view his arguments against the anti-semites might have laid him open to the charge of special pleading if he were seen to be speaking as a Jew. From a scientific point of view he needed to present himself as impartial: he wrote in the introduction to the pamphlet that the new methods of psychiatry and experimental anthropology and his own methods of positive scientific inquiry would safeguard him 'against the perils of partiality, so great in matters like this' (p.6), and one of the ways in which he could demonstrate his even-handedness was to show that, as well as suffering from the atavistic passions of non-Jews, the Jews gave their persecutors some good reasons for their anti-semitism. In social and political terms he sought to stand on the side of progress and reason (his Mazzinian, republican, secularising side) against anti-semitism – the product, he claimed, of inherited tradition and the stratification of memory – and this meant that he had to take his distance equally from those aspects of Jewish culture which were tied to the past, to dogma, superstition and ritual. Insofar as Lombroso could be said to have a Jewish self-identity it was a largely assimilationist one, strongly identified with scientific culture and a progressive secular political culture.

Seen in this light, the pamphlet still looks problematic but it does not look quite so perversely self-contradictory as it first appears. Rather, it falls into a wider pattern in this period of Jewish disidentification, or, if one prefers, Jewish self-hatred.[20] The 'ridicule and repugnance' which Lombroso describes as aroused by certain Jews is that typically experienced by the assimilated and secularised Jew, the rationalist or scientist, towards the practices of religious Jews. This attitude comes across most strongly in his remarks about the laying on of *tefillin* and circumcision, both of which he sees as atavistic practices, assimilating them respectively to primitive magic and prehistoric savagery:

> Now that even the lowliest doormen read thousands of lines of newsprint a day a written formula which is treated as magical is merely ludicrous, and it evokes squalid mysteries. But the worst thing is that they go even further. The true orthodox Jews (luckily they are few in number) do something stranger still: they wear woven on their prayer shawls the remnants of those *quippu* or knotted mnemonic threads which primitive people used (the Peruvian Indians, for instance), before ideographic writing, before the pictorial alphabet, and in the cruel practice of circumcision they go so far as to use, as well as their teeth, stone knives like our caveman ancestors.[21]

At this point I want to declare an autobiographical interest which will partly explain why I am drawn to discuss this pamphlet. My father, who died in 1992, was born in Budapest in 1914. His family on his father's side had emigrated to Hungary from Poland in the 1880s, when his own father (born in 1879) was still a small child; his mother came from a Transylvanian Jewish family named Haas. My father once described his own paternal grandfather to me, with black hat, ringlets and long beard, as the embodiment of that primitive world he himself had left behind. In the 1930s he went from Budapest to Paris to study medicine at the Sorbonne, then went to London to finish his training and practise as a doctor. He never joined a political party but he was close to the Labour left and used to attend public party meetings. His father died of natural causes in 1941; his brother and mother got out of Hungary and eventually settled in the United States. The remaining members of the two families died in the Holocaust. After the war, my father met and married my mother, who is English and who gets squeezed out of this particular narrative. He received British citizenship in 1951, and was proud to be British; he completely disavowed Judaism and rejected all forms of religion. He declared no interest in the development of the state of Israel and was politically pro-Palestinian. My one brother (who also became a doctor) and I were brought up as atheists. My father identified strongly with science and rationality, and with a neo-positivist model of scientific method (faith in experimental data, careful checking of results, trust in sense observation; distrust, even scorn for theories not admitting of empirical proof or refutation: he was a great admirer of Popper) but he also loved music and poetry, particularly Heine and Dante (as a child in Horthy's pro-Fascist Hungary he had been able to study Italian at school), and French literature, particularly Proust and Baudelaire. As a medical student in Paris he had read Freud and had once written him a letter, in German, to which Freud had replied. When I was about 14 he showed me the letter. I remember the small neat handwriting on two sides of blue paper. When I visited my parents years later in their new flat I asked him to show it to me again: he told me he had thrown it away, along with a lot of other old letters, when they had moved. He said he could never see the point of hanging on to relics of the past. On another occasion he told me he thought Freud was an example of poor science, even though he reckoned his work probably had some value as literature.

There is little in common between my father's particular brand of science (respiratory medicine) and Lombroso's theories of atavism and degeneration, but both of them had a medical training, both espoused scientific positivism in a broad sense, both identified with the values of a liberal-democratic, secular state and with a non-revolutionary form of socialism and both disavowed religious Judaism – and, to different degrees, Judaism *tout court*. Lombroso, in fact, at the end of his pamphlet, sees the way forward, out of and beyond anti-semitism, in an ever greater assimilation and integration of the Jews. In Italy the opening to Jews of all the professions, the education system and public administration allowed them to be identified with the state and the public sector and to break their links, still strong in other countries, with private commerce and financial speculation:

> Where all persecution is absent, as it is in Italy, the Netherlands and Britain, and where the Jew can spread with all his force in every direction, he is seen to throw himself, with the attraction one always experiences towards what had previously been forbidden,

immediately into politics, teaching, the army; and although some men were certainly not harmful to the country, others now abandon in large part that commerce, usury and gold dealing which made them so hated and, importantly, they also become poorer.[22]

The converse of this is exemplified for Lombroso by the negative situation of the Jews in Germany:

> When I think of the great Jewish medical geniuses in Germany, like Traube, Conheim and Casper, and of the stupid prohibition which prevents them from obtaining university chairs just because they are of Jewish blood, as if there were a Jewish cell theory and a Protestant one, or as if a scalpel produced different sections under the microscope in the hands of an orthodox Jew, I ask myself whether we are not well beneath the Middle Ages in many many things.[23]

If anti-semitism were to disappear, so, over five or six centuries, would Jews, because they would merge with the rest of the population. Anti-semitism, by this logic, tends to produce a result opposite to the one it desires, because by persecuting Jews it perpetuates their separateness:

> If anti-semitism were to triumph it would achieve an end diametrically opposed to the one it seeks, unless it were to destroy the Jews completely, something which is impossible in Europe in our time, if not in Russia. But by persecuting them, by closing off all other routes to them, it refines them in commerce and it pushes them ever more towards the observance of those ridiculous rites from which, in becoming secularised, they would gradually separate.
>
> I believe that if anti-semitism ceased to exist, gradually, in five or six hundred years, the Jew would disappear, and there would remain just a small number of observers in barbarous and remote countries.[24]

The correct path for the future according to Lombroso is not Zionism – in response to Birnbaum's pamplet *Zionismus* (Vienna, 1893) he says why go and settle in a desert? and anyway, if many Jews settle in Palestine, the other religious groups in Jerusalem, who get on at present with 'the apathetic Muslim' ('l'apatico mussulmano'), will not take kindly to a religion which opposes their fanaticism with its own (p.104) – but, rather, greater integration in those countries where Jews are already living. This attitude to Zionism is of a piece with Lombroso's repugnance at Jewish atavism and his pro-modernism:

> If there has to be emigration, let it be towards the more modern
> centres, like Australia, North America, even South America. The
> pseudo-idyllic colonies of Palestine can be kept for those old
> fanatics from the Slav lands who reject all modernity and still dream
> in earnest of the kingdom of Zion.[25]

He is pessimistic about overcoming anti-semitism because it is rooted,
as an atavistic phenomenon, in the passions, and is therefore amenable
neither to the reasoning of science nor to the rule of law, since mass
democracy tends towards the prevalence of the passions over reason:

> Unfortunately, since anti-semitism is an atavistic phenomenon,
> rooted in the basest and most squalid passions of man, I fear that it
> will pay little attention to scientific opinion and will not be much
> affected by the increase in civilisation, which may act upon the
> intellect but has precious little effect on the passions.
>
> So much the more where government based on universal
> suffrage tends increasingly to let the lower stata prevail over the
> upper strata.[26]

If Jews can be fully integrated (not just by giving them full political
rights but also by removing the absurd restrictions on certain professions,
such as the bar to university posts for Jewish doctors in Germany, and by
favouring mixed marriages, hospitals and cemeteries) and if they can
abandon their backward religious practices, then they might converge
with Christians in a common 'religion' of socialism, progress and
modernisation. The progressivist social-Darwinist implications of this are
transparent:

> The most complete solution would be if Jews and Christians could
> rise together out of their common prejudices and converge in a new
> religion, which would be neither that of the Vatican nor ancient
> Judaism, which would respect the new scientific discoveries and
> indeed would take up the new social ideas, already promoted by
> Christ, as its banner; in other words, if a new socialist Christianity
> could be formed which would absorb, without shame and without
> coercion, the Jews stripped of their old ridiculous rituals and the
> Christians freed from their hatred and anti-scientific superstitions.[27]

Lombroso's essay is, finally, an important piece of evidence of the self-
image of a significant number of Jews in Italy between unification and the
Fascist anti-semitic legislation of 1938, the so-called 'laws for the defence
of the race'. The identification throughout this period, particularly
among educated middle-class Jews, with the secular Italian state was very

strong, and it was facilitated by the opening of professional careers, including careers in science and public administration, to Jews and the absorption of a significant number of Jews into Italy's ruling elites.[28] The patriotic attitude shared by many educated Italian Jews was typically expressed by Arnaldo Momigliano: 'We have had this patriotism, this devotion to the new Italy of the Risorgimento, in our blood since the time of our great-grandparents and our fathers'.[29] Antonio Gramsci, commenting in his prison cell on some observations by Momigliano on Judaism in Italy, claimed that the nationalisation of the Jews had involved a 'dejudaisation' parallel to the secularisation of non-Jews. He claimed that their strong attachment to the Italian nation was a consequence of the weakening both of their religious 'cosmopolitanism' (similar to that of the Catholics) and of their 'particularism', their attachment to a local community. For this reason, Gramsci claimed, 'Anti-semitism does not exist in Italy'.[30] He wrote this in 1933. By 1938 he was dead, the racial laws had been promulgated and Momigliano was preparing to leave Italy with his family for England.

Not all Jews went as far as Lombroso in envisaging a total disappearance of Judaism. Many of them nurtured a 'dual identity' – Italian and Jewish – wherein a strong identification with the Italian state in the public sphere was combined with a maintenance of Jewish identity in the private sphere. For some this dual affiliation would be compatible, after the rise of Zionism at the end of the 1890s, with a dual Zionist and Italian nationalism, whereas for the liberal critics of Zionism identification with a Jewish homeland was appropriate only to eastern Jews living under oppressive regimes, not to those in 'cultured states' like Italy.[31]

Lombroso, in conclusion, was like many other Italian Jews of his generation in pursuing a professional career, espousing socialism and rejecting the 'ancestral rituals' of Judaism. His early socialism involved a belief in evolution from lower to higher social forms and was consistent with his own views on degeneration and racial inferiority. On his imaginary map of the new Italy, Jews were faced with a choice. They could either move through assimilation to the centre, or they could remain on the periphery, marked, along with other groups such as brigands, prostitutes and anarchists, by certain bodily characteristics of atavism.

NOTES

1. Cesare Lombroso, *L'antisemitismo e le scienze moderne* (Turin and Rome: Roux, 1894), p.9 ('un soffio gelido, d'odio selvaggio, percorre i popoli anche più civili d'Europa, dando luogo a scene che mal si sarebbero credute possibili nel Medio Evo; è il soffio dell'antisemitismo che prese nome ed abbrivio in Germania, ma che sotto altri appellativi meno scientifici aveva divampato nelle epoche anteriori e covava latente nei bassi strati dei

popoli Europei'). Subsequent references to this pamphlet are given by page numbers in parentheses in the text of this article, except where (as here) a longer passage is quoted, in which case the page reference is given in the notes followed by the original Italian text.

2. Quoted in Daniel Pick, *Faces of Degeneration: A European Disorder, c.1848–c.1918* (Cambridge: Cambridge University Press, 1989), p.122.

3. Edmond Picard, *Synthèse de l'antisémitisme* (Brussels: Larcier and Paris: Savine, 1892), p.56.

4. Ibid., p.82.

5. Ernest Renan, 'De la part des peuples sémitiques dans l'histoire de la civilisation', in *Mélanges d'histoire et de voyages* (Paris: Calmann Lévy, 1878), pp.1–25. The statement about perfectibility is quoted by Lombroso (*L'antisemitismo*, p.59) from Renan's *Mélanges* without a page reference.

6. Louis Figuier, *Les Races humaines* (Paris: Hachette, 1872), pp.195–6: 'Les Juifs ont conservé quelque chose de leur physionomie propre. Ils se distinguent des nations parmi lesquelles ils sont dispersés, par des traits particuliers, que l'on reconnaît facilement dans plusieurs tableaux des grands maîtres. Cependant ils ont fini par prendre plus ou moins les caractères des nations au milieu desquelles ils ont séjourné longtemps ... dans les contrées septentrionales de l'Europe, les Juifs ont la peau blanche, les yeux bleus et les cheveux blonds. ...Dans les parties de l'Inde où ils sont établis depuis longtemps, c'est-à-dire dans la province de Cochin, sur la côte de Malabar, ils sont noirs et si complètement semblables, pour le teint, aux indigènes, qu'il est quelquefois difficile de les distinguer des Hindous.' Arthur Gobineau, 'Essay on the Inequality of Human Races (1853–55)', in *Selected Political Writings*, ed. by Michael D. Biddiss (London: Jonathan Cape, 1970), pp.102–3: 'The warlike Rechabites of the Arabian desert, the peaceful Portuguese, French, German and Polish Jews – they all look alike' (the passage is from Chapter 10 of Book One of Gobineau's *Essay*).

7. This sentence, and the discussion which follows it in this part of *L'antisemitismo*, of the variety of racial types among Jews, is reproduced verbatim by Lombroso from his earlier work *L'uomo bianco e l'uomo di colore. Letture sull'origine e le varietà delle razze umane* (Padua: Sacchetto, 1871), pp.106–9.

8. *L'antisemitismo*, p.14 ('Questo conservatorismo si rinforzò con quello religioso, e non solo delle grandi linee teistiche, ma perfino dei riti che stuonano coi nostri tempi. ...così il selvaggio uso della circoncisione, che, come Spencer dimostrò, è un vero rudimento simbolico dei sacrifizi umani; così gli stupidi riti delle azime Pasquali; i quali, divergendo da tutti quelli in uso fra i popoli in cui vivono, destano naturalmente il ridicolo e la ripugnanza che cresce coll'esagerata importanza che gli ortodossi vi annettono.')

9. *The Jewish Encyclopaedia* (1904), VIII, 154.

10. Gina Lombroso-Ferrero, *Cesare Lombroso. Storia della vita e delle opere narrata dalla figlia* (Turin: Bocca, 1915), p.11.

11. *L'antisemitismo*, p.100, footnote; David Levi, *Il semitismo nella civiltà dei popoli* (Turin: Unione Tipografico-Editrice, 1884), pp.10–12.

12. The recollection is in the introduction Lombroso wrote to Criminal Man, according to the classification of Cesare Lombroso, briefly summarised by his daughter Gina Lombroso-Ferrero (New York: G.P. Putnam's Sons, 1911), pp.xiv–xv.

13. Giuliano Pancaldi, *Darwinism in Italy: Science across Cultural Frontiers* (originally published as *Darwin in Italia. Impresa scientifica e frontiere culturali*, Bologna: Il Mulino, 1983), transl. by Ruey Brodine Morelli (Bloomington and Indianapolis: Indiana University Press, 1991), pp.142–6.

14. Pick (see note 2), p.112.

15. See Cesare Beccaria, *Dei delitti e delle pene,*, ed. by Franco Venturi (Turin: Einaudi, 1965). The discussion of property and fines is in Chapter 22, on theft.

16. See for example Leopoldo Franchetti, *La Sicilia nel 1876.* Vol. I, *Condizioni politiche e amministrative della Sicilia* (Vallecchi, 1925); *Inchiesta Zanardelli sulla Basilicata* (1902),, ed. by Paola Corti (Turin: Einaudi, 1976); Alfredo Niceforo and Scipio Sighele, *La mala vita a Roma* (Turin: Roux Frassati, 1898); Matilde Serao, *Il ventre di Napoli*, Bianco,

Rome, n.d. [1885]. I discuss some of this work, insofar as it relates to cities, in my article 'Imagined Bodies: Rhetorics of social investigation in late nineteenth-century France and Italy', *Journal of the Institute of Romance Studies*, 1.1 (1992), 375–94. Among the studies in this period of the camorra and the mafia are Angelo Umiltà, *Camorra e mafia* (Neuchâtel: James Attinger, 1878) and two works by Giuseppe Alongi, *La mafia nei suoi fattori e nelle sua manifestazioni. Studio sulle classi pericolose della Sicilia* (Turin: Bocca, 1886) and *La camorra. Studio di sociologia criminale* (Turin: Bocca, 1890).

17. See Cesare Lombroso, *Sull'incremento del delitto in Italia e sui mezzi per arrestarlo* (Turin: Bocca, 1879) pp.10–25. Lombroso also discussed the behavioural characteristics of the camorra without attributing them to atavism or physical characteristics in his short text 'Sulla camorra nel 1875', reproduced as an appendix to *L'uomo delinquente*, first published in 1876. See *L'uomo delinquente in rapporto all'antropologia, alla giurisprudenza ed alle discipline carcerarie*, Vol.II, *Delinquente epilettico, d'impeto, pazzo e criminaloide*, third edition (Turin: Bocca, 1889), pp.501–5.

18. Pick (see note 2), pp.113–14.

19. Cesare Lombroso and R. Laschi, *Il delitto politico e le rivoluzioni* (Turin: Roux, 1890); Cesare Lombroso and Guglielmo Ferrero, *La donna delinquente, la prostituta e la donna normale* (Turin and Rome: Roux, 1893).

20. See Sander L. Gilman, *Jewish Self-Hatred: Anti-Semitism and the Hidden Language of the Jews* (Baltimore and London: Johns Hopkins University Press, 1986). The expression was originally popularised by Theodor Lessing's short book *Der jüdische Selbsthass* (Berlin: Jüdischer Verlag, 1930).

21. *L'antisemitismo*, p.15: 'Ora che fin gli ultimi portinai leggono migliaia di righe in un giorno nei giornali, una formola scritta che si tenga per qualche cosa di magico fa ridere, o desta l'idea di tristi misteri. Il peggio è che essi rimontano ancora più su; il vero ortodosso Ebreo (fortunatamente ve ne son pochi) giunge a qualcosa di più strano, a portare ricamati nei suoi manti religiosi gli avanzi di quei veri *guippu* o nodi mnemonici in filo che avevano gli uomini primitivi, i Peruviani, per es., prima della scrittura ideografica, prima dell'alfabeto a pittura; giunge ad adoperare nella crudel pratica della circoncisione insieme ai denti i coltelli di pietra come i nostri proavi delle caverne.'

22. *L'antisemitismo*, p.98: 'Si noti infine che dove manca ogni loro persecuzione, come in Italia, Olanda, Inghilterra, dove l'Ebreo può esplicare tutte le sue forze in tutte le direzioni, esso si vede, con quello slancio che si dà alla cosa già proibita, gettarsi immediatamente nella politica, nell'insegnamento, nella milizia; e mentre vi dà degli uomini che certo non furono dannosi al paese, abbandona in gran parte il commercio, specie l'usuraio, il commercio dell'oro, che lo rese così odioso, e diventa, cosa importante, anche più povera.'

23. *L'antisemitismo*, p.107: 'Quando penso ai grandi genî medici germanici ebrei, come Traube, Conheim, Casper, e allo stupido divieto che non permette che nemmeno uno diventi professore ordinario, solo perché di sangue ebreo, quasi vi fosse una teoria cellulare ebraica ed una protestante, e quasi il microtomo desse delle sezioni diverse nelle mani di un ortodosso, io mi domando se noi non stiamo di sotto al Medio Evo in molte e molte cose.'

24. *L'antisemitismo*, p.98: 'Per cui se l'antisemitismo vincesse, raggiungerebbe un fine perfettamente opposto a quello cui mira, a meno che, cosa impossibile nei nostri tempi in Europa, non dico in Russia, non distruggesse completamente gli Ebrei. Ma il perseguitarli, il toglier loro ogni altra via, certo li raffina in quella commerciale, e li spinge sempre più all'osservanza di quei riti ridicoli da cui secolarizzandosi a poco a poco si separerebbero. Io credo che se l'antisemitismo cessasse, a poco a poco, in 5 o 6 secoli, l'Ebreo scomparirebbe, restandone un piccolo numero di osservanti nei paesi barbari e remoti.'

25. *L'antisemitismo*, p.106: 'Se emigrazione dev'esservi, essa deve esser spinta verso i centri più moderni, nell'Australia, nell'America del Nord e anche del Sud. Potranno riserbarsi solo per queste pseudo idilliche colonie di Palestina quei vecchi fanatici delle terre slave che rifiutansi ad ogni modernità e che sognano ancora sul serio il regno di Sionne.'

26. *L'antisemitismo*, p.108: 'Ma, pur troppo [sic], essendo l'antisemitismo un fenomeno

atavistico, che ha le basi nelle passioni più basse e più tristi dell'uomo, temo che, poco curandosi dei pareri della scienza, non sentirà grande effetto dall'aumento della civiltà, che può agire sull'intelletto ma ben poco sulle passioni. Tanto più che il governo a base di suffragio universale tende sempre più a farvi prevalere gli strati bassi sopra gli strati più elevati.'

27. *L'antisemitismo*, p.109: 'La soluzione più completa si avrebbe se gli ebrei e i cristiani elevatisi contemporaneamente dai comuni pregiudizi, convergessero in una religione nuova, che non fosse nè la vaticana, nè l'antica giudaica, che rispettasse le scoperte nuove scientifiche, e prendesse anzi per bandiera le nuove idee sociali, che già Cristo aveva palleggiate; se si formasse, insomma, un neo-cristianesimo-socialistico in cui si potesse riunire senza vergogna e senza coercizione gli ebrei spogliatisi dai riti vecchi e ridicoli, come i cristiani scevri dagli odi e dalle superstizioni antiscientifiche.'

28. See Fabio Levi, 'Gli ebrei nella vita economica italiana dell'Ottocento', in *Storia d'Italia. Annali, ed. by* Corrado Vivanti, XI, *Gli ebrei in Italia*, tomo II, *Dall'emancipazione a oggi* (Turin: Einaudi, 1997), in particular pp.1180–85, 1188–90, 1209–10.

29. Arnaldo Momigliano, *Pagine ebraiche* (Turin: Einaudi, 1987), p.134.

30. Antonio Gramsci, *Quaderni del carcere,,* ed. by Valentino Gerratana (Turin: Einaudi, 1975), p.1801. The article that occasioned Gramsci's comments was a review by Momigliano of Cecil Roth's book on the Jews of Venice which appeared in *La Nuova Italia* on 20 April 1933. Gramsci died in April 1937 after ten years as a political prisoner and just days after being granted unconditional liberty on the grounds of his deteriorating health. 'Why anti-semitism does not exist in Italy' ['Perché l'antisemitismo non esiste in Italia'] had also been the title of a proposed editorial of a special issue in 1910 of the periodical *La Voce*, edited by Giuseppe Prezzolini, which was never published but of which a description survives in a contemporary letter from Prezzolini to Alessandro Casati: see Alberto Cavaglion, 'Tendenze nazionali e albori sionistici', in *Storia d'Italia*, ed. by Corrado Vivanti, *Annali*, XI, *Gli ebrei in Italia*, tomo II, *Dall'emancipazione a oggi* (Turin: Einaudi, 1997), p.1303.

31. Cavaglion (see note 30), pp.1297–300. The expression 'paesi di cultura', for Italy and similar countries, is used in an article by Rabbi Eude Lolli in *Il Vessillo Israelitico* of 1898, quoted by Cavaglion, p.1300.

'Barbarous and Mediaeval': Jewish Marriage in Fin de Siècle English Fiction

NADIA VALMAN

An editorial in the *Jewish Chronicle* in January 1889 noticed that in common with the rise of intra-communal strife in Anglo-Jewry,

> There is another kind of Jewish criticism of Jews which has begun to be unpleasantly frequent recently. Jewish *litterateurs*, finding a ready interest in descriptions of Jewish life among the general novel-reading public, have gone to the point of renewing their acquaintance with Jewish society for a few weeks in order to obtain local colour. On the strength of this, they produce superficial sketches of the aspects of Jewish manners that strike them unpleasantly. In non-Jewish authors this might be innocuous, especially as want of sympathy invariably results in faulty art not likely to win belief. But with the outside world the effect of such performances by Israelites is the more deleterious as it is impossible for the general public to know on what superficial knowledge of Jewish society such ill-natured sketches are founded.[1]

The editorial was identifying what Bryan Cheyette has termed the 'novel of revolt' against the tradition of apologia which had characterised Anglo-Jewish public representation in the Victorian period.[2] Inaugurated by Amy Levy's *Reuben Sachs: A Sketch* (1888), a spate of novels by assimilated Jewish writers at the fin de siècle evinced satirical depictions of Anglo-Jewish materialism, social ambition and bodily grotesqueness in terms more reminiscent of the racial representations of Anthony Trollope. Rather than insisting on the worthiness of the established Jewish community, the novel of revolt deployed 'a Jewish idealist – a persona of the novelist – [who] is represented as an example of a moral Jewish self which opposes official Anglo-Jewry'.[3] In Cheyette's account of *Reuben Sachs*, official Anglo-Jewry is represented by the ambitious barrister Reuben, while his cousin, the Cambridge student Leo Leuniger stands as the novel's moral Jewish self, deploring the acquisitive, philistine ethos of the Jewish community. Levy's text is thus not, as the *Jewish Chronicle* would have it, uniformly hostile but instead bifurcates its Jewish figures into 'good' and 'bad' Jews – a pattern typical of the ambivalence of liberal discourse regarding Jews.[4] This ambivalence was also, I will argue, repeatedly expressed in terms of gender. In *Reuben Sachs*, for example, the moral vacuity of the materialistic hero is counterposed not only against the articulate, intellectual Leo, but also, more significantly, against the earnest, cultured but repressed heroine Judith Quixano. Indeed, as this article explores, the Anglo-Jewish novel of revolt was crucially characterised by a focus on the subjection of women within Jewish society and the iniquities of Jewish matrimony. In this respect, it reflected widespread discussion in the period of the 'failure of marriage' – a controversy that was to make the heterosexual love plot a particularly effective form for examining the effects of capitalism on gender relations.[5]

The discontents of late-Victorian Jewish women were described in 'Middle-Class Jewish Women of To-Day', an 1886 article for the *Jewish Chronicle* now generally attributed to Amy Levy. Here, the author laments the destiny of the modern Jewess, who is taught to suppress 'her healthy, objective activities, ... her natural employment of her young faculties' and 'to look upon marriage as the only satisfactory termination to her career'.[6] In this she is governed by mercenary concerns, since Jews 'have not been educated to a high ideal of marriage'. Levy imagines Jewish women as unhappily imprisoned in the past, 'beating themselves in vain against the solid masonry of our ancient fortifications, long grown obsolete and of no use save as obstructions'. Jewish society, in this account, resists and impedes modernity; it is 'more Oriental at heart than a casual observer might infer ... a society constructed on ... a primitive basis'.[7] As Emma Francis puts it, in Levy's writing 'Middle-class Anglo-Jewry is presented as an overdetermined version of Victorian patriarchy'.[8] Whereas the *Jewish Chronicle* editorial of 1889 regarded her perspective as an example of Jewish self-hatred, recent research has provided a context for Levy's analysis in her liberal intellectual upbringing and her location in a circle of feminist writers and activists in London.[9] Indeed, I will argue, the terminology that she deploys for explaining the continuing subjection of women in Jewish life draws on the language of ethnography that pervaded discussion of gender relations in the late 1880s.

In her celebrated article on 'Marriage', published in the *Westminster Review* in August 1888 when Levy was still working on *Reuben Sachs*, Mona Caird asserted that 'Our common respectable marriage, upon which the safety of all social existence is supposed to rest ... is ... the worst, because the most hypocritical, form of woman-purchase'. Under the present organisation of sexual relations, she insisted, in which women were economically dependent on men, there was 'no reasonable alternative' to mercenary marriage. In this case, it was impossible to sustain the conventional contrast between the oppression of women in the East and the elevation of women in modern Western cultures; the only difference was that 'We like to have our survivals of barbarous old doctrine expressed with true refinement'.[10] A similar analogy is made by William Booth in his diagnosis of urban degeneration *In Darkest England and the Way Out* (1890): 'The lot of a negress in the Equatorial Forest is not, perhaps, a very happy one, but is it so very much worse than that of many a pretty orphan girl in our Christian capital?'[11] For Booth, the danger posed to young women in modern London was an emblem for the terrifying regression of contemporary society towards the law of the jungle. Comparing the status of pagan and Christian women was also a move made by the anti-feminist Eliza Lynn Linton, who, conversely, saw the advent of gender equality as an aspect of Western racial decline. Linton attacked missionaries to India who 'would incite the women to revolt against the rule of seclusion, which has been the law of the land for centuries before we were a nation at all ... we hold it to be an ethnological blunder, as well as a political misdemeanour, to send out these surging apostles of disobedience and discontent to carry revolt and confusion among our Indian fellow-subjects'.[12] Linton regarded the Oriental 'seclusion' of women not as 'barbarous old doctrine' but as a model – and condition – for domestic and imperial order. The Eastern woman, however, was a reference point for all of these discussions of the position of women in late-Victorian England.

In this context, Levy's 'Oriental' Jews, whose women live under 'the shadow of the harem', represent what would have been for liberal feminist thinkers a paradigmatic 'survival' of 'barbarous' society. To some extent, she argues, in 'Middle-Class Jewish Women of To-Day', the wrongs of Jewish society replicate those of the wider collective: the commodification and social restriction of women is an 'evil ... common to all commercial communities'. But, she continues, amongst Jews it is perpetuated 'with more vigour, more pertinacity, over a more wide-spread area, with a deeper root than in any other English Society'.[13] 'No prayer goes up from the synagogue with greater fervour than this,' proclaims *Reuben Sachs'* narrator of the 'pride of sex' affirmed daily by Jewish men: 'Blessed art Thou, O Lord my God, who hast not made me a woman'.[14] It is in these terms that Levy's novel offers its analysis of contemporary Anglo-Jewry, focusing on the plight of the dowryless heroine Judith Quixano, who, despite 'her beauty, her intelligence, her power of feeling, saw herself merely as one of a vast crowd of girls awaiting their promotion by marriage' (p.209). Levy presents 'woman-purchase' in the Anglo-Jewish marriage market as an aspect of the Jews' primitive concern with physical existence, diagnosed in the novel by Leo Leuniger. For him, Judaism is 'the religion of materialism. The corn and the wine and the oil; the multiplication of the seed; the conquest of the hostile tribes – these have always had more attraction for us than the harp and crown of a spiritualized existence' (pp.238–9). Here, Leo argues for a theological basis for the Jews' fixation with the acquisition of material wealth and power rather than more civilised, aesthetic interests.

Reuben Sachs, however, also locates the failings of Anglo-Jewry in the opportunities and dangers of modernity. The novel relates the rise and fall of the eponymous aspiring young barrister, who abandons his love affair with Judith because he needs a wealthy wife to aid his political career. Recognising both the depth of this betrayal and her powerlessness to avert it, Judith obeys the directive of her rich relatives, marries a spineless but aristocratic English convert to Judaism and finds herself passively 'borne on dividing currents' away from the Jewish community (p.289). Reuben, meanwhile, is elected to Parliament but dies of a heart attack soon after taking office. Reuben's bodily weakness is the most striking manifestation of a physical malaise that afflicts Anglo-Jewry more generally. His doctor, echoing the established medical opinion of his age, confides: 'More than half my nervous patients are recruited from the ranks of the Jews' (p.198). The theme of racial degeneration in Ashkenazi Jewry was prevalent in social scientific and medical discourse of the 1880s and 1990s throughout Europe, and ascribed variously to inbreeding, city-dwelling and the effects of the struggle for emancipation.[15] In Levy's novel, Anglo-Jewry is a dying race – physically and morally degenerate and heading, in Leo's words, for 'disintegration ... absorption by the people of the country' (p.239). This trajectory is impelled by its disregard for the values of culture and breeding in the pursuit of social advancement. It is because in Jewish society 'as elsewhere, the prestige of birth had dwindled, that of money had increased' that Judith Quixano's physical beauty and intellectual heritage as a Sephardic Jew are undervalued and ultimately lost to the Jewish community (p.208). In this pessimistic Darwinian view, as Emma Francis has argued, the thwarting of Judith and Reuben's mutual desire is presented as 'equally a racial and sexual failure ... in which the subjection of Judith exacts the price not just of her individual suffering, but also that of the degeneration of her people'.[16]

Noting the novel's shift of focus away from the consciousness of Reuben Sachs and towards that of Judith Quixano, a number of excellent recent essays have demonstrated that Amy Levy's representation of Jews is inextricable from her feminist politics.[17] Critics have emphasised the way that Levy's hostile portrait of Anglo-Jewry is produced in the context of the struggle for self-fulfillment of 'an intelligent woman in an inhospitable milieu'.[18] Less investigated, however, have been the ways in which other Jewish novelists of the 1890s took up and reworked Levy's preoccupation with the relationship between female subjection and racial degeneration. Levy's analysis of the plight of the Jewish woman as a sign of the atavism of Anglo-Jewish society was driven by her liberal feminist perspective, but the same tension between the possibility of 'progress' and the determinism of 'race' also animates the fiction of Cecily Sidgwick and Leonard Merrick.

Appearing only a few months after *Reuben Sachs* and brought out by the same publisher, Cecily Sidgwick's first novel, *Isaac Eller's Money* (1889), published under the pseudonym Mrs Andrew Dean, was described by the *Jewish Chronicle* as 'a clever performance in the style of Reuben Sachs, but less intentionally offensive'. In common with Levy's novel, the reviewer considered, *Isaac Eller's Money* 'selects from the many types of Jewish life some of the least favourable and holds them up to the public at large as the prevalent types'.[19] Sidgwick occupied an even more marginal position in relation to the established Jewish community than Amy Levy. Born Cecily Ullmann, the daughter of a German-Jewish immigrant, she was brought up as an Anglican and, like her father, married a gentile.[20] Sidgwick's family was typical of the Victorian Jews of German origin described by Todd M. Endelman, whose 'prior acculturation to gentile standards and habits or partial estrangement from Jewish beliefs and customs, as well as their exposure to the pervasive anti-Semitism of their homeland, profoundly influenced their communal and religious behaviour once settled in England', resulting in frequent disaffiliation from formal identification with Judaism.[21] It is this radically assimilationist perspective that informs Sidgwick's writing, which encompasses both polemical attacks on anti-semitism and an uncompromising depiction of the shallow materialism of the German-Jewish community of west London, reminiscent of *Reuben Sachs*. The stockbroker Louis Sampson is one such example: 'All day long he was absorbed in money-making, and most of his evenings were devoted to throwing it away... Though he looked quite young he was nearly bald, and he spoke in a discontented voice, and with much quick and restless movement'.[22] Sampson's dissatisfaction, reflected in his ailing physique, stands for the more widespread malaise of a community for which ostentatious consumption is an end in itself, 'calculated to excite the envy that is a pleasing tribute to prosperity' (p.43).

Sidgwick's novel begins with the wealthy German-born businessman Isaac Eller disinheriting his son Bernard when he marries a gentile woman. Subsequently, Michael Goldberg, an ambitious employee of Eller's, insinuates himself into Eller's favour and becomes recognised as his substitute heir apparent. Some years later, after Bernard's death, Eller becomes reconciled with his grandson Meredith and arranges his marriage to Goldberg's daughter Valerie in order to achieve his dream of founding a family firm. But Meredith is attracted to Barbara Lassen, Goldberg's poor but cultured niece, who also loves him. Despite opposition from his grandfather, the Goldbergs, and the wider Jewish community, Meredith marries Barbara and the revelation kills Eller. In his deathbed delirium, however, he confesses his ambivalence at the estrangement from his son. The novel ends with Meredith and Barbara becoming social successes among the German-Jewish community.

Like *Reuben Sachs*, Sidgwick's text creates its impact through intertwining religious with sexual politics. Indeed, within the first few pages Sidgwick is repeating Levy's observation of the liturgical and cultural basis of Jewish patriarchalism: 'Mr. Goldberg's other children were girls, and had been received with a faint welcome. The Jew who thanks God every week [sic] that he is not a woman is consistently ungrateful when Heaven sends him daughters. Mr. Goldberg felt the shackles of his faith as little as any man; but when his first girl was followed by half-a-dozen more he began to rival the orthodox in his small opinion of her sex' (p.14). Goldberg's denigration of women is here used to underline his vulgarity and to demonstrate how it is a function of his ambitious materialism (since daughters drain rather than augment their father's wealth). Moreover, the novel's narrative strategy also resembles *Reuben Sachs* in that the iniquities of Jewish social life come into focus through the point of view of Barbara Lassen, Goldberg's impoverished niece. Barbara and her brother David, a struggling painter, have been brought up in the bohemian neighbourhood of Bloomsbury, apart from the German-Jewish 'colony', by an unmaterialistic, philosophy-reading father thoroughly disapproved of by Goldberg, and they are left penniless when he dies. Barbara's experience as a poor female relative in the house of the Goldbergs recalls that of Judith Quixano; it is through her consciousness that Jewish society is mediated critically. In their drawing room, seated outside the family circle, Barbara observes that 'her aunt was dressed with sober elegance, and that her hair was as well arranged as the wig of a hairdresser's model, but her manner, voice, and laugh were not as subdued in tone as her costume. All was loud and artificial' (p.49). Through Barbara's eyes, the novel reveals the corporeal signs of a Jewish lack of refinement that cannot be concealed by wealth.

In a similar move to Levy's novel, *Isaac Eller's Money* allegorises its representation of Jewish society through the symbolism of the body. Thus, despite her social marginalisation, Barbara's physical superiority to the Jews around her frequently displays itself. At a ball, when she has been forbidden from dancing, 'she would have been the most conspicuous figure present, and perhaps she was hardly less so sitting there amongst those dark-haired elderly Jewesses' (p.140). In contrast to the German-Jewish women, Barbara has English pre-Raphaelite looks – blue eyes, 'heavy red gold waves' of hair – as well as cultivated manners and a devotion to music (pp.34, 53, 78). The Englishness of her physique and temperament find their match in the half-Jewish Meredith Eller, who is also described in distinction from the Jewish men who surround him:

> Born of an English mother in an English town, bereaved of his foreign father when still a child, and spending all his early youth amongst English people, his Jewish origin scarcely betrayed itself. From his mother's side he had inherited his great stature, and the ease and strength of carriage for which Englishmen are so often remarkable. He had his uncle's square chin, and firm mouth too, and the Merediths' blue eyes. But no Meredith had ever before come into the world with eyes of just that shape and expression, and with such dark eyebrows and lashes to set them off. "Girl's eyes," some one at school had once contemptuously called them, and it was not a bad description. They were far too good for a man ... But what especially distinguished him from [Mr. Klein and Mr. Sampson] was a modesty of bearing, and at the same time a certain dignity of voice and manner. He was the only person in the room who spoke English without either a foreign accent or a cockney twang, and he was the only man in the room who looked well bred (pp.63–4).

It is only Meredith's 'girl's eyes' – his effeminacy – that 'betrays' his 'Jewish origin'. But while his solid stature and manly physiognomy temper his Jewish effeminacy, they also modulate Meredith's Jewish inclination towards ambition in business:

> The offspring of a romantic marriage, the son of an impractical and unworldly man, he seemed on all hands to give the lie to his origin. There was no doubt that he had inherited his grandfather's genius for commerce, a gift as admirable and peculiar (in the hands of an honest man) as an artistic faculty. His very appearance bore in it the promise of success. People saw it in the keen glance of his eyes, in his quiet self-contained manner, in his square chin, and even in the outlines of his large frame (p.150).

Meredith's English honesty is able to turn Jewish commercial acumen into an 'artistic faculty'. It is precisely this anglicised Jewishness that appeals to the refined, artistic Barbara, who notices the combination of English and Jewish physiognomic features in Meredith, 'his square face and his capable-looking brow, and the uncommon shape and colour of his eyes, from which his Jewish descent looked out' (p.103). Unlike Reuben Sachs, who cannot sustain the tension in his life between 'the democratic atmosphere of modern London' and 'the conservative precincts of the Jewish community', in Meredith Eller the English element triumphs over the Jewish.[23]

The crucial test of this triumph comes in Meredith's response to the plight of Barbara Lassen. Determined that Isaac Eller's heir should not escape their clutches, the Goldbergs conspire to force Barbara into a compromising position with a Mr Klein, whom they hope she will marry, leaving Meredith free for Valerie. But when he sees her on the eve of this scene of martyrdom Meredith's chivalric sensibility is touched: 'The picture of Barbara drooping under the cruel gossip of those Jewish tongues ... stung him like an outrage' (p.174). Barbara's vulnerable position as a dowryless woman is here augmented by the suggestion of racial violation. While the narrative voice suggests Barbara and Meredith's affinity by distancing both from 'those Jew[s]' around them, they are also linked by their capacity to redeem each other from Jewishness. When Meredith rescues Barbara by marrying her, defying his grandfather and thus sacrificing his commercial ambitions, he demonstrates 'hardness and determination ... a degree of resolve ... that she could no more vanquish than she could have vanquished his physical strength' (p.217). In striking contrast to Reuben Sachs, then, Meredith Eller devotes his manly business skills to the cause of love. In turn, Barbara saves Meredith from a mercenary marriage that 'would shut him out for ever from the depths of affection and companionship' (p.128); she liberates him from being controlled by the Jewish 'genius for commerce' that wrecked his grandfather's life. Their union is redemptive not only mutually but also for the Jewish community as a whole.

In this respect Sidgwick reverses the pessimism of Levy's novel. *Isaac Eller's Money* ends with the incorporation into Jewish society of Meredith and Barbara, whose instinct for romantic rather than mercenary marriage, and for cultured rather than parochial pursuits, marks them out as precursors of a more enlightened Anglo-Jewry. That attitudes to marriage, for Sidgwick, are the crucial signifiers of archaic and progressive Jewish identities is evident throughout. When Barbara turns down an offer from Klein, for example, the Goldbergs lament her ingratitude, insisting that 'in an earlier generation, and even now, in any country but this foolish

English one, a girl of their race could no more have stood up against her guardians, and refused the husband of their choosing, than a slave can stand up against his owner' (p.207). Isaac Eller is no less authoritarian in marriage matters; the novel opens with his transformation at his son's intermarriage from the 'urbane and benevolent favourite of the London colony' into 'a picture for a mediaeval Ghetto' (p.10). Eller's regression to barbarity is reversed on his deathbed, when, confusing his grandson Meredith with his dead son Bernard he casts on Meredith 'a look of love and anguish' (p.235). In this momentary glimpse of the emotional cost of orthodoxy the novel declares, as it has been suggesting throughout, that the narrow clannishness of the 'mediaeval Ghetto' – and likewise the un-English enslavement of daughters – can be sustained no longer. That the Jewish community finally integrates rather than ostracising the anglicised Meredith and Barbara suggests its own capacity for salvation through modernisation.

The vulnerable figure of the young property-less woman on the Jewish marriage market thus occupies a key rhetorical position in Sidgwick's writing. A number of stories in *Scenes of Jewish Life* (1904), a collection of pieces previously published in periodicals such as *Cornhill* and *Temple Bar*, take up this concern. 'An Arabian Bird' reiterates the plot of *Isaac Eller's Money* in depicting the powerlessness of a heroine whose personal aspirations are in conflict with the archaic mores of her society. Eva Minden is an elegant but poor governess who has fallen in love with her wealthy cousin Fred Trieste:

> She felt sure that he loved her, but she knew that he would have to give her up and marry someone who had money. An English girl in her place would not have made herself miserable by such forebodings; she would expect a man of Fred Trieste's years and fortunes to please himself when he married. But Eva had been taught to think that even grown-up people cannot marry without the sanction of their parents; and she had often heard of lovers who were parted from each other on this account ... She could not think of a case amongst her own people where the will of the elders had not prevailed.[24]

Both Fred's mother and Eva's brother try to persuade Eva to marry Joseph Lehmann, a middle-aged stockbroker and old family friend, who anticipates her cooking and cleaning for him, considering that such labour 'is pleasure. All good women think so' (p.154). But, like *Isaac Eller's Money*, the story ends with the hero's insistence on a romantic marriage and the capitulation of 'the elders' to English practice rather than Jewish tradition.

'Mr. Rosenthal', the final story in the collection, underlines the author's polemic in a less upbeat manner. The story is written in free indirect discourse representing the point of view of a London Jewish merchant, 'Poor Mr. Rosenthal', whose 'trials were always in connection with his children' (p.274). Viewing the ugliness of his elder daughter Helen with 'dismay', Rosenthal coerces her into marriage with a middle-aged man 'By judicious gibes, together with threats, bribes and prayers' (p.273-4). Although his younger daughter Thora is considered beautiful her looks are not to her father's taste: 'her waxen skin, her prominent light-blue eyes, her absurd thinness and her infirm mouth – the outward signs of the nervousness and weakness that made her so difficult to manage' (p.275). For Thora he selects the rich Mr. Joshua, who 'was small and thin and knock-kneed. His bald head, pallid face, and exhausted-looking eyes suggested that the pursuit of wealth had not exclusively absorbed him' (p.278). But Thora has been secretly meeting Thornton, a young clergyman's son whom she met at a dance where he was 'the only person in the room with an English face' (p.280). When she is introduced to Joshua as her future husband she is physically repelled and faints. The next part of the story takes Thora's point of view, revealing her romantic longing for Thornton and her desperate hope that 'he might ask her to be his wife – might even insist, when told of the dreadful fate awaiting her, that she should come to him for refuge, marry him clandestinely, and escape under his wing to Rio' (p.294). But her marriage, a lavish and ostentatious one, is arranged without her being able to intervene, and two days later she is found dead of an overdose of chloral. Unable to read his daughter's physiognomy as a sign both of her sensitivity and her Englishness rather than her 'weakness', Rosenthal has condemned her to suicide.

Yet while much of Sidgwick's work criticises the practice of arranged marriage as a specifically Jewish institution, her writing also became more overt in attacking hostility to Jews. In her ethnographic study *Home Life in Germany* (1908) the section on the Jews of Germany draws attention to the practice of marriage brokerage, a 'business-like' process which, she says, still continues today although 'It need hardly be said, perhaps, that the refined and enlightened Jews refuse to marry in this way... Amongst Christians marriages are certainly not arranged for girls in this matter-of-course way'.[25] Sidgwick here again sees arranged marriage as something that the 'enlightened' and 'Christians' do not do, but in this volume her disapproval is more strongly directed not at Jews but at German attitudes to them. The book's closing remarks conclude with a strong indictment of contemporary German anti-semitism, as if this is Sidgwick's final word on the general subject of home life in Germany: 'The social crusade against Jews is carried on in Germany to an extent we do not dream of here. The Christian clubs and hostels exclude them, Christian families avoid them, and Christian insults are offered to them from the day of their birth'. But this is not only a modern phenomenon; the Jewish race, she says, 'has lived for hundreds of years cheek by jowl with a dense, brutal race that has never ceased to insult and humiliate it'. In line with the intensified hostility to Germany in public discourse in the wake of the Boer War, Sidgwick reads anti-semitism as a sign of the savagery of the German 'race'; she ends the book patriotically contrasting German 'sympathy with the Russian persecution of the Jews' with 'the deep helpless genuine horror felt in England at the pogroms'.[26]

Sidgwick's fiction of the 1890s is also designed to illustrate these arguments about English and Germanic attitudes to Jews. If *Isaac Eller's Money* represented the majority of the German-Jewish community as vulgar and shallow, *Lesser's Daughter* (1894) ascribes such qualities not to Jews but to anti-semites.[27] Lesser Bremen, an introverted, rich, and 'distressingly plain' Jewish businessman is married to Corona, an elegant and ambitious Viennese manufacturer's daughter who reads French novels, cultivates friendships with pseudo-aristocratic decadents and 'held aloof from her husband's people with a violence that in England is quite unusual. She had brought traditions with her that twenty years of a freer, more generous air did not help her to throw off' (pp.13, 35). Accordingly, the narrative point of view does not take Corona's part, but portrays her hostility to Jews as 'barbarous and mediaeval' (p.40).

Whereas Corona's 'prejudice' is linked to 'her [Austrian] race' (p.52) Bremen longs for 'English' values to govern his family. He views Charley Redruth, the gentile fiancé of his daughter Aline, with a kind of suspicious respect: 'Mr. Bremen did not feel quite at home with the young Englishman, whose looks and ways were so unlike his own. But he had a keen appreciation of just those advantages he missed most bitterly in himself; and besides, in some important respects, he had reckoned on Charley as an ally ... He thought that if his child married this honest, simple-natured Englishman she might remain unspotted from the world herself, and therefore better content with her unornamental father' (pp.22–3). While Bremen trusts in Charley's 'simple-natured' Englishness as a bulwark against Germanic 'prejudice', his 'keen appreciation' is also a recognition of his own 'lesser' status; his 'ugly Jewish features, his insignificant body, and his clumsy manners', the fact that 'he had not ... been born a fighter' are all aspects of his incomplete masculinity (p.41). Bremen's quixotic project of reading through the great works of Western literature only serves to emphasise his sense of deficiency. And Charley himself feels ambivalent about Bremen and his social manners in a way that echoes Bremen's own unease: 'Aline's father puzzled him. He looked like a little money-lender, and he behaved with curious, incomprehensible alternations of shyness and familiarity. This morning, for instance, he came into the room with the air of a man who rather expects to be kicked out of it' (pp.23–4). While *Lesser's Daughter* clearly deplores the 'barbarous' Jew-hatred of Corona and 'her race', the shifts of the narrative into Charley's point of view push the reader also to share his disdain for Bremen. By marrying Charley, Aline is redeemed not only from her mother's Germanic 'prejudice' but also from her father's Jewish awkwardness.

The complicity of Jews themselves in the 'social crusade' against them is also the subject of Sidgwick's story 'The Powder Blue Baron' in *Scenes of Jewish Life*. Here, Esther, the spirited London-born protagonist, visits cousins in the German town of Eberheim where Jews are excluded from dances and cut in public by gentile acquaintances. Courted by the handsome, aristocratic and proudly anti-semitic Major Baron von und zu Amsing, who makes allowances for her because she is 'different' from her relatives,[28] Esther persistently refuses his advances while they obsequiously cultivate his acquaintance. For her, more shocking than the social crusade of the anti-semites is what Sidgwick describes in *Home Life in Germany* as the 'painful undesirable conviction that the brutes are their superiors ... the spectacle in Germany of Jews seeking Christian society instead of avoiding it'.[29]

Yet the narrative voice betrays a similar conviction even as the story condemns Germanic anti-semitism as medieval and un-English (p.35): in order to elevate its heroine and to underline her authority, the text relies on a vocabulary of racial physique. The elegant Esther is thus distinguished from Rosalie and Recha, her 'two stout swarthy' cousins who unlike her are 'clumsy on their [ice]-skates' (pp.6, 15). The narrator, regarding Esther as 'different' from Rosalie and Recha – less Jewish in body and mind – effectively takes the perspective of the anti-semite Baron Amsing (p.19). Indeed, Esther's departure from Eberheim is shown to be precipitated more by her relatives than by their tormentors; she 'began to find her position untenable, and it was her hosts who made it so. She could have dealt with Baron Amsing if they had had more dignity ... But to agree with your adversary about the defects of your official allies is always intolerable' (pp.23–4). If Esther's repulsion from the 'defects' of the German Jews she finds in Eberheim aligns her with her 'adversary', her only recourse is to return to England where Jews are 'well-dressed, well-mannered people' (p.34). Sidgwick's story constructs Esther's Englishness as both a physical attribute, rendering her elegant rather than clumsy, and a temperament, rendering her proud of her Jewishness rather than ashamed of it. She reprimands her cousins: 'How there is any kindness or any charity left amongst you I cannot understand. If I lived here a year, I should want to be like Samson, and slay ten thousand of them with one of their own jawbones' (p.25). Sidgwick's liberal critique of anti-semitism is, in this way, underpinned by a contradictory assumption about Jewish racial inferiority.

Esther's aspiration to the biblical violence of Samson contrasts strongly with the pusillanimity of the Jewish men in Sidgwick's fiction. In 'The Crime of Israel Leyden', for example, a father who is an accessory to the death of his brutal son-in-law cannot even celebrate his daughter's deliverance without feeling secretly guilty.[30] Sidgwick's narratives often ascribe the vulnerability of the Jewish daughter to her father's weakness, which is only redeemed through her freely chosen marriage to a worthier man. Thus each of her heroines asserts their independence only to discover a more appropriate dependence. In the climactic scene of *Isaac Eller's Money*, Barbara and Meredith come to recognise their mutual attraction when Barbara ventures into central London alone, finds herself lost on a foggy night in Oxford Street and is rescued by the fortuitous arrival of Meredith. She is impressed both with his masculine mastery of the hostile urban environment and with 'the power of a man with money in his pocket to carry off anything in a shop that takes his fancy'.[31]

The author's position on women's economic independence is made even clearer in *The Grasshoppers* (1895), one of Sidgwick's novels not on a Jewish theme. Here, Hilary Frere, a self-styled New Woman who claims to want to earn her own living, nevertheless expects her father's wealth to support what the narrator calls her 'extravagant' education and dilettante socialism'.[32] Hilary rejects a proposal of marriage from her devoted childhood friend Dick, informing him that 'women have grown and changed. We no longer find our only happiness in marriage. I want my life to be a wide one' (p.95). But when her father dies a bankrupt and she is forced to support herself financially she finds that her college education has equipped her for no useful work. She finally capitulates to Dick, who reassures her 'You shall never trouble your head about money again' (p.432). In *A Woman with a Future* (1896), the decadent Hesperia Madison uses the language of contemporary feminism to resist the authority of her serious, scholarly husband Philip Troy. The narrator meanwhile expresses a preference for Mrs Troy, Philip's mother, who 'had never talked big about the emancipation of women' but was one of those who 'do a great deal for their sex by gaining the respect of every man they know'.[33] Whereas for feminists like Mona Caird, Olive Schreiner and Amy Levy, female economic independence was a prerequisite for sexual autonomy, Sidgwick's defence of women's choice of marriage partner was not grounded in a feminist politics.

Instead, her narratives are resolved with the restoration of sexual and social order – and, in her Jewish stories, with the fantasy of racial order.

That the suffering of the heroine at the hands of Jews is a symbol of racial disorder is most forcefully expressed in another novel of the period, *Violet Moses* (1891) by Leonard Merrick (né Miller). The novel imitated Julia Frankau's 1887 satire *Dr Phillips* in describing the decadence of Maida Vale middle-class Jewish society through the perspective of a gentile woman.[34] Merrick's Christian protagonist Violet Dyas is the innocent object of exchange between her father, a swindler and drunk, and Leopold Moses, a Jewish stockbroker, on whose financial support he depends. Moses is attracted by Violet's culture: 'to listen to a girl who talked poetry and books, and had ideality in her eye instead of a carriage and pair, was a novel sensation to him'.[35] In comparison with Violet, the 'Oriental' appearance and social manners of the Jewish women of his circle are thrown into relief, rendered 'coarse and loud' (II.78–9). But their marriage begins badly with a honeymoon during which Violet looks out to sea and is 'possessed by a passionate yearning for comfort though she knew not what was her grief – an intense longing to hear passionate words and feel the strong embrace of her husband's arms'. His response – offering to teach her to play cards – is comically emblematic of his inadequacy as a husband (II.186). Grateful to possess her, it never occurs to him to 'wake her affections'; 'he was sluggishly content ... the knowledge that she belonged to him, gorged him mentally and physically, and he would have been astonished to hear there were reasonable grounds for supposing she might be unhappy' (II.175, 205). Through the lens of this marriage, the Jew is represented as acquisitive, grossly physical and emotionally insensitive.

The misery of Violet's marriage is underscored by two key scenes in the novel. In the first, Violet argues with her husband when he objects to her desire to go to church. Finally giving in to his wish not to make him look foolish by displaying his lack of domestic mastery, Violet 'comprehended that by this concession she was pledging herself to abstain from all public worship for years' but determines that the future conflict over the faith of their children will be 'a battle which she would fight with all the authority of the woman's belief' (II.212–13). Here the cruel enforcement of wifely submission as part of the marriage contract is made all the more horrifying to the reader because it entails Violet's compromising her Christian faith. Moses' wish not to be badly thought of by his co-religionists for intermarrying is made tantamount to a denial of Christianity; the relationship between husband and wife is given an undercurrent of religious antagonism.

In the second scene, the novel's most striking one, Violet reluctantly accedes to her husband's insistence that they attend a friend's card party, even though it is held on a Sunday. Indeed, for the Maida Vale Jews, 'gambling was almost the *Alpha* and *Omega* of the programme of amusement': cards have replaced God (II.242). The card party, mediated through the gaze of Violet, represents the worst of Maida Vale's depravity, which 'she contemplated ... in horror' (II.229). Violet watches as food is served late because the women cannot bear to leave the card table. She is shocked at the equanimity with which the men lose large sums of money, and at the lack of emotional restraint displayed by the women. By half past two 'the drawing-room ...looked like a gambling-hell, the women had grown noisier, the perpetual Babel accompanied by the clink of the coins, and at intervals culminating in a yell of triumph or despair, suggested to the disgusted girl another illustration for the "Inferno".' (II.231). The heat of the atmosphere takes its toll on the women's complexions: at first 'those of the women who were losing had ceased to rummage their pockets for their powder-puffs, and kept them lying beside their purses in readiness for use' but by half past four 'they did not have recourse to powder at all now, but sat with streaky faces glaring at the cards like so many nervous devils' (II.233–4). The card party stages a progressive stripping away of the veneer of civilised femininity: for Violet 'the naked hideousness of the thing frightened her' (II.244). When, at six in the morning, she and her husband go outside to find a cab to drive them home, 'the brute of beef and beer whom Mr. Moses hailed, grinned at the beauty of Violet with precisely the same mixture of contempt and admiration that he would have cast on a handsome "fare" he had picked up at the door of the "Cavour".' (II.236). Just as Violet's beauty is no longer a sign of her innocence but is easily mistaken for that of a streetwalker, Violet herself is implicated in the decadence of Jewish society because her mercenary marriage has made her no different from a prostitute. Merrick's scene of hysteria, primitive individualism and physical decomposition is rendered as an iconic image of modern Jewish racial degeneration, and, at the same time, set within a religious framework, invoking an older tradition of representing Jews as eternally reprobate or even satanic.

Violet's superiority to her husband and his friends is indicated by her moral response to their gambling, by her taste for high culture rather than the comic opera and burlesques they enjoy and by her physical response to Jews: 'Which of the fourteen-stone Jewesses in ruby velvet and black satin could ever develop into her friend!' (II.253). But the novel also represents the marriage of Jew and Christian as resulting in 'the repression of Violet's inner or truer self', a repression to which Moses is oblivious, since 'her docility and superficial complaisance rendered her a vastly more congenial companion to him than her natural disposition would have done' (III.3). It is to Violet's 'inner or truer self' that Allan Morris, a successful sensation novelist and former suitor appeals when he appears in the Maida Vale circle. Capable of literary discussion and disgusted by the 'disputatious women losing their money and their femininity simultaneously' at the card table, Morris recognises Violet's redemptive virtue and, unlike her husband, longs to be the object of it (III.39). But he also challenges the conservative principles of Violet's world. He protests against being cast in the role of the '"systematic scoundrel" of melodrama and fiction' because her marriage has intervened between them: 'He had not altered in the respect of his love; he was a villain because circumstances had altered, while he remained the same' (III.177). In this equation, Anglo-Jewish society, like the simplified moral vision of melodrama, represents an overdetermined version of bourgeois morality. As Violet's only friend Mrs Benjamin assures her: 'I'm not proud of that class of my co-religionists, though I'm proud of my religion; but whether I like them or not, I'll do all the women of Judaism the justice to say that an instance of a Jewess bringing disgrace on her family is so rare that it may almost be said to never happen' (III.159).

In contrast, the complexity of Violet's emerging subjectivity is revealed by her acknowledgement of an adulterous passion:

> To begin to doubt her power of resistance is the most appalling horror a woman's virtue ever confronts. Hell itself need hold no torture more devilish than the reviviscence and eternal prolongation of those minutes in the flesh, when it is as though her identity had slipped away from her – the "self" which was She gone, leaving her tottering with an alien's feet on the brink of a precipice, giddy with an alien's brain. It is no more, her former self; all, save consciousness of her peril, has fled. She stretches out her hands and calls for it wildly, the old self that was so strong and brave. She knows if she stumbles and crashes to the bottom, she will lie bathed in her own blood; but on the brink she is still a stranger to herself, and the stranger is too magnetized to retreat.
>
> It is a nightmare from which the sunshine will not rescue her. She is beset by danger, yet the "she" who has contended with it has forsaken her, leaving her with a new, unrecognizable individuality which is creeping dizzily nearer and nearer to the edge (III.181–3).

Despite the melodramatic register, Merrick's depiction of a woman's crisis of identity here approaches the agonised discourse of the New Woman novel. Like Amy Levy's Judith Quixano, Violet's struggle with 'a new, unrecognizable individuality' leaves her not triumphant but newly conscious of her capacity for desire and suffering. Her heroic resistance to Oriental foreignness notwithstanding, Violet finds herself, finally, rendered an 'alien'.

The novel is ambiguous in other ways about the moral crisis wrought in its heroine. The narrator expresses scepticism about the depth of Morris's love, which is seen as commonplace rather than heroic, and prefaces the lovers' final meeting with a premonitory scene in Hyde Park among soldiers and servant girls where 'vice was omnivagrant and reigned supreme' (III.200–201). But Merrick also finally confers a certain authority on Morris's cause. While Violet clings to her honour, despite her misery, Morris's persuasions draw on a number of images which recapitulate the novel's concerns. 'You have bartered yourself away for money as foully as the foullest', he accuses her, 'you are balancing the deference of Maida Vale against the claim of a Heaven-created love' (III.218, 221). He warns her that her conventional principles will later fall from her mind and leave her 'bowed in despair before the false gods to which her idolatry had sacrificed their lives' (III.230). In this way, the novel aligns the cause of love – even adulterous love – with moral righteousness and Christianity, in contrast to the mercenariness, conventionality and heathenism of Maida Vale Jewry. Although ostensibly applauding the heroine's steadfast virtue, *Violet Moses* opens up the possibility of readerly sympathy with adulterous desire by associating it with resistance to 'Jewish' values. Violet, who ends the novel wretched and without hope for the future, is as much a sacrifice to middle-class Anglo-Jewry as Judith Quixano; like Judith, her potential for redemption is suggested by the novel but goes unrecognised by its characters.

Violet Moses reveals most starkly of all the texts under discussion here the ways that representing the rights of women was imbricated with the discourses of anti-semitism. In Merrick's novel, female sexual autonomy is set in stark opposition to a Jewish world that is patriarchal, philistine and anti-Christian. Merrick's religious frame of reference is deployed in a similar way to Amy Levy and Cecily Sidgwick's use of the more contemporary language of race in order to moralise their romantic narratives. The plight of their idealised heroines gains force from a rhetoric of racial repulsion that demonstrates their distinctiveness from the decadence of Anglo-Jewry. Jewish writers, I have argued, far from being above such rhetoric, actively incorporate it into their work. Nevertheless, these elements are made to work for different ends in their novels. For Amy Levy, Jewish racial degeneration is both expressed in and exacerbated by Jews' disregard for the vital resource of women. Cecily Sidgwick's writing, on the other hand, suggests the redemptive potential of symbolic or literal intermarriage with English Christians.

For Leonard Merrick, in contrast, Jews are irredeemable and Jewish oppression of women is aligned with conservative 'conventional principles' and 'idolatry'. In each of these texts we can see the operation of an ambivalent semitic discourse in which Jewish men are irredeemably racialised, while the modern, cultured and healthy heroines are seen to transcend 'race'. Offering an exemplary narrative of female subjection linked on the one hand to the archaic structure of 'Oriental' societies and on the other to its modern manifestation in the capitalist marriage market, the novel of Jewish marriage displaced onto the Anglo-Jewish milieu broader fin de siècle preoccupations with the relationship between social progress and racial regression.

NOTES

1. 'Critical Jews', editorial, *Jewish Chronicle*, 25 January 1889, p.11.
2. Bryan Cheyette, 'From Apology to Revolt: Benjamin Farjeon, Amy Levy and the Post-emancipation Anglo-Jewish Novel 1880–1900', *Transactions of the Jewish Historical Society of England* 24 (1982–86): 253–65 (p.260).
3. Ibid.
4. Ibid., p.255.
5. Studies of New Woman fiction on this theme include Ann Heilmann, *New Woman Fiction: Women Writing First-Wave Feminism* (Basingstoke: Macmillan, 2000), and Sally Ledger, *The New Woman: Fiction and Feminism at the* fin de siècle (Manchester: Manchester University Press, 1997). See also *The Late-Victorian Marriage Question: A Collection of Key New Woman Texts*, ed. by Ann Heilmann (London: Routledge Thoemmes Press, 1998).
6. 'Middle-Class Jewish Women of To-Day: By A Jewess', *Jewish Chronicle* 17 September 1886, p.7. Melvyn New, in *The Complete and Selected Writings of Amy Levy 1861-1889*, ed. by Melvyn New (Gainesville: University Press of Florida, 1993), attributes this unsigned article to Levy. The similarity of phrasing and sentiment to Levy's other writing suggests to me that this is a correct assumption.
7. Ibid.
8. Emma Francis, 'Socialist Feminism and Sexual Instinct: Eleanor Marx and Amy Levy' in *Eleanor Marx (1855-1898): Life. Work. Contacts*, ed. by John Stokes (Aldershot: Ashgate, 2000), pp.113–27 (p.117).
9. See Linda Hunt Beckman, *Amy Levy: Her Life and Letters* (Athens: Ohio University Press, 2000) and Naomi Hetherington, 'New Women, New Testaments: Christian Narrative and New Woman Writing (Olive Schreiner, Amy Levy, Sarah Grand)', unpublished PhD thesis (University of Southampton, 2003), ch. 2.
10. Mona Caird, 'Marriage', repr. in *The Morality of Marriage and Other Essays on the Status and Destiny of Woman* (London: George Redway, 1897), pp.63–111 (pp.100, 99, 95). For a full discussion of the contours of the Marriage Question in the 1880s and 1990s see Lucy Bland, *Banishing the Beast: English Feminism and Sexual Morality 1885–1914* (Harmondsworth: Penguin, 1995), ch.4.
11. Extract reprinted in *The Fin de Siècle*, ed. by Sally Ledger and Roger Luckhurst (Oxford: Oxford University Press, 2000), p.47.
12. Eliza Lynn Linton, 'The Wild Women as Social Insurgents', *Nineteenth Century* 30 (Oct. 1891), 596–605 (p.603).
13. [Levy], 'Middle-Class Jewish Women' (see note 6).
14. Amy Levy, *Reuben Sachs: A Sketch* (London: Macmillan, 1888) repr. in *The Complete and*

Selected Writings of Amy Levy 1861–1889, ed. by Melvyn New (Gainesville: University Press of Florida, 1993), p.214. Further references to this edition will be included in the text.

15. See Sander L. Gilman, *Freud, Race, and Gender* (Princeton, NJ: Princeton University Press, 1993), p.100.

16. Francis (see note 8), p.122.

17. Francis (see note 8); idem, 'Amy Levy: Contradictions? – Feminism and Semitic Discourse', in *Women's Poetry, Late Romantic to Late Victorian: Gender and Genre 1830-1900*, ed. by Isobel Armstrong and Virginia Blain (Basingstoke: Macmillan, 1998), pp.183–204; Meri-Jane Rochelson, 'Jews, Gender, and Genre in Late-Victorian England: Amy Levy's *Reuben Sachs*', *Women's Studies* 25 (1996), 311–28; Deborah Epstein Nord, '"Neither Pairs Nor Odd": Women, Urban Community and Writing in the 1880s' in *Walking the Victorian Streets: Women, Representation and the City* (Ithaca, NY and London: Cornell University Press, 1995), pp.181–206.

18. Rochelson (see note 17), p.311.

19. 'New Books', *Jewish Chronicle*, 2 August 1889, p.12.

20. Todd M. Endelman, *Radical Assimilation in English Jewish History, 1656–1945* (Bloomington: Indiana University Press, 1990), p.123; and Endelman, 'German Jews in Victorian England: A Study in Drift and Defection', in *Assimilation and Community: The Jews in Nineteenth-Century Europe*, ed. by Jonathan Frankel and Steven J. Zipperstein (Cambridge: Cambridge University Press, 1992), pp.57–87 (pp.68–9).

21. Endelman, 'German Jews' (see note 20), pp.62–3.

22. Mrs Andrew Dean [Cecily Sidgwick], *Isaac Eller's Money* (London: T. Fisher Unwin, 1889), pp.59, 61. Further references to this edition will be included in the text.

23. Levy, *Reuben Sachs* (see note 14), p.200.

24. Mrs. Alfred Sidgwick [Cecily Sidgwick], *Scenes of Jewish Life* (London: Edward Arnold, 1904), p.140. Further references to this edition will be included in the text.

25. Mrs. Alfred Sidgwick [Cecily Sidgwick], *Home Life in Germany*, 3rd edn. (London: Methuen, 1908), pp.80–81.

26. Ibid., pp.319, 320, 321.

27. Mrs. Andrew Dean [Cecily Sidgwick], *Lesser's Daughter* (London: T. Fisher Unwin, 1894). Further references to this edition will be included in the text.

28. Sidgwick, *Scenes of Jewish Life* (see note 24), p.19.

29. Ibid., p.320.

30. Ibid., p.267.

31. [Sidgwick], *Isaac Eller's Money* (see note 22), pp.98, 99.

32. Mrs. Andrew Dean [Cecily Sidgwick], *The Grasshoppers* (London: Adam and Charles Black, 1895), pp.58, 8, 23.

33. Mrs. Andrew Dean [Cecily Sidgwick], *A Woman with a Future* (London: Adam and Charles Black, 1896), p.139.

34. For discussions of *Dr Phillips* see Bryan Cheyette, 'From Apology to Revolt' and idem, 'The Other Self: Anglo-Jewish Fiction and the Representation of Jews in England, 1875–1905' in *The Making of Modern Anglo-Jewry*, ed. by David Cesarani (Oxford: Basil Blackwell, 1990), pp.97–111; Michael Galchinsky, '"Permanently Blacked": Julia Frankau's Jewish Race', *Victorian Literature and Culture* 27.1 (1999), 171–83; Todd M. Endelman, 'The Frankaus of London: A Study in Radical Assimilation, 1837–1967', *Jewish History* 8.1–2 (1994), 117–54.

35. Leonard Merrick, *Violet Moses*, 3 vols (London: Richard Bentley and Sons, 1891), II.77. Further references to this edition will be included in the text.

Max Nordau and the Generation of Jewish Muscle

MARILYN REIZBAUM

In 1892, Max Nordau wrote in *Degeneration* [*Entartung*]: 'The *fin-de-siècle* state of mind is today everywhere to be met with.'[1] This is, it would seem, a statement true of every turning if we may judge by this latest millennial shift. In fact, Nordau begins his classic text with a denunciation of that state of mind, with the mood that he characterises as the 'impotent despair of a sick man': 'This fashionable term has the necessary vagueness which fits it to convey all the half-conscious and indistinct drift of current ideas. Just as the words "freedom," "idea," "progress" seem to express notions, but actually are only sounds, so in itself *fin-de-siècle* means nothing, and receives a varying signification according to the diverse mental horizons of those who use it.'[2] With all the renewed interest in Nordau, or, at least, in his *Degeneration* and its like, and with the recent urgency about questions of ethics, literary and otherwise, it seems that the beginning of the twenty-first century is firmly preoccupied with, even conceptually lodged within, the previous *fin de siècle*, fulfilling in Nordau's terms what he himself predicted for the twentieth century – that retrogression would be the ideal of those who (claim to) cherish progress.[3] Nordau would of course have given the idea of progress a very different value from some of us millennialists or Y2Kers, who in the best postmodern way have come to delimit progress as always already retrogressive, as a narrative with a bad attitude. This accusation against certain thinkers of his generation is, like so much of Nordau's condemnatory rhetoric, highly contradictory. When Nordau says that *fin de siècle* cases of degeneracy have a common feature – a contempt for traditional views of custom and morality – he implies that the best way to go forward is to look or stay back; this is, in a sense he seems to refuse, a description of the retrogression he will condemn. Nordau understands tradition as a safeguard against atavism, against disease itself, so loaded a term in this period, summed up in Nordau's era-characterising phrase – 'impotent despair of a sick man'.

'Impotence', 'despair', 'disease' – these are the qualities of the degenerate man that Nordau both identifies and tacitly disavows and/or displaces. There is remarkably no mention of Jews in these terms in Nordau's early work, either to confirm or protest (unlike Lombroso) the by then resonantly established Jewish stereotype of degeneracy. This omission, if that is what it is, might be read as pathological or logical (as self-hating, repressed, denial or refusal). Nordau's contradictory reading of the past, then, can be understood in terms of the cultural conundrum of his own history. In his backward glance, what he is longingly looking at or for is the image of the 'new Jew' he would project in his later Zionist tracts, derived from the image of manliness and restraint which together make the civilised man. This image is ironically modelled on the Aryan ideal, and would be produced in relief, or as relief by his own (and other) treatises on degeneration. This is what George Mosse means in his introduction to the 1968 reissue of the 1895 English translation of *Degeneration* when he suggests that Nordau portrays a negative strain throughout his ardent Zionism.[4] That is, his idealised figures of Jewish success are shot through with the spectres of the degenerate Jew, who is fashioned in their anti-image. Nordau would claim that oppression made him do it, or made Jews what they are, and he would write them out of the discourse of degeneration as a strategy of recuperation or defensiveness.[5]

What I want to examine here is Nordau's legacy for the twentieth and, at least thus far, the twenty-first centuries, how he and figures like him (Cesare Lombroso, his teacher) unwittingly contributed to a discourse of anti-semitism and racism that has dominated the century. Of course, the irony in the case of these figures lies in the fact of their own Jewishness (as distinct from the other major European figures associated with this arena – Havelock Ellis and Richard Kraftt-Ebing, for example). Nordau falls into line with the likes of Otto Weininger (though less pathologically, perhaps), as part of a documented and contested *fin de siècle* phenomenon of Jewish self-hatred. Unlike, let us say, their black counterparts in the United States, such as Booker T. Washington, who might have adopted the ideals of the white establishment, thereby appearing to buy into the images of superiority used against blacks, Nordau and Lombroso were busy constructing the degenerate and criminal men. However much one argues that these were their means of dissociation, the fact remains that these very images were then used to reinforce the negative stereotyping of Jews. At the same time, Nordau's retrogressive impulse in *Degeneration* eventually leads to a method of restoration and recovery in the later work, especially the Zionist tracts, these processes being closely related. Making it new was really making it old. Scholars of Nordau generally focus on one part or the other. (Mendes-Flohr and Reinharz's compilation, *The Jew in the Modern World*, does not even mention *Degeneration*, and the recent focus has been primarily on the early part.)[6] It seems Nordau's legacy for modernity reflects the continuities between the new and the old, despite what has been apprehended as a bifurcated sensibility. I shall come to a more specific discussion of such legacies in a moment, but first I want to lay out the historical ground of the continuities.

In keeping with his own contradictory logic, but also with the logic of contradiction that attends Jewish representation in the period, in *Degeneration* Nordau constructs the type – the slack artist figure – he would need to contest in his later work and for himself: this type evinces MADNESS (neurasthenia); MODERNITY (anarchism, uncertainty, stylistic innovation, the avant garde, emancipation, experimentation); EFFEMINACY, or in B.A. Morel's words, quoted here by Nordau, 'a morbid deviation from an original type', i.e., 'the Jew'.[7] The plot thickens as we encounter some of Nordau's detractors, among them most notably, George Bernard Shaw, who, in *The Sanity of Art: An Exposure of the Current Nonsense About Artists Being Degenerate* (1908), would characterise Nordau's assertions as not only inaccurate but hysterical, one of the typifying qualities Nordau claims for the degenerates. We are familiar with this characterisation as part of the discourse of anti-semitism, the symptom of the 'Jewish' diseases (that certainly Freud and perhaps here Nordau, too, however unconsciously, dissociate from as Jews). Shaw's remarks evince a kind of encoded anti-semitism: he describes Nordau as 'one of those remarkable cosmopolitan Jews who go forth against modern civilization as David went against the Philistines', a description Nordau would later contest in print (particularly ironic in light of his imminent Zionist profile).[8] Shaw's barb interestingly casts Jews, however cosmopolitan, as retrograde, anti-modern. And, of course, Nordau did situate the proletariat, with whom he identified, against the modern, a situation mocked here by Shaw in his equation of philistine with modern.[9] We are to read Nordau in this as pretentious, petit bourgeois, self-righteous, and just plain stupid. (Shaw goes on to compare Nordau's critical abilities to that of Gulliver's nautical skill). Whatever one's sentiments about Shaw's overall response to Nordau, he does mention Jews where Nordau does not, placing, one might say, the Jew into the text, or more provocatively, the 'jew who hates the jew in the jew', to borrow from Joyce's notes for the characterisation of his own dubious Jew, Leopold Bloom.[10]

Daniel Pick describes the discourse on degeneration of the period as an avalanche and sets out a substantive list in his *Faces of Degeneration*.[11] He sums up the concept of degeneration as constituting 'an impossible endeavour to "scientise", objectify and cast off whole underworlds of political and social anxiety'.[12] And if, as these 'scientists' were arguing, society was increasingly susceptible of the pathologies of degeneration (not only racial deviation but also social phenomena like crime, alcoholism, prostitution, suicide), then a theory or process of differentiation became necessary – an implicit product or motive of the studies and treatises so popular in this period – including Nordau's unconscious project of denial or defence.

At the same time that Nordau was perhaps leaving things out in *Degeneration*, he was filling them in (or filling them out), in his later Zionist tracts, most famously in 'Muskeljudentum', one of a series of short pieces he did for *Judische Turnzeitung* [*Jewish Gymnastic Times*] in 1903, which were later compiled as part of *Zionistische Schriften* [*Zionist Writings*], dislodging it thereby from its important original source with its doctrine of athleticism for the new Jew. In a concurrent work, *Von Kunst und Kunstlern* [*On Art and Artists*] (1905), mostly a diatribe against the 'decadent' and much misunderstood doctrine of 'art for art's sake', Nordau examines Rodin's artistic method and berates him for 'inventing muscles which do not exist and never did exist'. Mosse cites this observation as an example of Nordau's critique of the excesses of imagination and of the flouting thereby of the empirical. But when you read on in his critique of Rodin, you find an articulation of – to use his own word – 'discomfort' with the very revelation of the body (despite his insistence on material proofs and means). Here is Nordau on Auguste Rodin: '"The Thinker" excites in a spectator of uninitiated taste, not cheerfulness, but discomfort, which may give rise to loathing. "The Thinker" is not only naked, but also flayed. Its anatomy is executed with obtrusive importance, without the covering epidermis with its vital warmth. The enormous exaggeration of the muscles, the impossible assertion of strength which is expressed by the extreme contraction of all the muscles, therefore also of the counteracting muscles, are well-known features of sculpture in its worst period of decline'.[13]

How curious then that two years before this he would have produced the paradigm of Jewish muscularity, or muscle-Jews, where he suggests that Jews return to a *state* (a double entendre in this case) that was forcibly removed through oppression of body and soul, that of 'deep chested, sturdy, sharp-eyed men'. (Women seem decidedly excluded from the general discourse except in affective terms or as a set of contributory stereotypes. Feminism is often cited by recent critics of degeneration movements as a catalyst both to the movements and their antidotes.) If we go back to the essay itself, we see the same contradictions or at least some confusion there about the place or the meaning of the new Jew, or 'Jewish muscle'. On the one hand, Nordau places the historical rejection of body or bodily dissociation firmly in the Christian camp, by citing corporal mortification as a Christian virtue. He rather ironically suggests that Jews were engaged in such mortification, 'or rather, to put it more precisely – others did the killing of our flesh for us ... We would have preferred to develop our bodies rather than to kill them or to have them – figuratively and actually – killed by others.'[14] In the next breath, however, he seems to rationalise a rejection or disavowal of the body – 'if, unlike most other peoples, we do not conceive of [physical] life as our highest possession, it is nevertheless very valuable to us and thus worthy of careful treatment'. He argues that an appreciation of the bodily was an ancient and now suppressed value among Jews: 'Our new muscle-Jews [*Muskeljuden*] have not yet regained the heroism of our forefathers who in large numbers eagerly entered the sports arenas in order to take part in competition and pit themselves against the highly trained Hellenistic athletes and the powerful Nordic barbarians. But morally now the new muscle-Jews surpass their ancestors, for the ancient Jewish circus fighters were ashamed of their Judaism and tried to conceal the sign of the covenant by means of a surgical operation.'

Daniel Boyarin has written about the historical basis for this confusion about body in his essay on 'Goyim Naches, or Modernity and the Manliness of the Mentsch', wherein the wishful image of martial knightliness for Jews is cast as the wicked son in the Passover *Haggadah* or script, as against the scroll- or book-toting scholar who iconically comes to represent the righteous son. It is also important to note in Boyarin's analysis that antique Christian and Jewish males exchange places within this paradoxical spectrum of masculinity, religion defining itself against imperial power. Nordau taps into this historical paradox; on the one hand, he wants to rationalise the Jewish body by privileging the Jewish brain – the rational – but on the other he wishes to establish a tradition of bodily strength and beauty, Nordic and Greek more than biblical. In other words, he acts like his own version of Rodin, putting muscles where they perhaps do not and never did exist, but at once projects an empirical claim for what one cannot yet see (by going backwards), just as, conversely, he wishes new muscle-Jews to demonstrate moral mettle by showing what has been or is historically/stereotypically seen as the sign of their lack – their circumcised penises. The question is, of course, whether these moves are compatible. After all, the circumcised penis was the demarcator of unmanliness or effeminacy. Perhaps Nordau's discomfort about the body stems from this confusion about what is and is not there, what signifies Jewishly and what does not, what spectaclises difference. When he refers to the prototype of ancient Jewish athletes as *Zirkuskämpfer* or circus performers, he seems to refer to this spectacle, and reveal his anxiety about the freak status circumcision confers upon 'the jew' or the Jewish male body. Furthermore, in these terms – at least, for Jews – Nordau's definition of civilisation is unrealisable or at least paradoxical, since it would seem that restraint and manliness are mutually exclusive.[15] But I will come to more of that later.

Why this surge of interest in Nordau? His work is firmly part of a preoccupation with *fin de siècle* issues that haunt the present, in particular, questions about fitness: racial, sexual, national, social, categorical (aesthetic, etc). What twenty-first century scholars want to do, it seems, is undo the images or the retrogressive damage done in both ethical and social terms. Or perhaps, like Nordau in their own right, they have more atavistic aims. As I have already noted, it is primarily scholars of cultural studies, but not of Jewish culture studies, who are best acquainted with *Degeneration*; at the same time, they know little about or, at least, say little about Nordau's Jewishness and his mammoth contributions to modern Judaism or Jewishness. This seems strangely and inexplicably lacking, despite the fact of Nordau's own omissions. His Jewish readers, traditional or otherwise, rarely mention *Degeneration*, and yet that is the work that put him on the so-called cultural map. There are some notable exceptions, many of whom appear in Bryan Cheyette's and Laura Marcus's collection of essays, *Modernity, Culture and 'the Jew'*, among them, Daniel Boyarin, whose essay I have already mentioned, and Jean Radford, who discusses Dorothy Richardson's use of Nordau in *Pilgrimage*. Mosse and Pick are both suggestive about Nordau's motives for writing as he did by discussing his name change from Südfeld to the more Nordic Nordau ('northern meadow'). Israeli critics of this by now vague national icon in the minds of most of the general Israeli population, have, in many cases, sought a continuity between the two phases of his career and work.[16] But none of these treatments is particularly extensive.[17] As a way of grounding my own view of the relationship between the *fin de siècle* cultural scientist and the Zionist, I will examine a few twentieth-century artistic legacies of Nordau's work, ones that either directly or indirectly acknowledge that inheritance. The individual texts were written or produced long after the publication of *Degeneration*, but not beyond the reach of its impact. They span the twentieth century in English letters.[18] Each of them is concerned with looking back as way of clarifying the present – to examine and comprehend from a contemporary vantage point what haunts – but not with retrograde correctives. They are, in reverse chronological order, Pat Barker's *Regeneration* (1991), a kind of handbook on the topic of degeneration, Hugh Hudson's *Chariots of Fire*

(1981 – the film version of the handbook, you might say), and James
Joyce's *Ulysses* (1922).

   Degeneration's final chapter is called 'The Twentieth Century' and
begins this way: 'Our long and sorrowful wandering through the hospital
– is ended.'[19] The subheading of the first part of the chapter is 'prognosis',
of the second part, 'therapeutics'. Nordau, the self-appointed and (at the
time generally acknowledged) cultural diagnostician is making this
prediction for the twentieth century: even if we have yet to find the cure
for what ails us, at least we have found the cause. This rhetoric is a bit
reminiscent of Hugo (whom Nordau aligns with Zola as romantically
decadent) in its ironically emphatic inaccuracy, and is ironic, too, in its
invocation of Jewish wandering which here acts as metaphor for the
passage Nordau will make from the conclusion of this work to his work
on Zionism. This resonant idea of wandering through the hospital is
particularly apt for a discussion of Barker's *Regeneration*, set in
Craiglockhart War Hospital in Scotland during the period of the First
World War. Nordau's descriptions or even prescriptions of mental
disorder have chilling relevance here. Mental disorder is the domain of
the degenerate, who has a brain incapable of normal working.
Degenerates lisp and stammer, instead of speaking. They manifest
'feebleness of will, inattention, predominance of emotion, lack of
knowledge, absence of sympathy or interest in the world and humanity,
atrophy of the notion of duty and morality'. This reads as a diagnosis of
the condition of the shellshocked soldiers who are the subject of Barker's
Regeneration, for whom fitness or degeneracy is at stake.

   Choosing the war poet Sassoon for her primary soldier/subject is a
stroke of brilliance, a stroke much like Joyce's in the creation of Leopold
Bloom. It seems an unlikely choice for making a certain kind of
assessment of the twentieth century, at least of Englishness, through the
figure of 'the Jew' – a surprise to everyone inside the texts and out. And
Siegfried Sassoon is the perfect kind of Jew, right down to his name (he
tells Wilfred Owen in the novel that he was named Siegfried because his
mother liked Wagner).[20] He cuts a confusing and disturbing figure as
signifier, a confusion mirroring Nordau's own – a Jew and somehow not
Jew-ish. (Sassoon was born of a first-generation English, Sephardic Jewish
father and English Anglican mother.) One of the self-conscious ironies of
this novel and this assessment is that despite, or maybe because of, its
setting in a psychiatric context/hospital, the modus vivendi of the men
within it and even the narrative that governs them is denial, denial most
emphatically of the implications of the figure that Sassoon represents and
of the homosociality of this world. At the conclusion of the novel he is
described by the establishment members of the board judging his fitness

to return to the front as having a physique you rarely see 'even in the so-called upper classes' – Nordau would be proud – but quickly assessed or maybe dismissed as the product of 'hybrid vigour'.[21] 'Vigour' was a term used often both to characterise or even euphemise excess and to describe a needed quality for the regeneration of the race, a kind of positive atavism.[22] This image of the vigorous Sassoon would counter that conjured by his declaration of conscientious objection to the war, produced on the first page of the novel, and tantamount to a declaration of his unmanliness which is fortified by the hint throughout the novel of his homosexuality – in this historical moment another marker of effeminacy. The excess becomes the other side of lack; the display of muscle at once signifies its lack, as in the case of Rodin's thinker, Sassoon's poetry, and, as in the case of the circumcised penis, the signifier of Jewishness.

Could this be the 'new man'? Despite these representative establishment members' concern with eugenics – we are informed of their interest by Rivers, the chief physician and consciousness of the novel, based on Dr W.H.R. Rivers – they observe Sassoon with a kind of longing admiration, however grudging. In fact, Sassoon is the novel's – and perhaps in Barker's notion, the period's/culture's – discreet object of desire. He is everything to every*body* – uncontainable – but strangely nothing to himself. Or, at least, his wish to return to the front may be interpreted as a willingness, more than a wish, to die which is equated in the novel with manliness. That these should be equated disturbs the concept of generation, technically (if not ideologically) becoming degeneration. These equations and their implications stir up much. 'Fitness' in racial and sexual terms, then, would in the context of the war forecast the end of the race – the human race. (Whereas that is the role typically assigned to homosexuality, to its literal degenerative effect in the heterosexual narrative. But here, admission of homosexual desire would render one in the camp of life.) The members of the board would not wish to disprove Sassoon's fitness by acknowledging his sexuality (mirrored in their admiration/desire); in acknowledging his race, they condemn him to their deathwish for him – that hybrid vigour must be expunged – rather than his own. At the end of the novel, Sassoon is sent back to the front.

Perhaps Barker is not thinking of Nordau when she chooses the subject and title of her book, but she is certainly thinking of his subjects: how the medical experiments of regeneration were inflected by the philosophies of war and militarism, national fitness and scientific progress, and led to the pathologisation of art and artists. This conflictual site takes on sexual proportions in the dream world/work of the doctor, who always remarkably denies the sexual reading in his interpretations. Rivers, who struggles with his role as doctor, a displacement in a sense from his repressed sexuality, makes the connection between these realms in a number of ways throughout the novel, particularly in his dreams. He feels complicity in the men's death by helping to recover their fitness, and fears any other response – like that of Sassoon – for fear of uncovering his empathy with Sassoon's position, his identification with him, his own lack of fitness. That explains why he wishes Sassoon to return to the front and why in the end he sees that return as a deathwish on Sassoon's part. But the pronouns exchange places, I believe, or, at the very least, merge. Here he is just before his first major dream, musing on what becomes the catalyst for his dream: 'His irritation, groping for an object, fastened on Sassoon. Sassoon made no secret of his belief that anybody who supported the continuation of the war must be actuated by selfish motives, and yet if Rivers had allowed such motives to dominate, he'd have wanted the war to end tonight.'[23] Rivers disguises the true meaning of his fixation – his groping and fastening on the object Sassoon – with his belief that he wishes to leave the hospital in order to return to his research. But that wish becomes his nightmare in this first dream of the novel; all his dreams chart the modus vivendi of denial and the underbelly of the war effort.

In the dream, Rivers recalls an experiment done with a colleague on the regeneration of nerves after injury. The experiment and the dream centre on the radial nerve of the forearm, and make Rivers the recipient of such an injury in what he believes is a symbolic act of reciprocity. He understands it as an act of self-punishment, a 'wish' to practise upon himself what he is practising upon his patients. But he refuses to see the real meaning, and he even tells us so through a statement of rationalisation: 'He didn't believe such a dream could be convincingly explained as wish fulfillment, unless, of course, he wished to torture one of his closest friends. No doubt some of Freud's more doctrinaire supporters would have little difficulty with that idea, particularly since the form of torture took the form of pricking him, but Rivers couldn't accept it. He was more inclined to seek the meaning of the dream in the conflict his dream self had experienced between the duty to continue the experiment and the reluctance to cause further pain.'[24] As with later dreams the physical site of torture or pain or regenerative experiment is a displacement from the symbolic site, mentioned here in a seeming throwaway remark at the end of the passage.

> In a moment or two an orderly would tap on the door and bring in his tea. He put the notebook and pencil back on the bedside table.

Henry would be amused by that dream, he thought. If wish fulfilment had been involved at all, it was surely one of Henry's wishes that had been fulfilled. At the time of the nerve generation experiments, they'd done a series of control experiments on the glans penis, and Henry had frequently expressed the desire for reciprocal application of ice cubes, bristles, near-boiling water and pins.[25]

When Rivers dreams about the epicritic and protopathic sensations of the forearm, that would, in retrospect, seem to be dream language for the glans penis with or without foreskin. That itself becomes the signifier for Jewish Sassoon – a double displacement, the actual or latent symbolic site – whose relevance for the dream Rivers considers momentarily. What he cannot accept and/or understand at this point and maybe never is that his retrogressive methods of dream analysis and therapy will be anything but regenerative. By making the men fit, he is teaching them to suppress their emotions again; the fitness or manliness training they have all had is restored to them. 'His patients might be encouraged to acknowledge their fears, their horror of war – but they were still expected to do their duty and return to France. It was Rivers' conviction that those who learned to know themselves, and to accept their emotions, were less likely to break down again.'[26] But we see how carefully Rivers himself guards against such knowledge and refuses the interpretation that would implicate his feelings, for Sassoon, for men. Barker adds a lovely detail by telling us that his current issue of *Man* is next to his bed, still in its envelope (A Journal of the Royal Anthropological Institute, extant in one incarnation or another since the eighteenth century, then officially described as 'a paper ennobling the species'). One can read Rivers at the end of the novel as being more in tune, less repressed and retrogressed, but it seems to me that with every step of recognition he takes comes another backwards: 'Rivers saw that he had reached Sassoon's file. He read through the admission report and notes that followed it. There was nothing more he wanted to say that he could say. He drew the final page towards him and wrote: *Nov. 26, 1917. Discharged to duty.*'[27]

Sport does not figure in the realm of fitness and militarism in *Regeneration*, but was nevertheless a major feature of the propositions of manliness and racial/national fitness associated with these discourses. Sport is the ostensible subject of *Chariots of Fire*. Its trope of motion is running rather than wandering, though the latter is implicated both as a kind of backdrop to the lives of its main figures, a Jew and a Scot, and as a threat to the nation which is wandering off-course in the aftermath of the First World War. As many recent essays on the national imperatives of Englishness have delineated for us, the nineteenth century was a period of national renewal for England, even, as one critic put it, 're-racination'.[28] One might suggest that, as with the dubious centrality of sport in the film, these figures are just as marginal to it: England would be the real protagonist.

The film begins chronologically in the late 1970s and remembers back to the time of the 1924 Paris Olympics. The only survivor of those games in the present tense of the film is the upper-class English classmate, an inferior athlete but a good sport. The Olympics and running become the proving ground for Harold Abrahams, the proto-Jew, and Eric Liddell, the 'muscular Christian', a popular term of the period used in the film to describe Liddell. Muscular Christianity was a movement of the second half of the nineteenth century thus dubbed by a reviewer of Charles Kingsley's novel, *Two Years Ago*. Kingsley, who did not like to have the term applied to him (he preferred 'manly Christian'), was fixated on the degraded body and its symbolic import for Englishness.[29] The notion of muscular Christianity which he espoused and which was widely accepted was resonant of the doctrine of the elect, in that an outward display of 'vigour' became the sign of spiritual and moral and eventually national fitness. The rhetoric of such regeneration of the nation included the necessary combination of 'Godliness and manliness', the formula for moral regeneration and spiritual nationhood. This idea of vigour that we have seen in Barker's novel is an unstable property, deriving from a hybrid product meant at first to idealise the combination of the feminine with masculine qualities or to romanticise the 'primitive', the 'noble savage', which would, as many colonial philosophies imagined or rationalised, rejuvenate the nation. These 'primitive' cultures are metonymous with the feminine in this equation; finally neither god, man nor country could stand the threat of the pollution of the body or the intrusions into the body politic. (The Irish or Celts, for example, were never suitable for this role of noble savage, being finally uncivilisable, as Kingsley rehearses in his work; nor were the Jews, for that matter, often aligned with the Celts in these terms.) In Kingsley's work, including his novels *Alton Locke* and *Westward Ho!*, as C.J.W.-L. Wee tells us in his excellent essay on this general topic, the 'original English vigor' is recuperated or 'resuscitated as Teutonic'.[30] 'What Kingsley, the historian J.A. Froude, and other imperialist writers of the mid-nineteenth century manage to do is to wrench or perhaps capture the narrative of progress for their own purpose: "progress" now means strengthening the nation-state as an end in itself.'[31] 'Englishness can be reclaimed only in its glorious past.'[32] It would seem, therefore, that the romantic rationale for the missionary and the coloniser is disturbed, and that some uneasy alliance between the primitive and the modern is again made. We see here, as with Nordau, that the 'narrative of progress', the civilisation of the twentieth century, is by nature retrogressive, that progress as such is delimited against modernity, as, ironically, a deterrent narrative.

All of this is the backdrop for the England that sponsors Liddell and Abrahams, figures who are generally understood as counterpoised in their relation to the nation, since both in the film and in history Liddell was hugely celebrated for his success and tolerated in his religious zealotry. In fact, as the film suggests in its biographical endnote, Abrahams, too, was celebrated, and he capitalised on his fame, though it does not appear that way in the film narrative. The film wishes to savour the irony in the fanfare that attends the victory of the humble Scot as against the deafeningly silent welcome Abrahams receives after his winning run. It perhaps manipulates history a bit at the Scot's expense, dramatising his internal conflict, not so much between God and country, but over the quiet victories of the religious devotions and the triumphalism of muscularity. The Jew is rendered more noble by his outcast status.

In fact, Liddell and Abrahams are on par in the spectrum of Britain's insider/outsiders. Each is on a mission to reverse the degenerate claim on them. The empire that is England is present in the hallowed halls of Cambridge and in the royal presence at the Olympic Games. We are introduced to both in running mode, Abrahams seeking to break the record and win for the first time at the traditional run around the inner court of the college by the strike of the clock. But while he seems to be making history in keeping with the tradition, those masters of the college who watch from their windows make it clear that he has broken something much more cherished than a record and that he is a 'primitive' agent to be guarded against rather than assimilated. As Abrahams observes when he is trying to explain this need to run – 'England is Christian and Anglo-Saxon and so are her corridors of power and those who stalk them guard them with jealousy and venom.' It is unclear to both the powers and Abrahams whether he is running for or against England and which of these scenarios, finally, might be in his or their own best interests. Whatever the answer, he is certainly running scared, as the scene between him and the coach, himself an outsider (Italian-Arab) demonstrates.[33]

Upon our introduction to him at a running meet in Scotland, Liddell claims that he will always be a Scot, 'whilst I breathe'. This may already be seen or unseen as ironic since his parents and most of his family are missionaries and live out their Scottishness in remote places such as

China. Such a display of nationalism might seem to define his conflict
with the nation – the English establishment – but since that national
fervour is conjoined with the religious one, they can be realised as one
master and he the servant of him, not England. But is he a humble
servant? Liddell enjoys flexing his Christian muscle, and the film asks us
to consider whether this hubris is sublimated into 'good' works, and
what may be perceived as the connections between missionary work and
acts of colonisation, or, to use the more polite term, civilizing the natives,
harnessing the primitive energies for the nation, for God. Again, the two
masters are conflated into one. We are reminded here of Boyarin's point
about the proper image of the Jew (and Kingsley's dilemma about the
image of the Christian), as to whether such physical flexing, such bodily
or worldly ostentation is ethical, whether there should be an equation
between bodily/manly strength and moral rectitude, or whether they are
antithetical. Furthermore, in the way the film dramatises the relationship
between Liddell and his devout sister, who is extremely distressed over
her brother's seeming desertion from missionary work for his passion for
running and the Olympic trial, one can only think that her investment is
as sublimated or displaced as his. His flexing muscle seems to be some
kind of grotesque display of sexuality, either a reminder of what must be
repressed or a flexing in another direction, away from her. In keeping
with the clichés, the film presents the sexual issues that attend the Scots
in rather more oblique form than with the Jew, whose sexual conquest
and relationship with the beautiful and distinctly Christian actress seem
almost beside the point. (Though the fact of her stage career is, it seems
to me, part of the cliché. She's just *less* than respectable.) Nevertheless, the
same questions about the ethics of the bodily attend Abrahams' case.

Chariots of Fire was a very popular film when it was released and one
would suppose that its (however misunderstood) subject of
sport/winning was the reason for that. Certainly, it had a different kind
of appeal for its British audience. The most memorable part of the film
for many of its viewers seems to be the wrapping, the part that introduces
and concludes the film. We see the British team running on the beach in
France, presumably in practice. The running is shown in slow motion
with the award winning score by Vangelis playing to crescendo. There is
something about that scene that sums it all up. The music is romantic and
has notes of both melancholy and victory. The men are running forward
towards their hopes for success, but they are also running in place in that
they are fixed in an image of the glorious primal, their bodies in perpetual
motion but necessarily fixed in time. And this is reinforced in the final
scene of the film itself, when Aubrey Montague, the survivor, now old
and quite decrepit, can remember back to the image that began the film.

Of course, it is also the Christian Anglo-Saxon, to use Abrahams' description, who is the surviving body. (I am not sure how to read his decrepitude here – perhaps as a commentary on the fallen empire. Whatever one wants to make of it, one has to contend with the import of the flashback frame.) If, as we must surmise, the film is projected through his memory, then while it is a benevolent recollection – he does not, after all, revise the events in his favour – it is in his hands. In a certain way, the fates of both Abrahams and Liddell were in those Christian Anglo-Saxon hands, since Andy (the effetely generous Lord Lindsay) makes it possible for Liddell to run by giving up his weekday spot to him, and thereby for both Abrahams and Liddell to win by not having to race against each other in that first Sunday heat. History is aided here by the empire that pits against each other these outsiders who finally cannot cancel each other out as 'unacceptable models of alterity'.[34]

The Dublin papers between 1888 and 1904 reveal a great deal of discussion about nation building, the idea of the nation literalised in the image of the 'fit body'. James Joyce's *Ulysses* takes notice. The metaphor is extended in a Cyclopian interpolation, a parody of a newspaper account of the minutes of an organisation of the period, *Sluagh na h-Eireann* [The Army of Ireland – akin to the Gaelic Athletic Association], described as a patriotic society whose aim it was to revive ancient Gaelic sports and to emphasise the importance of physical culture, as understood in ancient Rome and ancient Ireland, for purposes of the *development* of the race.[35] This idea of nation building as body building, articulated in the chapter through the equation of Irish sports with Irish character ('racy of the soil'), is resonant of Nordau's contemporaneous Zionist theories, and also by implication of his theories of degeneration.[36]

There are many ways to approach Joyce's use of this material in *Ulysses*. I suspect he knew Nordau's work since he knew Herzl's, and Otto Weininger's, too, among others of the 'degenerationists'. Joyce was certainly concerned with the narratives of both degeneration and the so-called 'degenerate'. Wilde is present and so are his and other contemporary theories of art. But, as I have argued elsewhere, his own aesthetic and form were heuristically engaged with these questions, and his emblematic figure of degeneration was 'the Jew'.[37] *Ulysses*, set in 1904, could only foresee the Great War, the meeting point of many millennial backward glances. The war that comes up resonantly if not extensively in these terms is the Boer War (a current centenary preoccupation) and I use that as my way in here, because of the confusion it engendered over the question of national fitness. Although the Boer War was over by 1902, it seems to haunt *Ulysses*. It becomes an emblem (like 'the Jew') of split allegiances and ambivalent national assertions. The Irish support for the right of the Boers in South Africa was more anti-English than pro-Boer, a battle cry of national aspiration. But the analogue is clearly misplaced or even displaced, since the record of Afrikaner treatment of the indigenous populations of the lands they had, after all, occupied was far worse than that of the English there. By 'displaced', I mean that in supporting the Boers, the Irish can achieve a kind of double or semi-position of colonised and coloniser, of underdog and imperialist. For as we see in *Ulysses*, the identification with the Boers as against the 'native' is tantamount to a kind of self-hatred, ironically displaced onto Leopold Bloom, the Jew, the exemplary object of hatred and exemplar of self-hatred; and therefore a form of disavowal is at work in the alliances formed here.[38]

Arthur Griffith was the father of the Sinn Fein movement, proponent of Irish nationalism and editor for a time of the *United Irishman* – in short, a well-known figure in this period, whose journalistic campaigns in favour of the Boers were laced with anti-semitic sentiment, something for which he was notorious in general. The English were 'uitlanders' [outsiders], as were the Jews, their financiers (of course, in the rhetoric of the Boers or the Afrikaners, so were the Irish). In many essays during this period, his anti-semitism became virulent, almost hysterical, and I believe that the shift in valence from one characterisation to the other is culturally relevant here. He conflated Jewish support of the British in the Transvaal where British subjects may be, as he put it, 'any Jew, swindler, or murderer who can buy for a small sum the full and right title of a Britisher in South Africa', with what he called the Anglo-Saxon anti-French sympathies of the Jewish supporters of Dreyfus (another emblematic figure in the discourse of degeneration).[39] Through these alignments we see the shifting positionality, determined by the fixed property of anti-Britishness. Ironically, but also illustratively in this context, Nordau, in a speech made in London in 1900, compared the Maccabean Revolt to the struggle of the Boers against British imperialism, identifying the Jews with what he perceives to be the underdog Boers in the search for national realisation, just as Griffith does with the Irish.[40] But the metonymy of Jew or Jewishness for Griffith finally does not besmirch the English as much as it reinforces, in Joyce's configuration, a 'hysterical' relationship between the Jews and the Irish, regardless of the aggressive attempt at virulent self-possession on the part of those like Griffith. Griffith, like Nordau, contributed to a rhetoric of fitness in nationalist and/or racial terms that instantiated the contradictions, the fissures in the very holistic images they wished to create.[41]

In the section of Cyclops (Chapter 12) where the *Sluagh na h-Eireann* is invoked and parodied, some of these mixed allegiances become palpable. Joyce has the parodies of the chapter confuse games, or, as in an earlier chapter, 'natives'. One of the tropes of the novel is the anachronistic foot and mouth disease that caused the embargo and slaughter of Irish cattle (the nearest reported case in Ireland was in 1912). In the Nestor chapter where we are introduced to this trope and to Mr Deasy's obsession with the embargo and its unfairness to the native Irish, the diseased cattle are conflated with Jews in Deasy's confused apprehension of each.[42] In Cyclops, the complaint that Gaelic games are disallowed in local parks while English, or as they are called 'shoneen', games (gentlemanly – i.e., polo, tennis) are permitted is superimposed on to the protest about the slaughter of the self-same cattle. The confusion suggests an alignment among diseased bodies, unfit for public display or consumption. And while the permission for such display arguably is denied from without (the English establishment), the confusion is perpetrated from within.

> Nannan's going too, says Joe. The league told him to ask a question tomorrow about the commissioner of police forbidding Irish games in the park. What do you think of that, citizen? The *Sluagh na h-Eireann*...
>
> Mr Cowe Conacre (Multifarnham. Nat.): Arising out of the question of my honourable friend, the member of Shillelagh, may I ask the right honourable gentleman whether the government has issued orders that these animals shall be slaughtered though no medical evidence is forthcoming as to their pathological condition?
>
> Mr Allfours (Tamoshant. Con.): Honourable members are already in possession of the evidence produced before a committee of the whole house. I feel I cannot usefully add anything to that. The answer to the honourable member's question is in the affirmative.
>
> Mr Orelli O'Reilly (Montenotte. Nat.): Have similar orders been issued for the slaughter of human animals who dare to play Irish games in the Phoenix park?
>
> Mr Allfours: The answer is in the negative.
>
> Mr Cowe Conacre: Has the right honourable gentleman's famous Mitcheltown telegram inspired the policy of gentlemen on the Treasury bench? (O!O!)
>
> Mr Allfours: I must have notice of that question.
>
> Mr Staylewit (Buncombe. Ind.): Don't hesitate to shoot. (Ironical opposition cheers.)
>
> The speaker: Order! Order! (The house rises. Cheers)[43]

The seeming reference to Balfour, who was British prime minister in 1904, signals such confusions or conflations as are parodied here – a Scot in service of the British government (in servitude as suggested by his depiction as 'allfours'), originally opposed to intervention in the Transvaal and the Boer War, and undersigner of the 1917 Balfour Declaration outlining British support for a Jewish homeland in Palestine. For some a knight in shining armour, for others a coward. (One might like to locate a continuity in his position on nativism in these two opinions. However, in his role as chief secretary for Ireland, 1887–91, he supported the policy of coercion through which all overt Irish nationalist sentiment was suppressed.) Furthermore, the narrative of progress here, of building up the nation, is duly framed by 'the revival of the ancient Gaelic sports and the importance of the physical culture, as understood in ancient Greece and ancient Rome and ancient Ireland, for the development of the race'.[44] But this backward reach at glory produces a mixed bag of associations. Apart from its mirroring of the Yeatsian retrievals of 'authentic' forms of Irishness, there are the homoerotic implications of the Hellenic ideal of the masculine body; the gladiatorial culture of savage physical prowess, projections of empire that implicate the Irish in postures they refuse to see, or at least, its parodied myopic representative(s) cannot see. The new army of Ireland and the Irish gladiators do not historically mix, yet in the context of these colonial circumstances they are interchangeable.[45] In Joyce's parody they are mostly mirrored in the impotence they would attribute to their displaced representative Bloom, and by extension to the English, and that mirror is two-way. In rendering their enemies impotent, they indict themselves. By assuming the gladiatorial position, they project a victorious image, but one which finally serves the empire as both image and act. We are reminded of Nordau's *Zirkuskämpfer*, who cannot shake off their historical associations with the humiliated subject.

As historian Thomas Pakenham has pointed out, 'contemporaries talked of the Boer War as a "gentleman's war" and a "white man's war"'.[46] Through much of the recent critical inquiry into colonialism, postcolonialism, nationalisms and sexualities, the complex of contradictions that inhere in such conceptual relationships as that between gentlemanliness and imperialism has been foregrounded.[47] Many English liberals became proponents of the Boer side precisely because of this contradiction – you cannot be a bully and a gentleman at the same time – without recognising an analogous problem in their own election of the Boers. They might, however unconsciously, reconcile their choice along class lines. We are reminded here of Nordau's exhortation of the necessary ingredients for civilisation – manliness and restraint – which, like the combination of the feminine and the masculine in a 'new' concept of vigour, become incompatible. Gentlemanliness would become antithetical to manliness and therefore such a characterisation (as that of the Boer War) along with whiteness would come to suggest impotence and sterility. As both *Regeneration* and *Chariots of Fire* certainly suggest, the English historically have had to juggle these contradictions, often finessing their imperialism with their gentlemanliness. (Nordau's new Israelis would encounter this same dilemma; their muscularity or muscle would eventually forfeit them moral ground.)

In *Ulysses* Joyce develops the relationships among jingoism, militarism and athleticism on the question of fitness, a topic one might argue the novel is consumed by. Nordau might disparagingly have said of it what he mocked in other 'modern' novels of the *fin de siècle* – that they had to be obscure to be good. Whatever else we have learned from *Ulysses*, we have not, I would argue, learned well enough its propositions about reading and form, and relatedly, its critique of the idea/l of progress, a lesson that would among other things help us to read Joyce's work. *Ulysses* admonishes against retrograde thinking with its play on the notion of teleology as a governing narrative principle, implicating 'forward thinking' along the way. Nordau's retrograde vision of the modern may be exemplary of modernity in ways we have yet to consider. His idea of the modern and its relation to the future might be seen in the terms of futurity that Lee Edelman lays out, as necessarily conservative, a reproduction of the past in certain terms.[48] The historical debates over how to read Bloom's and the novel's *nostos*, its arrival at a conclusion, its fantasy about a dead child withal, illustrate these points or questions about the directional cruxes of modernity. As we turn at the advent of this new century to the new imperatives about social and aesthetic ethics, I fear that Nordau's predictions for the last century have come too ironically true – that we are becoming the retrograde, or should I say, futuristic arbiters of a new millennium.

NOTES

1. Max Nordau, *Degeneration* , trans. from the second edn of the German (Lincoln and London: University of Nebraska Press, 1993).
2. Ibid., p.3. In his work on Nordau, Hans-Peter Söder marks Nordau's use of the term *fin de siècle* as a rhetorical heading for a 'socioliterary typology' of modernism. 'Disease and Health as Contexts of Modernity: Max Nordau as a Critic of Fin-de-Siècle Modernism', *German Studies Review*, 14.3 (1991), 473–87 (p.473).
3. 'Atavism', primitivism, 'darwinism', are all implicated in the idea of progress. See Pick's discussion of the recent treatment of the history of the idea of progress. Daniel Pick, *Faces of Degeneration: A European Disorder, c.1848–c.1918* (Cambridge: Cambridge University Press, 1989), p.120. Nordau speaks of atavism as 'one of the most constant marks of

degeneracy' (Nordau, p.555). Using evolutionary principles, he chides those whom he claims draw a false distinction between these qualities or postures (throwbacks are go-backs, as it were). He associates retrogression with the property of illness or disease, by referring to the movement as 'relapse'. But in his chide about these states or impulses as 'a good example of the confusion which a word is capable of producing in the muddled or ignorant brain', he unwittingly outlines his own muddle about his retrogressive dicta. In all of this he conflates what Daniel Pick calls overlapping but separate conceptions of the degenerate and degeneration (Pick, p.9). As Pick explains, degeneration was perceived as an invisible and perhaps even inevitable process of decline confounding the diagnostics of the degenerate type which would distinguish the healthy from the sick.

4. George Mosse, 'Introduction' to Nordau (see note 1), p.xxvii.
5. Söder speaks to this issue of Nordau's incompatible early and late views. He suggests that in Nordau's resistance to modernism he mistook the anti-Enlightenment outlook of, for example, the Decadents, as a religious renaissance which would thereby sabotage his project for a secular, enlightened world in which the legacies of Judaism would no longer be an issue'. Söder (see note 2), pp.481–2. This provides a compelling argument for continuity in Nordau's views since Nordau, in line with Herzl and other foundational Zionists, was a secularist (though, unlike Herzl, he sought a holistic alternative to assimilation). It also aligns him with Lombroso. But even Lombroso addressed the topic of Jews; Nordau's omission of Jewish figures of any kind from his treatments of the subject of degeneration is not compatible with Söder's view that he 'did not suspend or negate his Jewish identity' (p.479). See also Jacques Le Rider, *Der Fall Ottoweininger: Wurzeln des Antifeminismus und Antisemitismus*, translated from French by Dieter Mornig (Vienna: Löcker Verlag, 1985).
6. *The Jew in the Modern World: A Documentary History* ed. by Paul R. Mendes-Flohr and Jehuda Reinharz (New York: Oxford University Press, 1980).
7. Nordau (see note 1), p.16. In line with a certain romanticisation of the primitive or primeval or pastoral (e.g. Rousseau), Nordau's contradictory logic would elect the peasant as the 'original type', as against the effete upper classes.
8. George Bernard Shaw, *The Sanity of Art: An Exposure of the Current Nonsense About Artists Being Degenerate* (London: The New Age Press, 1908), p.4.
9. In an editorial remark appended to an exchange between Shaw and Siegfried Trebitsch on the subject of Nordau and Shaw's commentary on him, Samuel Weiss writes:

   Nordau struck back in an open letter to Shaw in *Frankfurter Zeitung* (24 November [1907]), ironically using Shaw's title: 'Wie Shaw den Nordau demolierte' professing surprise at being destroyed. He then accused Shaw of anti-semitic bias in referring to him as 'one of those remarkable cosmopolitan Jews' who attack modern civilization. Shaw, in the *F.Z.* on December 14, regretted the misunderstanding and explained that his reference was not pejorative, that in England one's Jewishness aroused favorable interest, and that the existence of Marx, Lassalle, and Nordau supported Shaw's concept of cosmopolitan Jews opposed to modern civilization. In *Bernard Shaw's Letters to Siegfried Trebitsch*, ed. by Samuel A. Weiss (Stanford, CA: Stanford University Press, 1986), p.127.

   Despite Shaw's protestations, as Weiss reports, this would not be the last time he would be accused of anti-semitism.
10. *Joyce's 'Ulysses' Notesheets in the British Museum*, ed. by Phillip Herring (Charlottesville: University Press of Virginia, 1972), p.119.
11. Pick (see note 3), p.20.
12. Ibid., p.10.
13. Max Nordau, *On Art and Artists*, trans. by W.F. Harren (London: T. Fisher Unwin, 1907), p.289.
14. Mendes-Flohr and Reinharz (see note 6), p.434.
15. Daniel Boyarin's essay appears in *Modernity, Culture and 'the Jew'*, ed. by Bryan Cheyette and Laura Marcus (Stanford, CA: Stanford University Press, 1998). The German word

Nordau uses – *Zirkuskämpfer* – is translated by J. Hessing in the Mendes-Flohr and Reinharz volume as 'circus fighters'. The rhetoric seems volatile here as Nordau moves suggestively between the representation of Jews as heroic and as victims – 'die Heldhaftigkeitder Vorfahren wiedererlangt, die sich massenhaft in die Arena drängten ... die alten jüdische Zirkuskämpfer schämten sich ihres Judentums' [Nordau, *Zionistische Schriften* (Köln und Leipzig: Jüdischer Verlag, 1909), pp.380–81]. Nordau is trying to suggest that the new 'muscle Jews' are worthier than these predecessors who sought to disguise their Jewishness, even to the point of operating on their circumcised penises. But the rhetoric reveals the fissures, since even the characterisation as 'heroic' suggests some extraordinary act, perhaps of valour, perhaps of sacrifice, something more Roman than Greek in context. To invoke the Hellenic period, though, is also to suggest some necessary link between such prowess and the relinquishment of Jewishness.

16. While many Israelis may be unable to place Nordau's particular contributions to the Zionist 'state', he is assessed within the Israeli academic community in terms of his whole oeuvre. Hamutal Bar-Yosef, for example, argues that many early modern Hebrew writers perceived Nordau's Zionism as a kind of remedy for the 'Jewish illness' [translated from the Hebrew]. The effect of this pathologisation of the Jewish psyche was, in turn, to pathologise Jewish writing, deemed decadent because of the melancholy nature it reflected. In Hamutal Bar-Yosef, *Decadent Trends in Hebrew Literature: Bialik, Berdychevski, Brener* (Jerusalem: Bialik Institute, 1997), p.30. I would like to thank Professor Hannan Hever for his direction in this matter.

17. See note 15 for Cheyette and Marcus; Jean Radford's essay is called 'The Woman and the Jew: Sex and Modernity'. I would also mention here of Hans-Peter Söder's work, and Shlomo Avineri's *The Making of Modern Zionism* (London, 1981); Meir Ben-Horin, *Max Nordau: Philosopher of Human Solidarity* (New York, n.p., 1956); David Biale, 'Zionism as an Erotic Revolution', in *People of the Body: Jews and Judaism From an Embodied Perspective*, ed. by Howard Eilberg-Schwartz (Albany: State University of New York Press, 1992), pp.283–308; George Mosse has perhaps the most extensive treatment of this intersection in his essay, 'Nordau, Liberalism and the New Jew', *Journal of Contemporary History*, 27.4 (1992), 565–82; Jacob Press's essay on 'Same-Sex Unions in Modern Europe: *Daniel Deronda, Altneuland* and the Homoerotics of Jewish Nationalism', in *Novel Gazing: Queer Readings*, ed. by Eve Kosofsky Sedgwick (Durham, NC: Duke University Press, 1997).

18. The works span the twentieth century in publication but are all set within the first two decades of the century, all with a *fin de siècle* sensibility, and in the case of Barker and Hudson, with a view to the interaction between that sensibility and the First World War. I would also note that all the works are English or 'British' (i.e., Irish) while most of the degenerationists – certainly the Jewish ones – were not. Daniel Pick suggests that 'there is no real sense of a 'founding text' of degeneration in England, like Morel's *Treatise* (1857) or Lombroso's *Criminal Man* (see note 3, p.176), though he discusses several relevant figures – eugenicists, such as Francis Galton, Henry Maudsley and Edwin Ray Lankester – and brings to mind Havelock Ellis, who, apart from his probably best-known work on the psychology of sex, wrote *The Criminal* and *The Problem of Race-Regeneration* in 1911. William Greenslade lays out the debates around this topic in England in his *Degeneration, Culture and the Novel* (Cambridge: Cambridge University Press, 1994).

19. Nordau (see note 1), p.536.

20. Pat Barker, *Regeneration* (New York: Plume, 1991), p.217.

21. Ibid., p.247.

22. C.J. W.-L. Wee, 'Christian Manliness and National Identity: The Problematic Construction of a Racially "Pure" Nation', *Muscular Christianity: Embodying the Victorian Age* , ed. by Donald E. Hall (Northridge: California State University Press, 1994). Wee discusses the idea of vigour in this compelling essay on the muscular Christian movement, especially as embodied by the mid-nineteenth century English author Charles Kingsley: 'A primitive vigor and character could be recovered either from non-European lands – from someone else's culture – where manly energy was unconstrained by modern life, or from English historical precedents, where a united nation existed (p.68).

23. Barker (see note 20), p.45.
24. Ibid., p.47.
25. Ibid., p.48.
26. Ibid., p.48
27. Ibid., p.250.
28. In his discussion of Kingsley's *Westward Ho!*, a novel which posits the New World as the primitive or primeval source for regeneration, Wee suggests that the literary conflation of England with that landscape constitutes a rejection of the other as the cure for what ails Englishness: 'Perhaps the Englishman doesn't *need* non-European primitivism; perhaps he need only look inside his own culture for renewal; perhaps it is internal 're-racination' rather than reinvigoration that is at issue here' (Wee [see note 22] p.82).
29. In a sermon on King David, Kingsley complains that the expression 'muscular Christian' belies the feminine aspect present in the manly Christian. See Wee's note on this sermon (ibid., p.86, note 2).
30. Ibid., p.73.
31. Ibid., p.71.
32. Simon Gikandi, *Maps of Englishness: Writing Identity in the Culture of Colonialism* (New York: Columbia University Press, 1996), p.102.
33. In the scene between the coach and Abrahams just after he wins, their mood is elated but sombre. There is a sense of something monumental, but also dreadful. In the same way that Abrahams worries that his life will lose meaning if he stops running or winning, so too winning seems to deprive them both of a sense of purpose even with the poignant sense of satisfaction it brings. The scene aligns them familially as outsiders. And just a note on Abrahams's use of the word 'venom' in the scene with Aubrey – according to Wee, that word was used specifically by Kingsley to designate savagery or some uncivilising property in, for example, the Irish. It seems Abrahams turns that back on those who might use it to degrade him (Wee, p.78).
34. Ibid.
35. All parenthetical citations of James Joyce's *Ulysses* refer to chapter and line in the 1986 Random House/Vintage Books edition of the corrected text, edited by Hans Walter Gabler with Wolfhard Steppe and Claus Melchior. In this passage, L. Bloom is singled out as the naysayer, who receives a mixed reception and is shut down by the chairman of the meeting, in this instance the Citizen, a nationalist bully. The parody rehearses not only such meetings in the public domain, but the passage just before this, in which Bloom takes on the cautionary role with respect to over-exercise. Bloom becomes the flabby/flappy one, exercising one muscle over the other, as it were. In the parody, the grammatical elision fuses Bloom with the Citizen, typical of the chapter throughout: 'L. Bloom, who met with a mixed reception of applause and hisses, having espoused the negative the vocalist chairman brought the discussion to a close.'(ch.12, ll.912–14).
36. *Ulysses*, ch.12, l.890. A note to the chapter glosses this phrase as 'characteristic of a people or a country (usually of Ireland)', in Don Gifford with Robert J. Seidman, *Ulysses Annotated: Notes for James Joyce's Ulysses*, (Berkeley: University of California Press, 1988), p.342. Certainly this definition coincides with the general definition of the word 'racy' as distinctive or flavourful, regardless of the claim about Irish idiomatic particularity.
37. See Bryan Cheyette's work on Joyce's emblematic use of 'the Jew', in, for example, *Constructions of 'the Jew' in English Literature and Society: Racial Representations, 1875–1945* (Cambridge: Cambridge University Press, 1994), and my own, in Reizbaum, *James Joyce's Judaic Other* (Stanford: CA: Stanford University Press, 1999).
38. Theodor Lessing's *Jüdischer Selbsthass* (Berlin: Zionistischer Bücher-Bund; Jüdischer Verlag, 1930). The term 'Jewish self hatred' is attributed to Lessing.
39. See Griffith's essay, 'The Pirate the Jew' in *The United Irishman*, 23 September 1899, where, in addition, he identifies the pirate, the Jew and the freemasons as the 'three evil influences of the century – marauders of all kinds, who threaten the true and decent forces'. See also Griffith's *The Resurrection of Hungary: A Parallel for Ireland* (Dublin:

James Duffy, 1904), a pamphlet published separately which collects a series of articles that appeared in the *United Irishman* around this topic.

40. Shlomo Avineri discusses Nordau's speech, 'On the Maccabean War and the Boer War' (*Zionistische Schriften*, see note 15), in *The Making of Modern Zionism* (see note 17), p.111: 'At the time, the resistance of the Boer republics to British colonialism was viewed by most European liberal opinion as the heroic struggle of a small people against an enormous and rapacious empire. This attempt by Nordau to equate the Maccabean Revolt with the first anti-imperialistic struggle of the twentieth century is another aspect of his innovative and revolutionary Zionist ideology, which had begun to reread Jewish history in the light of modern world history.'

41. Chapter 2 of *James Joyce's Judaic Other* (see note 37) has a discussion of the contradictory logic in Griffith's thinking about race and nativism. For example, he believed in the concept of a Jewish homeland – perhaps cynically, but, at least, in part because of the analogues that were extant between the ancient Hebrews and the Irish. The modern Jew bore no relation to his dignified ancestor.

42. Also in Chapter 2 of *James Joyce's Judaic Other*, I discuss the trope of foot and mouth disease and Deasy's connection to it. This trope provides yet another avenue for the mirroring of Jews and Irish (see in particular pp.37–8).

43. *Ulysses*, ch.12, ll.857–79.

44. *Ulysses*, ch.12, ll. 899–901.

45. *Ulysses*, ch.12, l.968.

46. Thomas Pakenham, *The Boer War* (London: Weidenfeld & Nicolson, 1979).

47. See, for example, Jonathan Rutherford's *Forever England: Reflections on Masculinity and Empire*.

48. Lee Edelman, 'The Future is Kid Stuff: Queer Theory, Disidentification, and the Death Drive', *Narrative* 16.1 (1998), 18–30. Those certain terms are reproduced within a promise of a future that is, as Edelman puts it, 'reborn each day to postpone the encounter with the gap, the void' (p.29).

Textual and Tribal Assimilation: Representing Jewishness in *A la Recherche du Temps Perdu*

EDWARD J. HUGHES

Proust's insistence on the purely mental character of reality has tended to reassure those who wish to see in his work a downgrading of the social and a promotion of the private and the introspective: 'seule la perception grossière et erronée place tout dans l'objet, quand tout est dans l'esprit' (RTP, IV, 491) [it is only a clumsy and erroneous form of perception which places everything in the object, when really everything is in the mind (T, III, 950)].[1] But the same pages of *Le Temps retrouvé* where Proust issues this corrective also examine the momentous events and mass prejudices of the author's times, typically the Dreyfus Affair and anti-semitism and, a decade later, the First World War and Germanophobia. As Proust reflects incisively, to understand the shifts in *national* prejudice and opinion is not dissimilar to comprehending the whims and inconsistencies that characterize our *private* lives. Thus, just as Marcel has had several loves and a commensurate string of loyalties and resentments, so at a collective, social level the same discontinuities are visible. The supporters of Dreyfus, Proust reflects, who, a couple of decades earlier, had been branded as more treacherous than the Germans with whom they were allegedly in league, are seen, in the First World War, as patriots, while the German enemy is relegated to the position of lowest of the low (RTP, IV, 491–2). Labelling these fluctuations as a form of perversion (ibid.), Proust's Narrator sees these ephemeral allegiances and vilifications as being essential elements in the ideological apparatus of society.

Among the string of prejudices that are listed at this point in the novel, the Narrator reflects on the widespread belief in the 'impossibilité de la race juive à se nationaliser' (RTP, III, 492) [it is impossible for the Jewish race to be assimilated into a nation (T, III, 952)]. The line is a direct borrowing from the discourse of anti-semitism made popular by Edouard Drumont, whose *La France juive* (1886) attracted a massive readership in late nineteenth-century France.[2] Drumont insists on what he labels the Jewish threat to nationhood and to family morality.[3] He constructs the rival typologies of the Jew, seen as neurotic, sickly, and introspective, and as shunning nature, and the Aryan, whose supposed good nature and love of legend and combat are all commended. Conflating the Jew with would-be Universalism and Cosmopolitanism, Drumont galvanises a form of cultural paranoia, in which the French nation is seen as being especially vulnerable to what Drumont terms 'La Conquête juive' [The Jewish Conquest]. A whole nation, he asserts, risks being subjugated by the Jew, just as the Saxons of England were ousted by 60,000 Normans under William the Conqueror.[4]

Proust was well aware of Drumont's diatribe, and there are references to *La France juive* in both *A la recherche* and the correspondence.[5] Significantly, the novel itself incorporates the discourse of cultural invasion: it accommodates virulent anti-semitism; it puzzles over Frenchness and flirts with the xenophobic instinct; and it toys with the popular prejudice that calls for vigilance in respect of Jewish infiltration of society. The purpose of this essay is to reflect on Proust's use of Judeophobic and philosemitic rhetoric, to consider the ambiguous nature of much of his reflection on ethnic specificity, and to suggest that such ambiguity reflects a strategy designed to create a space of cultural hybridity in which a homogenised and in a sense totalitarian ethnicity can be resisted and undone.

Looking back on the visits of boyhood friends to his home, Proust's Narrator reflects on his grandfather's habit of concluding that the invited friend was inevitably Jewish: 'Aussi quand j'amenais un nouvel ami il était bien rare qu[e mon grand-père] ne fredonnât pas: *"O Dieu de nos Pères"* de *La Juive* ou bien *"Israël, romps ta chaîne"*, ne chantant que l'air naturellement (Ti la lam ta lam, talim), mais j'avais peur que mon camarade ne le connût et ne rétablît les paroles' (RTP, I, 90). [And so whenever I brought a new friend home my grandfather seldom failed to start humming the 'O, God of our fathers', from *La Juive*, or else 'Israel, break thy chains', singing the tune alone, of course, to an 'um-ti-tum-ti-tum, tra-la'; but I used to be afraid that my friend would recognise it and be able to reconstruct the words (T, I, 98)]. Marcel's fear is that the intertexts (in this case Eugène Scribe's libretto for Fromental Halévy's hugely popular nineteenth-century grand opera, *La Juive*, and Ferdinand Lemaire's text as set to music by Saint-Saëns in *Samson et Dalila*) and the brutal ethnic conflict that these works enact in such melodramatic fashion, will surface. The impression of a vigilant but benign grandfather, able to identify Jews – isn't Swann, of Jewish origin, one of his old friends, the text tells us – is reinforced in his indirect interrogation of Marcel's friends:

> Si c'était le patient lui-même déjà arrivé qu[e le grand-père] avait forcé à son insu, par un interrogatoire dissimulé, à confesser

ses origines, alors pour nous montrer qu'il n'avait plus aucun
doute, il se contentait de nous regarder en fredonnant
imperceptiblement:

> De ce timide Israélite
> Quoi, vous guidez ici les pas!

ou:

> Champs paternels, Hébron, douce vallée.

ou encore:

> Oui je suis de la race élue. (RTP, I, 90-91)

[If it were the victim himself who had already arrived, and had been
unwittingly obliged, by subtle interrogation, to admit his origins,
then my grandfather, to show us that he had no longer any doubts,
would merely look at us, humming under his breath the air of

> What! do you hither guide the feet
> Of this timid Israelite?

or of

> Sweet vale of Hebron, dear paternal fields,

or, perhaps, of

> Yes, I am of the chosen race (T, I, 98-99)].[6]

The cultural codes work in ways that are both obscure and obvious,
secretive and yet also – to Marcel's embarrassment – close to being
revealed as crassly bigoted. An intertext (which incidentally reproduces
the discourse of pious, unadulterated affiliation to the tribe of Israel) may
go unnoticed by Bloch, while the reader is given a glimpse of it in the
form of the brief transcription. Given that the same text has the status of
a known frame of cultural reference for Marcel's family, the boy's
instinct is to censor a work of art in which antagonistic Christian and
Jewish identities provide the framework for stylised conflict.

Scribe's libretto for *La Juive* is also quoted later in the novel to
help evoke Nissim Bernard's secretive pursuit of homosexual pleasure
in the corridors of the hotel at Balbec. His furtive passion, the
Narrator comments with mocking grandeur, 'faisait penser à ces vers de
La Juive:

> O Dieu de nos pères,
> Parmi nous descends,
> Cache nos mystères
> A l'oeil des méchants!' (RTP, III, 239)

[put one in mind of those lines in *La Juive*:

O God of our Fathers, come down to us again
Our mysteries veil from the eyes of wicked men! (T, II, 874)]

The intertext here carries its own provocation, since in their original
context – which is significantly not reproduced in the *Recherche* – the
words are those of the Jewish *paterfamilias*, Eléazar, who, against a
backdrop of rampant, Christian-led persecution (the Christians are the
méchants), has assembled family and friends in his home to celebrate a
Passover meal. The motif of the concealment of religious ritual from the
enemy Christians ('*Cache nos mystères*') becomes, with Nissim Bernard,
the covering up of homosexuality, as though one form of flagrant social
marginalisation significantly begets another exclusion obtaining at the
level of private, sexual orientation. While the link between
homosexuality and Jewishness has been carefully explored by critics, I
want to consider further Proust's preoccupation with the signs of Jewish
identity, and more particularly with their occultation and revelation.[7]

If the grandfather plays riskily with these signs in his humming
routines, his allusions are part of a much more copious intertextuality,
extending not only to *La Juive* and *Samson et Dalila*, but also to Racine's
tragedies *Athalie* and *Esther*, as well as to the Old Testament Book of
Esther, to which the latter play harks back. The effect of this textual
networking is to provide Proust with a number of interfaces on which to
project contrasting perspectives on Jewishness. Central to these
reflections is the impression of cultural hybridity – of being both inside
and outside a tradition – that Proust is keen to convey. For Marcel's
grandfather, young Bloch's visit to their home imparts a feeling of
comfortable superiority, in which Jewishness, seen as peripheral and
outlawed, encroaches on a culturally dominant Christianity.

Proust was alert to the Christian ability to collapse cultural difference
by assimilating pre-Christian myth and belief in pursuit of its own
illustriousness. The church of Combray, for example, described at some
length in the opening volume of the novel, contains two tapestries
depicting a scene from the Book of Esther: 'Deux tapisseries de haute lice
représentaient le couronnement d'Esther (la tradition voulait qu'on eût
donné à Assuérus les traits d'un roi de France et à Esther ceux d'une dame
de Guermantes dont il était amoureux)' (RTP, I, 60). [There were two
tapestries of high warp representing the coronation of Esther (tradition
had it that the weaver had given to Ahasuerus the features of one of the
kings of France and to Esther those of a lady of Guermantes whose lover
he had been) (T, I, 65)].

If, in the Book of Esther, the union of Jewish queen and Persian king
stands against a backdrop of ethnic intolerance and impending genocide

directed against the Jews, the two figures in the Combray church undergo radical cultural assimilation, forming part of an apparently homogenised French aristocratic culture. The seemingly effortless assimilation of Esther into the Christian fold recalls the reflections of Julia Kristeva in *Etrangers à nous-mêmes* on the incorporation into the Jewish tradition of Ruth the Moabite. Pointing to the need of the faithful to assimilate the outsider, Kristeva explores the psychology that informs the assimilation of the *étranger*:

> Les fidèles dévorent l'étranger, l'assimilent et l'intègrent sous la protection du code moral de leur religion, auquel l'intégrant et l'intégré adhèrent tous deux. Couverts par ces idéaux religieux, les fantasmes dévorateurs ne s'expriment pas, et la culpabilité qu'il pourrait susciter est écartée. Plus encore, sous la protection des idéaux moraux propres à la religion, l'étranger incorporé travaille le fidèle lui-même de l'intérieur, mais à titre de "double" – appelant une identification au "bas", à l'"excès" et au "hors-la-loi", qui est offerte en permanence au croyant et qui stimule la dynamique de sa perfection. Si David est *aussi* Ruth, si le souverain est *aussi* une Moabite, alors la quiétude ne sera jamais son lot.

> [The faithful devour the outsider, assimilating and integrating him; they envelop him in the moral code of their religion, to which the assimilator and the assimilated adhere. Masked by these religious ideals, the devouring fantasies are driven underground and the guilt that such fantasies might awaken is avoided. Moreover, protected by the moral ideals that are proper to religion, the outsider, once incorporated, troubles the believer from the inside, but in the form of a 'double' – calling up an identification with what is base, excessive and beyond-the-law that the believer never loses sight of and that drives forward his quest for perfection. If David is *also* Ruth, if the sovereign is *also* a Moabite, then he will never experience quietude].[8]

The picture of subterranean tension between infidel and believer painted by Kristeva has a direct bearing on the cultural clash in the *Recherche*. For behind Proust's apparently bland statement about this uncontested appropriation (*la tradition voulait que* ... signals deftly an ostensibly idealised, uncontentious absorption of the kind that Kristeva mentions), there is clear evidence he was alert to the cultural aggression that the icons of Esther and Ahasuerus betray. As explored in *A la recherche*, then, cultural assimilation entails a zone in which recrimination, disloyalty and the sublimation of aggressive instincts are all part of a psychological bedrock.

Proust envisaged invoking the figure of Esther with its provocative religious associations in more than one way. In *La Prisonnière*, Albertine plays Esther, fearful about entering the room of the imperious Narrator/Ahasuerus without his prior knowledge and consent. Seen in this light, their cohabitation not only signals the jealous suspicion of two obsessive lovers in a secular setting but also awakens archaic biblical memories of tribal conflict. Intriguingly, in one of the early preparatory manuscripts, it is Marcel's mother who plays the role of Esther daring to enter the room of the alien king.[9] In the same *cahier*, the mother sings the choruses of Esther set to music by Reynaldo Hahn: 'Et les belles images de son visage juif, tout empreint de douceur chrétienne et de courage janséniste en faisaient Esther elle-même' (RTP, I, 1130). [And the beautiful images of her Jewish face, imbued with Christian sweetness and Jansenist courage, meant that she was Esther herself]. The mother thus not only embodies hybridity of an explicitly religious kind, in the allusion to Racine's *Esther*, but also bears a visible Christian trace or imprint (*tout empreint*) on her face.

The same preoccupation with religious hybridity is featured in the preface to Proust's *Contre Sainte-Beuve*, where Marcel speaks about his writing projects, enjoining the Mother/Esther not to delay entering his/Ahasuerus's room, which for others is out of bounds:

'Mais non, ma petite maman.
   Esther, que craignez-vous, suis-je pas votre frère?
   Est-ce pour vous qu'on fit un ordre si sévère?

[But no, my dear mother.
   Esther, what have you to fear? Am I not your brother?
   Is it for you that such a severe injunction was passed?][10]

Proust's suggestive quotation alludes to a sense of fraternal alliance, collapsing the categories of filial and maternal and simultaneously eliding the distinction between Self and ethnic Other. Intertextual allusion thus provides Proust with the space in which the contradictions of cultural identity can be inscribed and accommodated.

This earlier version of the encounter with a modern-day Esther displays greater closeness to the Jewishness of both Esther and the mother. Pierre-Louis Rey and Jo Yoshida point out that the tapestries representing the coronation of Esther and Ahasuerus in *Combray* are Proust's vehicle for the hidden Jewishness of the mother, adding that Proust's parents were the owners of a Franken le Jeune painting, *Esther et Aman*.[11]

It is clear that successive layers of composition have erased the traces of Proust's own biography: son of a Jewish mother and a Christian father. But these raw data only begin to explain the energy with which Proust's Narrator addresses the question of Jewish identity. The historical moment at which Proust was writing in France, in the immediate aftermath of the Dreyfus Affair, provides a feverish political context in which to read and understand his deft engagement with questions of tribal loyalty.[12]

At the heart of the biblical story of Esther lies the issue of her Jewishness, hidden ('Esther ne fit connaître ni son peuple ni sa naissance' [Esther disclosed neither her people nor her birth] (*Esther*, II, 10)) and later revealed, with momentous consequences, in that her heroic intervention with King Ahasuerus secures the protection of Jews threatened with persecution. The casting of the mother as Esther has a number of resonances in the context of motherhood and ethnic separateness. Maman/ Esther's mythical power is as great as the vulnerability of those Jewish subjects she intervenes to protect. By immersing the mother in the Esther myth as reworked by Racine, Proust conjures up numerous intersections and hybrids. Working between Jewess and Persian, Jewess and Christian, mother and son, supplicating Queen and powerful King, Old Testament and Racine, Proust celebrates those interstitial spaces and frontiers around which identities and power relations are being negotiated, and he scrutinises what Kristeva terms 'la quête permanente pour l'accueil et le dépassement de l'autre en soi' [the permanent quest for the welcoming and the outstripping of the other in oneself].[13]

Of immediate relevance are those moments when the Narrator fantasises about forms of culture that are imagined as homogeneous and unbroken: as, for example, when he enthuses about the church of Saint-André-des-Champs: 'Que cette église était française! Au-dessus de la porte, les Saints, les rois-chevaliers une fleur de lys à la main, des scènes de noces et de funérailles, étaient représentés comme ils pouvaient l'être dans l'âme de Françoise' (RTP, I, 149). [How French that church was! Over its door the saints, the chevalier kings with lilies in their hands, the wedding scenes and funerals were carved as they might have been in the mind of Françoise (T, I, 164)]. The protestations of national specificity in this essentialised portrait (the servant Françoise, employed by Marcel's family, stands for a closed, unquestioning patriotism) eschew cultural relativism and signal a seamless integration. Yet despite the would-be inviolable Frenchness of the location, Proust's Narrator insists on another space that breaks the idyll of sameness: 'Devant nous, dans le lointain, *terre promise ou maudite*, Roussainville, dans les murs duquel je n'ai jamais pénétré, Roussainville, tantôt, quand la pluie avait déjà cessé pour nous, continuait à être châtié comme un village de la Bible par toutes les lances de l'orage qui flagellaient obliquement les demeures de ses habitants, ou bien était déjà pardonné par Dieu le Père' (RTP, I, 150; my italics). [Before our eyes, in the distance, a promised or an accursed land, Roussainville, within whose walls I had never penetrated, Roussainville was now, when the rain had ceased for us, still being chastised like a village in the Old Testament by all the slings and arrows of the storm, which beat down obliquely upon the dwellings of its inhabitants, or else had already received the forgiveness of the Almighty (T, I, 166)].[14] Within a self-congratulatory Christian hegemony, Proust's Narrator thus invokes as counterpoint a shunned Jewishness, seeing in Roussainville the location of religious and ethnic otherness and thus confirming the paradigm of access to Jewishness in *A la recherche*.

If the beauty of the mother's Jewish features serves as a reminder of the reverence that such evocations can trigger, crucially the same Jewishness is often demonised. By eventually placing the Esther mantle on the shoulders of the unreliable Albertine, the Narrator gets beyond any pious commemoration of origins. On the battlefield of their claustrophobic love relationship, the encounter with the Other/ Albertine/Esther is fraught with ambivalence. But the return to Jewishness is perhaps at its most spectacular and disruptive in the meeting with Rachel, whom Marcel first encounters in the brothel to which his Jewish friend Bloch introduces him.

Bloch has earlier confounded Marcel by saying that all women think about is love, throwing in for good measure the outrageous suggestion that Marcel's great aunt had been a prostitute and 'publiquement entretenue' (RTP, I, 92) [notoriously kept] in her earlier years. In vaunting the merits of Rachel, the brothel-keeper invokes the latter's Jewishness: '"C'est une Juive. Ça ne vous dit rien?" (C'est sans doute à cause de cela qu'elle s'appelait Rachel.) Et avec une exaltation niaise et factice qu'elle espérait être communicative et qui finissait sur un râle presque de jouissance: "Pensez donc, mon petit, une Juive, il me semble que ça doit être affolant! Rah!"' (RTP, I, 566) ["She's Jewish. How about that?" (It was doubtless for this reason that she called her Rachel.) And with an inane affectation of excitement which she hoped would prove contagious, and which ended in a hoarse gurgle, almost of sensual satisfaction: "Think of that, my boy, a Jewess! Wouldn't that be thrilling? Rrrr!" (T, I, 620)]. In the brothel-keeper's outburst, pleasure accrues from two mutually reinforcing sources: a hackneyed racism and a degraded sexuality. Unlike the earlier virtuous model of the mother as Esther, the brothel-keeper here settles for an unimaginative typecasting, in the figure of the lascivious Jewess.

The pendulum swing of vice and virtue is something the Narrator consciously prolongs when he admits to donating the furniture inherited from his aunt Léonie to the brothel: 'dès que je les retrouvais [les meubles], dans la maison où ces femmes se servaient d'eux, toutes les vertus qu'on respirait dans la chambre de ma tante à Combray, m'apparurent, suppliciés par le contact cruel auquel je les avais livrés sans défense! J'aurais fait violer une morte que je n'aurais pas souffert davantage.' (RTP, I, 568) [as soon as I saw [the pieces of furniture] again in the house where these women were putting them to their own uses, all the virtues that pervaded my aunt's room at Combray at once appeared to me, tortured by the cruel contact to which I had abandoned them in their defencelessness! Had I outraged the dead, I would not have suffered such remorse (T, I, 622)].

Proust's Narrator thus configures familial piety and prostitution and toys with the prospect of violent moral transgression. But to the tidiness of these opposites, we need to add the complicating factor of Jewishness, here associated with Rachel and the brothel and thus desecrating the virtues of a Christian Combray. Whereas the figure of Esther is morally uplifting when applied to the mother, that of Rachel deliberately tarnishes the biblical stereotype. In this dialectic of opprobrium and adulation, then, we have an ambivalent, unpredictable account of Jewishness in which Proust shows not just overdetermined deference but also a willingness to destabilise its pieties.

This pattern of moral undecidability forms a corollary to the regular imbrication of what is Jewish and Christian in *A la recherche*, a link confirmed by the allusive play of associations resulting from Marcel's nicknaming of Rachel as 'Rachel quand du Seigneur' [Rachel when from the Lord]. This quotation-become-name comes from an intertext that we have already considered, Halévy's *La Juive*, a work familiar to Marcel and a mystery to the brothel-keeper (just as it was earlier known to the former's grandfather but not to Bloch). The renewed insistence on the source text calls for further explanation of its religious intrigue at this point.

Taking as its backdrop the Council of Constance of 1414, the action in Scribe's libretto revolves around a dominant Christian community, with, on the fringes, the Jewish merchant Eléazar and his daughter Rachel. Unlike her namesake in Marcel's brothel, Scribe's young Jewess is a figure of impeccable virtue and religious orthodoxy who, with her stereotypically grasping father, regularly runs the gauntlet of hostile Christians. The theme of religious intolerance pervades *La Juive*. While Eléazar sings of the Christian community 'O race imbécile' [O stupid race], (Acte I, sc.ii), the Chorus insists in respect of Eléazar and Rachel who are later to fall foul of the Christian law:

> Pour eux point de grâce!
> Que de cette race

Le nom détesté
S'efface et périsse!

[No mercy for them!/
Let this race's/
hateful name/
be wiped out and die] (Acte I, sc. v)

The manichean workings of tribal allegiance dominate the intrigue, as each community reasserts its religious prestige and authority. The linkage of cultural sameness and moral probity occurs with brutal directness, as when the Chorus calls for vengeance:

Au lac! Au lac! Oui, plongeons dans le lac
Cette race rebelle et criminelle! ...
Les enfants d'Isaac.

[To the lake, yes, let us throw in the lake/
this rebellious and criminal race ...
these children of Isaac] (Acte 1, sc.v).

Proust, like the many other contemporary *aficionados* of grand opera, was clearly aware of the stylised sectarianism of *La Juive*. He also knew the work's climactic finale, when, as Rachel falls to her death into the cauldron, her supposed father, Eléazar, before joining her, discloses to the Christian prelate Brogni overseeing the joint execution, that Rachel is in fact Brogni's long lost *Christian* daughter. Melodramatically, then, the opera ends with a story of anagnorisis, the correction of which significantly transcends – and collapses – the seemingly inviolate separation between Jew and Gentile, Same and Other. Indeed, the figure of Rachel, perceived throughout the drama as the infidel by Brogni, turns out to be a figure of virtue (just as, in reverse, the furniture of Tante Léonie's home finds its way into Rachel's brothel). We can reflect on the fact that Scribe's Rachel, rescued by Eléazar from the flames that engulfed Brogni's home in Rome, grows up in a Jewish environment, estranged from her roots. Two constructed alterities thereby intersect, and with the adoptive Jewish identity comes an intolerance of the Christian Other that she herself once was as the daughter of Brogni (the latter, believing his daughter to be dead, enters holy orders). *La Juive* thus provides Proust and his contemporaries with the melodramatic inseparability of Self and Other, and a dense entanglement of Christianity and Jewishness. Indeed what we might see as the Proustian paradigm of reversibility is already operational in Halévy's opera.[15] Here the echoing of the Judaic in the Christian is conveyed structurally in the regular overlaying of Gentile and Judaic voices. In the Finale, for example, the adoptive and natural fathers, Eléazar and Brogni, form part of a sextet of voices lamenting the plight of Rachel. In these simultaneous vocal performances, we have a precursor of the rival perspectives on Jewishness – hostile, supportive and detached – that make themselves heard in *A la recherche*.

Proust's intertext, once unravelled, thus delivers up an imbrication of identities. But even within the pages of *A la recherche* and without any knowledge of *La Juive*, we see that the prostitute 'Rachel quand du Seigneur' has an important double identity. When Marcel next meets her, she is the pampered mistress of Saint-Loup, prompting Marcel to reflect long and hard on the enigma of human identity and on the workings of human perception: 'je sentis que l'inquiétude, le tourment, l'amour de Saint-Loup s'étaient appliqués jusqu'à faire – de ce qui était pour moi un jouet mécanique – un objet de souffrances infinies, ayant le prix même de l'existence' (RTP, II, 456) [the anxiety, the torment, the love of Saint-Loup had been concentrated in such a way as to make, out of what was for me a mechanical toy, the cause of endless suffering, the very object and reward of existence (T, II, 160–61)]. A typical example of these alternatively sacred and profane evaluations of Rachel occurs when the Narrator refers to Saint-Loup's adulation of Rachel 'dont la personnalité [était] mystérieusement enfermée dans un corps comme dans un Tabernacle' (RTP, II, 456) [whose personality [was] mysteriously enshrined as in a tabernacle (T, II, 160)]. The religious metaphor extends the gulf between the rival perceptions of Rachel in *A la recherche*, and indirectly evokes the place of sacrilege in *La Juive*, where Rachel is idolised by her adoptive Jewish father Eléazar and vilified by the Christians. If, in the opera, a monolithic Christianity and a peripheral Jewishness find their point of contiguity in the vulnerable figure of Rachel, the Narrator conceives of Marcel's and Saint-Loup's responses to Rachel's slim facial features in terms of two atmospheres in collision: 'L'immobilité de ce mince visage, comme celle d'une feuille de papier soumise aux colossales pressions de deux atmosphères, me semblait équilibrée par deux infinis qui venaient aboutir à elle sans se rencontrer, car elle les séparait. Et en effet, la regardant tous les deux, Robert et moi, nous ne la voyions pas du même côté du mystère' (RTP, II, 458). [The immobility of that thin face, like that of a sheet of paper subjected to the colossal pressure of two atmospheres, seemed to me to be held in equilibrium by two infinites which converged on her without meeting, for she held them apart. Looking at her, Robert and I, we did not both see her from the same side of the mystery (T, II, 162)]. Proust thus displaces onto physics the would-be mutually exclusive twin orders that underpin *La Juive*. If Rachel thus becomes an emblem of undecidability, the image of the face as a sheet of paper provides us with a metaphor for Proust's writing itself, as it holds in tension the rival value-systems of Judaism and Christianity. Nor is it coincidental that, reflecting on the power of the human imagination, Proust should rekindle the seme of misrecognition by evoking the celebrated confusion of Mary Magdalen, who, seeing the figure of the risen Christ, mistook him for the gardener (ibid.). Proust's 'Rachel quand du Seigneur' constitutes, then, a busy crossroads on the map of self-identity. For not only do we have the intersection of sacred and profane, veneration and denigration. But also central to the anagnorisis in *La Juive* is the axis linking Jewish fringe and Christian orthodoxy.

'Deux infinis qui venaient aboutir à [Rachel] sans se rencontrer' [two infinites which converged on [Rachel] without meeting]: the clash between Marcel's and Saint-Loup's contrasting reactions to Rachel acquires significant additional resonance when read alongside Halévy. For the latter throws up a naked sectarian interface, strewn with fractured images of tribal belonging and casualties such as Rachel herself. The 'Rachel quand du Seigneur' intertext also highlights a complex paternity case, and Eléazar's celebrated aria in Act IV of the opera not only provides Proust with his nickname for the prostitute but also encapsulates Eléazar's paternal possessiveness in respect of the child Rachel placed in his care.

> *Eléazar*
> Rachel! quand du Seigneur la grâce tutélaire
> A mes tremblantes mains confia ton berceau,
> J'avais à ton bonheur voué ma vie entière,
> O Rachel! ... et c'est moi qui te livre au bourreau!
> Mais j'entends une voix qui me crie:
> 'Préservez-moi de la mort qui m'attend;
> Je suis si jeune! et je tiens à la vie
> O mon père, épargnez votre enfant!
> ... J'abjure à jamais ma vengeance,
> Non, Rachel, tu ne mourras pas!
>
> *Choeur, en dehors.*
> Au bûcher les Juifs! qu'ils périssent!
> La mort est due à leurs forfaits!
>
> *Eléazar*
> Quels cris de fureur retentissent!
> Vous demandez ma mort, chrétiens! ... et moi j'allais

Vous rendre mon seul bien, mon trésor! ... non, jamais!
Israël en est fière, Israël la réclame.

[*Eléazar*
'Rachel, when the Lord's saving grace/ committed your cradle into
my hands/ I made your happiness the avowed aim of my whole life/
and it is I who am sending you to your execution!/ But I can hear a
voice calling to me: / save me from the death which awaits me!/ I
am young and I cling to life!/ O my father, spare your child! ... I will
give up my vengeance for ever./ Rachel, no, you shall not die!

Chorus (offstage)
To the stake with the Jews/ Death is the reward for their crimes.

Eléazar
What cries of hatred ring out!/ You Christians call for my death! ...
and I was going to/ Return to you my one and only treasure! ... No,
never!/Israel is proud of her. Israel claims her] (Acte IV, sc. v).

It emerges forcefully in the denouement that Eleazar was never the father
of Rachel, who in turn was never Jewish.[16] Yet the non-father speaks
passionately of his paternal instincts, while the once-Christian Rachel
grows up to be an ardent defender of Judaism. The effect of Proust's
intertext, taken with the varied responses to Rachel in *A la recherche*, is to
demonstrate that fiction, misrecognition, and inaccuracy lie at the heart
of these fanatically-held convictions about race, religion, vice and virtue.
The bases of difference are thus whim, amnesia and misperception and
the myth of a unitary, homogenised culture is shattered.

Taking this a stage further, the twists and turns of the Proustian text
create, as Jeanne Bem argues, the impression of a negation of difference.[17]
To this we can add Proust's rejection of the tribalism that is predicated
on such difference. Writing of the author's intransigent individualism,
Kristeva asserts that Proust regularly counters the prevailing doxa of clan
and nation, that he flirts with the attractions of perversely tribal
identification but insists on its ultimate impossibility.[18] Hence Proust's
predilection for the figures who resist assimilation, often adrift from
consensus and orthodoxy, at an intermediate point between rival world
views. By the same token, in exploring society's peripheral spaces, Proust
identifies those who aspire to social incorporation and who covet the
sado-masochistic pleasures of belonging to the clan.

Of particular relevance here is the figure of Bloch, the snobbish and
insecure Jew overheard by Marcel on the beach at Balbec mouthing crude

jibes 'contre le fourmillement d'Israélites qui infestait Balbec' (RTP, II, 97) [against the swarm of Jews that infested Balbec (T, I, 793)]. The internalisation of anti-semitic discourse by the Jew reflects the perverted outlook of the *étranger* and social climber, pushing against all the odds, the Narrator says, in the hope of finding social acceptance. Just as he apes the language of his would-be Christian denigrator, so in apparently trivial details of pronunciation is triggered an analogous criss-crossing between social exclusion and inclusion, incorrectness and correctness. As Bloch persistently mispronounces the English term *lift* as *laïft*, and Ruskin's work becomes in his mouth *The Stones of Venaïce*, Saint-Loup anticipates his Jewish friend's *later* embarrassment and blushes: '[Saint Loup] se sentit coupable comme s'il avait manqué de l'indulgence dont il débordait et que la rougeur qui colorerait un jour le visage de Bloch à la découverte de son erreur, il la sentit par anticipation et réversibilité monter au sien' (RTP, II, 99). [[Saint Loup] felt as guilty as if he had been found wanting in the indulgence with which, as we have seen, he overflowed, so that the blush which would one day dye the cheek of Bloch on the discovery of his error, Robert already, by anticipation and reversibility, could feel mounting to his own (T, I, 795)]. Here, the Narrator's hypothesising about *la réversibilité* rapidly transcends any narrow preoccupation with *savoir faire*. For *laïft* and *Venaïce* become passwords for momentous social exclusions and inclusions. Likewise, Saint-Loup's blushing cheek – like the figure of Rachel in *La Juive* – becomes the signifying surface on which is inscribed the interpenetrability and exchangeability of Jewish and Christian emotion. We can contrast this picture of cultural porosity with another cameo in the novel when the Narrator vindictively sums up Bloch's chances of social advancement:

> Bloch était mal élevé, névropathe, snob et appartenant à une famille peu estimée supportait comme au fond des mers les incalculables pressions que faisaient peser sur lui non seulement les chrétiens de la surface, mais les couches superposées des castes juives supérieures à la sienne, chacune accablant de son mépris celle qui lui était immédiatement inférieure. Percer jusqu'à l'air libre en s'élevant de famille juive en famille juive eût demandé à Bloch plusieurs milliers d'années. Il valait mieux chercher à se frayer une issue d'un autre côté (RTP, II, 99).

> [Bloch was ill-bred, neurotic and snobbish, and since he belonged to a family of little repute, had to support, as on the floor of the ocean, the incalculable pressures imposed on him not only by the Christians at the surface but by all the intervening layers of Jewish castes superior to his own, each of them crushing with its contempt

the one that was immediately beneath it. To pierce his way through to the open air by raising himself from Jewish family to Jewish family would have taken Bloch many thousands of years. It was better to seek an outlet in another direction (T, I, 799)].

In Proust's merciless psychology of social *arrivisme*, the fantastic metaphors drawn from oceanography energise the reconstruction of society's hierarchies. While the Christians occupy the surface of the ocean, the Jews, far from any promised land, must content themselves with a submerged existence. The *incalculables pressions* recalls the 'colossales pressions de deux atmosphères' (RTP, II, 458) [colossal pressures of two atmospheres] that we saw earlier impinging on Rachel as a result of the radically different perceptions of her held by Saint-Loup and the Narrator. The logic of the metaphorical transposition is that powerful, enveloping atmospheres exert real impact by conserving ethnic specificity, privilege and prejudice. Equally potent in the punitive analysis of Bloch is the force of atavism. Thus, in spite of strenuous efforts to secure assimilation, Bloch is hard pushed to shed his ethnic origins. As the Narrator writes, with a combination of witty detachment and sadistic pleasure at the sight of persisting ethnic traits:

> Mais Bloch n'ayant pas été assoupli par la gymnastique du 'Faubourg' ... restait, pour un amateur d'exotisme, aussi étrange et savoureux à regarder, malgré son costume européen, qu'un Juif de Decamps. Admirable puissance de la race qui du fond des siècles pousse en avant jusque dans le Paris moderne, dans les couloirs de nos théâtres, derrière les guichets de nos bureaux, à un enterrement, dans la rue, une phalange intacte, stylisant la coiffure moderne, absorbant, faisant oublier, disciplinant la redingote, demeurée en somme toute pareille à celle des scribes syriens peints en costume de cérémonie qui à la frise d'un monument de Suse défend les portes du palais de Darius (RTP, II, 488).

> [But Bloch, not having been limbered up by the gymnastics of the Faubourg ... remained for the lover of the exotic as strange and savoury a spectacle, in spite of his European costume, as a Jew in a painting by Decamps. How marvellous the power of the race which from the depths of the ages thrusts forward even into modern Paris, in the corridors of our theatres, behind the desks of our public offices, at a funeral, in the street, a solid phalanx, setting their mark upon our modern ways of hairdressing, absorbing, making us forget, disciplining the frock coat which on the whole has remained almost identical with the garment in which Assyrian scribes are

depicted in ceremonial attire on a frieze of a monument at Susa before the gates of the palace of Darius (T, II, 194-95)].

The Narrator vigorously maps out this cultural battleground, in which the forces of social assimilation join combat with what Proust depicts atavistically as a persistent ethnicity. Proust may be parodying the commonplace fostered by Renan that modern Jews were unchanged descendants of ancient 'Semites' and certainly the review of cultural rivalry is here set in a very specific historical context, the Narrator alluding on the same page to the anti-Dreyfus cyclone that was raging and to further turns in the social kaleidoscope. In light of the force of rabidly nationalist discourse that such anti-semitism released (and Drumont's *La France juive* is symptomatic of that cultural configuration), we need urgently to reconsider the anthology piece on the church of Saint-Hilaire in *Combray* which can be read, retrospectively and provocatively, as a form of triumphalist cultural propaganda, in which the appeal to Frenchness is preserved: '[l'église] déployant à travers les siècles son vaisseau qui ... semblait vaincre et franchir ... des époques successives d'où il sortait victorieux' (RTP, I, 60) [the church, extending through the centuries its ancient nave, which ... seemed to stretch across and conquer ... each successive epoch from which it emerged triumphant (T, I, 66)].[19] Seen against the backdrop of anti-Dreyfusard rhetoric that was rampant in the Third Republic, the much-touted victory over time scored by the eleventh-century church becomes, at a deeper level, a triumph over cultural heterogeneity. In the same vein, the millennial appeal of 'l'église! Familière ... simple citoyenne de Combray' (RTP, I, 61–2) ['the church! Homely and familiar ... a simple citizen of Combray' (T, I, 67)] suggests a provincial domesticity while simultaneously displacing a still more ancient, yet now pointedly discarded Hebrew culture.

These embodiments of Frenchness and Orientalness are promoted as guarantees of cultural specificity and conservatism. Yet while they underline important distinctions in the Narrator's hierarchy of cultural value, Proust is nevertheless cautious about offering essentialised ethnic portraits: 'parler de permanence de races rend inexactement l'impression que nous recevons des Juifs, des Grecs, des Persans, de tous ces peuples auxquels il vaut mieux laisser leur variété' (RTP, II, 488) [to speak of racial persistence is to convey inaccurately the impressions we receive from the Jews, the Greeks, the Persians, all those people whose variety is worth preserving (T, II, 195)]. It is tempting to see the equivocal language as reflecting the contradictions in Proust's own position, as he oscillates between cultural narrowness and pluralism. Yet in reality, this cultivation of ambiguity has a highly determinate function. For in the promotion of hybridity, we see the Narrator moving between cultural sites and resisting tribal assimilation. Thus Combray is both charming and claustrophobic, its codes both comforting and xenophobic, its clannishness an important source of sado-masochistic tension in the novel.[20] Describing Françoise, the trusted provincial servant of the household whose simple-mindedness and sureness of instinct constitute for Marcel a form of reassuring *racial* continuity, Jeanne Bem writes: 'Etre aussi FRANCAIS que FRANCOISE, consécration suprême chez Proust.' [To be as French as Françoise is the ultimate recognition in Proust's novel].[21]

More problematically, the spectacle of Bloch's Oriental features is simultaneously cause for denigration and a source of wonder. Contact with Bloch involves a time warp, spelling access to the soul of the ancient Hebrews that has been 'arrachée à une vie tout à la fois *insignifiante et transcendantale*' (RTP, II, 489; my italics) [torn from a life at once insignificant and transcendental (T, II, 195)], and the overall effect of this reappearance in Parisian high society is of a disconcerting pantomime (ibid.). Behind the language of unsettling mimicry, we have the conflation of the insignificant and the transcendent. It is precisely this ambivalence that the Narrator embraces strategically in his staging of Jewishness in *A la recherche*. And in the logic of that prevarication, a medievalised Françoise captures emblematically the longevity of Frenchness, while an Old Testament Bloch stands uneasily as a figure both of derision and of wonder.

The road from exclusion to social acceptance is one that Proust's Narrator regularly surveys, as he reviews the 'progress' of those such as Bloch who might 'make it'. Hence in *Le Temps retrouvé*, where many of the major socialites in the novel reappear on stage for a last time, transformed by the passing years, Bloch's would-be transformation stands not as a function of the fullness of time but rather as the satisfaction of a desire to see his ethnic features transformed. His inclusion in this final roll-call of the novel's characters reminds us of Proust's persisting preoccupation with ethnicity, and extensive quotation here will help demonstrate the traces of Bloch's evolution that are inscribed on his body and audible in his speech:

> J'eus de la peine à reconnaître mon camarade Bloch, lequel d'ailleurs maintenant avait pris ... le nom de Jacques du Rozier, sous lequel il eût fallu le flair de mon grand-père pour reconnaître la 'douce vallée' de l'Hébron et les 'chaînes d'Israël' que mon ami semblait avoir définitivement rompues. Un chic anglais avait en effet complètement transformé sa figure et passé au rabot tout ce qui se pouvait effacer. Les cheveux, jadis bouclés, coiffés à plat avec une

raie au milieu, brillaient de cosmétique. Son nez restait fort et rouge, mais semblait plutôt tuméfié par une sorte de rhume permanent qui pouvait expliquer l'accent nasal dont il débitait paresseusement ses phrases... Et grâce à la coiffure, à la suppression des moustaches, à l'élégance, au type, à la volonté, ce nez juif disparaissait comme semble presque droite une bossue bien arrangée. Mais surtout ... la signification de sa physionomie était changée par un redoutable monocle ... il s'installait derrière la glace de ce monocle ... ses traits n'exprimaient plus rien (RTP, IV, 530–31).

[I had difficulty in recognizing my friend Bloch ... who had now assumed the name of Jacques du Rozier, beneath which it would have needed my grandfather's flair to detect the 'sweet vale of Hebron' and those 'chains of Israel' which my old schoolmate seemed definitely to have broken. Indeed an English *chic* had completely transformed his appearance and smoothed away, as with a plane, everything in it that was susceptible of such treatment. The once curly hair, now brushed flat, with a parting in the middle, glistened with brillantine. His nose remained large and red, but seemed now to owe its tumescence to a sort of permanent cold which served also to explain the nasal intonation with which he languidly delivered his studied sentences... And thanks to the way in which he brushed his hair, to the suppression of his moustache, to the elegance of his whole figure – thanks, that is to say, to his determination – his Jewish nose was now scarcely more visible than is the deformity of a hunchbacked woman who skilfully arranges her appearance. But above all ... the significance of his physiognomy had been altered by a formidable monocle ... behind the lens of this monocle Bloch was now installed ... his features never now expressed anything at all (T, III, 995–6)].

If the overall evocation is constructed around a commonplace in Proust's novel, namely *detection* of the figure of the Jew, the metaphor of planing away suggests a conscious but only ever on-the-surface transformation. While the myriad of subterfuges employed betrays Bloch's desire for a form of self-obliteration, the effect is one of grotesque distortion. Indeed in the implied loss of authenticity and naturalness, expression and particularity have given way to ontological void. Contrast this with the figure of Swann, whose social assimilation is such that he avoids the caricature and recrimination heaped upon Bloch. Indeed the former's social prestige is superior to that of Marcel's unsuspecting family, who delight in the assumption of their social superiority.[22] Significantly, in the story of Bloch's perverse transformation, we see the Narrator's backhand endorsement of faithfulness to ethnic type. In this corner of the novel at least, atavism becomes the antidote to *arrivisme* and social assimilation spells an incongruous and perverse evolution.

The revamped Bloch (he who seemed condemned to oceans of social obscurity in the earlier mischievous account) thus surfaces at the *bal costumé*, the reception at the Guermantes where the masks come courtesy of the ravages of time on those who wear them. While others go grey and face death, Bloch declines into facial and mental ridicule, the monocle supplanting the quirky and intimate friend whose debate and companionship Marcel had previously enjoyed. Focusing almost obsessively on Bloch's nose, Proust summons up a hackneyed marker of cultural difference that acts stereotypically as a focus for racial abuse. The appeal to phylogenesis is thus an ambiguous one: harbinger of an age-old anti-semitism, and yet suggestive, in these pages of general nostalgia for *le temps perdu* in the last volume of the novel, of a longing for 'la permanence de la race' (RTP, II, 488) [the permanence of the race] that at one level so intrigued Proust.

Bloch's self-anaesthetising is thus not only an object of derision but also, ambiguously, a source of regret. But if his record in *Le Temps retrouvé*, which incidentally includes the charge of plagiarising Marcel's work, is one of pretension and feckless mimicry, we should not lose sight of the earlier endorsement of him.[23] The Narrator makes the point that, with the demise of what he terms unselfconsciously 'la race de Combray, la race d'où sortaient des êtres absolument intacts comme ma grand-mère et ma mère' (RTP, II, 105) [the race of Combray, the race from which sprang creatures as absolutely unspoiled as my grandmother and my mother (T, I, 801)], the stark choice is between the company of dull, loyal plodders and those like Bloch who 'tant qu'ils sont auprès de vous vous comprennent, vous chérissent, s'attendrissent jusqu'à pleurer, prennent leur revanche quelques heures plus tard en faisant une cruelle plaisanterie sur vous, mais vous reviennent, toujours aussi compréhensifs, aussi charmants, aussi momentanément assimilés à vous-même' (RTP, II, 105) [so long as they are with you understand you, cherish you, grow sentimental to the point of tears, then make up for it a few hours later with some cruel joke at your expense, but come back to you, always just as understanding, as charming, as in tune with you for the moment (T, I, 801–2)]. While the endorsement of Bloch is provisional, the verb *assimiler* has its own resonance given the subtext of ethnicity here. Moreover, the diagnosis of evasion and hypocrisy may be read as part of the Narrator's own reflections on Jewishness when we remember that this same combination of charm and deviousness was the stock-in-trade of Drumont, who writes derisively in *La France juive* of the Jew's conversation switching rapidly from Schumann to business: the voice, from being a caress, a murmur of the Aeolian harp, resumes its guttural whistle.[24]

From the solemn evocation of the Mother's graceful Jewish features to the disdainful recall of Bloch's insecurity and social-climbing, we see the polyphonic range of responses to the representation of Jewishness: the Narrator, now scathing, now fawning, curious about archaic tradition and simultaneously dismissive of ethnic pieties, exploring social *arrivisme* and regretting the betrayal of roots it represents, displays a fundamental ambivalence. Moral typologies acquire a geographic corollary too. At one level, Combray occupies the moral high ground, even if, as we have seen in our analysis of the icon of Esther in the Saint-Hilaire church, a Judaic component has been internalised in an apparently seamless way within a medieval French Catholic context. Yet if, as the novel itself demonstrates, *la race de Combray* is an idyllic moral order that cannot be perpetuated, filial piety still requires Marcel to preface any encomium to deviousness – in the person of Bloch – with an invocation of the *êtres intacts* and their moral probity. Similarly, any concession made to a socially vilified Jewishness has to come in the wake of homage paid to the codes and virtues of Christian Combray. In reading *A la recherche* as a drama of tribal assimilation, we see how it articulates the religious and ethnic tensions of the Third Republic.

From the standpoint of hybridity that he occupies, Proust is keenly aware of the social inclusions and exclusions that these tensions generate and his Narrator is caught in an endlessly ambiguous negotiation with these forces. In this light, ambiguity becomes a strategy with an entirely unambiguous function. For in the varied cameos of Jewish and Christian identity that Proust offers, we see the biographical and more broadly cultural significances of these representations. Proust himself does not shy away from the invective of the anti-semite and there are pages of his novel that mimic the crass sectarianism of a Drumont. Yet if the Jewish anti-semitism of Bloch on the beach at Balbec suggests a longing for social integration, we also see in *A la recherche* the appetite to resist cultural homogenisation. In Proust's ambivalent representation of tribalism, we detect a capacity for dissidence and a will on the part of the *transfuge* to live and articulate the in-betweenness that grows out of cultural hybridity. In this way, the cultivation of ambiguity becomes a way of living and a style of writing in an age of ethnic intolerance. As Kristeva reminds us, 'if David is *also* Ruth, if the sovereign is *also* a Moabite, then he will never experience quietude'.[25]

ACKNOWLEDGEMENTS

An earlier version of this paper was presented to the 50th annual conference of the Society for French Studies (UK and Ireland) held at the Sorbonne, Paris, September 1997. I am grateful to Marshall Brown and Ritchie Robertson for invaluable advice and suggestions about the arguments deployed here.

NOTES

1. Page references are to the four-volume Pléiade edition of *A la recherche du temps perdu* (Paris: Gallimard, 1987–1989) and are indicated as RTP, followed by the volume and page numbers. The English translations are drawn from the three-volume *Remembrance of Things Past*, trans. C.K. Scott Moncrieff and Terence Kilmartin (London: Penguin, 1983). References to the translation are indicated thus: T, followed by volume and page number.

2. *La France juive* was, in the words of Albert Lindemann, 'one of the best-selling books in the history of French publishing before World War I', Albert Lindemann, *The Jew Accused: three anti-semitic affairs: Dreyfus, Beilis, Frank, 1894–1915* (Cambridge: Cambridge University Press, 1991), p.83.

3. See, for example, 'Que veut dire Patrie? Terre des pères', Edouard Drumont, *La France juive: Essai d'histoire contemporaine* (Paris: Marpon & Flammarion, 1886), 2 vols., I, 58.

4. Drumont defines his writing project in his Introduction, where he boasts: 'Taine a écrit la *Conquête jacobine*. Je veux écrire la *Conquête juive*' [Taine wrote his *Jacobin Conquest*. I want to write the history of the Jewish Conquest [of France]], *La France juive*, I, v–vi. He adds that the *patrie* has no meaning for the Jew: 'le juif … est d'un *inexorable universalisme*' [the Jew is of an inescapable universalism], I, 58 (the emphasis is Drumont's).

5. See RTP, II, 586 and III, 551 and *Correspondance de Marcel Proust*, ed. by Philip Kolb (Paris: Plon, 1970–93), 21 vols., VI, 65, 67 and XIV, 135.

6. The Pléiade editors identify the line 'Champs paternels, Hébron, douce vallée' as belonging to Méhul's sacred opera *Joseph* (1807), a new version of which was performed at the Paris Opera in 1899, but are unable to identify sources for the two other quotations here. In *La Juive*, Eléazar asks rhetorically 'Ne suis-je pas fils d'Israël', which is echoed indirectly in the line 'Oui je suis de la race élue'.

7. See, for example, Julia Kristeva, *Le Temps sensible: Proust et l'expérience littéraire* (Paris: Gallimard, 1994), especially 'Proximités de Bloch', pp.52–65 and 'Questions d'Identité', pp.178–203; Jeanne Bem, 'Le Juif et l'homosexuel dans *A la recherche du temps perdu*: fonctionnements textuels', *Littérature*, 37 (1980), 100–112; Bernard Brun, 'Brouillons et brouillages: Proust et l'Antisémitisme', *Littérature*, 70 (1988), 110–28; Marion A. Schmid, 'The Jewish Question in *A la recherche du temps perdu* in the Light of Discourses of Race', *Neophilologus*, 83 (1999), 33–49, and 'Ideology and Discourse in Proust: The Making of "M. de Charlus pendant la guerre"', *Modern Language Review*, 94, 4 (1999), 961–77; and Edward J. Hughes, 'Sexual Topographies in Proust's *Recherche*: The Place of Xenophobia', *Journal of the Institute of Romance Studies* (University of London), 3 (1994–95), 205–14.

8. Julia Kristeva, *Etrangers à nous-mêmes* (Paris: Gallimard, 1991; first published Librairie Arthème Fayard, 1988), p.111. The italics are Kristeva's and the translation of Kristeva is my own.

9. Extracts from Cahier 2 are reproduced at RTP, I, 1130; see editor's note 2 to RTP, I, 60.

10. Proust, *Contre Sainte-Beuve* (Paris: Gallimard, 1971), p.217. The quotation is from Racine's *Esther* (lines 637–8).

11. See the editors' note, RTP, I, 1130. For an incisive examination of Proust's use of both philosemitic and antisemitic discourses, see Marion Schmid's *Neophilologus* article referred to in note 7 above.

12. For a discussion of Jewish identity and anti-semitism in the Third French Republic, see Michael Sprinker's *History and Ideology in Proust: A la recherche du temps perdu and the Third French Republic* (Cambridge: Cambridge University Press, 1994).

13. Kristeva, *Etrangers à nous-mêmes* (see note 8), p.111.
14. Reflecting on the Narrator's portrait of Swann's daughter as 'la petite fille rousse' [the red-haired girl], Jeanne Bem associates the colour with Jewishness and sees the place-name Roussainville as a 'cryptogramme de la judéité' [a cryptogram of Jewishness], Bem (see note 7), pp.104–5.
15. Reflecting on the celebrated case of the Princesse Sherbatoff who is taken to be a prostitute, and on the swing from heterosexuality to homosexuality in the novel, Barthes argues: 'Le renversement est une loi' [Inversion is a principle of the novel], Roland Barthes, 'Une idée de recherche' in R. Barthes et al., *Recherche de Proust* (Paris: Editions du Seuil, 1980), pp.34–9 (p.38).
16. See André Tubeuf, Halévy, *La Juive* (Philips Classic Productions, 1989), 41.
17. Writing with reference to Proust's treatment of Racine's *Esther*, Jeanne Bem refers to connections between dejudaicisation and transsexuality and to the more general splicing of questions of religious and sexual identity, Bern (see note 7), p.109.
18. Kristeva, *Le Temps sensible* (see note 7), pp.202–3.
19. Drumont rails against what he terms provocatively the desecration of Catholic churches by Jews who merely enter them in *La France juive*.
20. Kristeva, *Le Temps sensible* (see note 7), pp.202–3.
21. Bem (see note 7), p.103. The capitalization is Bem's.
22. Yet as Kristeva points out, it is Swann who is on the receiving end of the grandfather's anti-semitism in early versions of the novel, hence Kristeva's reference to the provenance of Bloch as 'sorti de la cuisse de...Swann' [issued from the thigh of Swann], *Le Temps sensible* (see note 7), pp.52–3.
23. Bloch's plagiarism could be read as a variant on the anxiety of radical assimilation and loss of ethnic and religious identity.
24. Drumont, *La France juive* (see note 3), II, 268.
25. See note 8 above.

Péguy, the Jews and the Jewish Question

NELLY WILSON

In his appreciation of the magnificent tribute Péguy paid to his Jewish friend Bernard Lazare (1865–1903) in *Notre Jeunesse* (1910),[1] Gershom Scholem noted: 'Nothing in German literature corresponds to those unforgettable pages in which Charles Péguy, the French Catholic, portrayed Bernard-Lazare as a true prophet of Israel.'[2] I would add that there is nothing comparable in French literature, and this applies not only to *Notre Jeunesse*, the most concentrated and significant of his writings on Jews, but also to his philo-semitism in general.[3] How this descendant of a long line of peasants, illiterate down to his grandmother who helped to bring him up, with a traditional early Catholic education, Republican schooling, with a loathing for capitalism and modernity, an intense patriot with a nostalgia for 'la vieille France', how such a man not only escaped the anti-semitic air one breathed in turn-of-the-century France but actually loved Jews, almost because they were Jews, has remained something of a mystery.

By way of providing at least part of the emotional background to Péguy's reflections on the Jewish Question, I would like to spend a little time probing the origins of a mysterious philo-semitism seemingly coming from nowhere, and contrary to what one might have expected from someone so remote from anything Jewish. Friendship, commonly regarded as the source and beginning of it all, goes some way towards explaining things. It is a fact that from an early stage Péguy positively surrounded himself with Jews, much to the bafflement and at times dismay of the non-Jews in his entourage. However, I would argue that the heavy Jewish presence in both his personal and professional life represents the concrete effect of a previously formed attachment, the second stage in a growing involvement. Two prominent traits in Péguy's psyche and personality, itself decidedly out of the ordinary but well attested, shed light on his conduct: a rebellious and fiercely independent mind and a compassionate heart, an instinctive, passionate pity for and readiness to identify with the victim, the sinner, the persecuted, the poor, all the damned of the earth excluded from salvation.[4] The victim on his own doorstep when the aspiring young scholar settled in Paris in 1894 was the Jew, crucified in the person of 'the traitor' Dreyfus.

Whatever contact Péguy may have had with individual Jews prior to the Affair, it was in the crucible of the anti-Jewish hysteria unleashed on that occasion that the initial attachment to an eternally victimised and excluded people was first forged. Accompanying it was the vehemently-expressed break with Christianity and Christian teaching, in contrast to an earlier, quiet exit from the Church because it was a place for the rich. During the height of the Dreyfus Affair riots in 1898 and 1899 Péguy lived with the fear of a massacre of the infidel. And the most devastating part of the experience was the thought of the collective crime being committed by the faithful without faith, by ordinary people not motivated by any strong beliefs nor acting on the order of a fanatical ruler or preacher. The crowds clamouring for 'the blood of this Jew to fall on our heads and those of our children' merely remembered what they had been taught way back in their childhood.[5] Péguy must have been familiar with that teaching and he rebelled against it, hence, perhaps, the vehemence with which he publicly declared his soul to be free from any trace of centuries of Christian teaching.[6]

He was mistaken, as he would realise before long; but the very violence of the reaction is a measure of his pity for all the damned, including an unloved people whom he wished to rehabilitate from centuries of contempt by respecting them and loving them for what they are, not least of all for their obstinacy to remain Jewish.

This is the point where friends and collaborators enter the story, providing living proof that all was well, that Jews were still Jews, each in their own way. Throughout its thirteen-year existence, Péguy's review, the *Cahiers de la Quinzaine* (1901-14), published the most diverse writers, and though not all of them were bold enough or Jewish enough to affirm their identity, a fair number testified to the post-Dreyfus Affair revival of Jewish consciousness.[7] To Péguy, who encouraged such expressions, this was a source of great comfort.

The most striking feature of Péguy's philo-semitism expressed itself in his preoccupation with the continuity of the Jewish people as a people and its ongoing role in history. That, for him, was the essence of the Jewish Question. I propose to examine this theme and its progressive widening into a critique of the modern world on the basis of parallel texts as presented in the *Cahiers*: Jewish fictional stories focusing on the modern Jew's dilemma and Péguy's widely ranging amplifications inspired by that dilemma. I shall also consider the survival strategies discussed in *Notre Jeunesse* and, finally, the Jewish Question as perceived by Péguy in the light of his rediscovered faith.

The Dreyfus affair riots to which reference has already been made held another important lesson for Péguy. Faced with such an unpredictable return to barbaric times, a hundred years after the French Revolution, he began to question what he had been taught by progressivistic teachers. Here we have a first, brief brush with the dominating philosophy of progress which was to loom large in subsequent discussions. For the moment, however, his response to the much-debated Jewish Question was to categorically affirm, as did other progressive liberals, that the Jewish Question did not exist in a Republic of equal citizens.[8] Before long, probably under the influence of Jewish friends, he realised that implicit in the denial of the Jewish Question was a rejection of the only valid point anti-semitism had to make, namely that Jews constituted an ethnic group with its own distinct cultural identity.

Henceforth the Jewish Question would be perceived as a kind of David–Goliath battle between a minority, and indeed all minorities anxious to preserve their cultural or spiritual identities and, on the other side, a formidable combination of forces denounced by Péguy as the 'modern world': a godless, soulless, metaphysic-empty world with no sense of historical continuity, suspicious of diversity, difference and uniqueness in the name of order and equality, and given to condemning to the graveyard past cultures and civilisations in the name of progress, albeit with respectful inscriptions recording the contributions made by the dead. Thus, in the Jewish context, good republicans believed that the Jewish people as a people had happily disappeared, at least in France, thanks to a hundred years of successful acculturation, of emancipation *from* Jewishness, from national aspirations fostered in the past by religion. For their part, historians and philosophers of religion argued that Judaism had lost its *raison d'être*, its role having been surpassed long ago. It was a spent force, worthy of academic study or a place in a museum but with no relevance to modern life. The same fate awaited Christian culture, only in this case anticlerical governments thought it advisable to speed up the process of dechristianisation by law, by a series of oppressive educational measures against which Péguy, then a self-professed atheist, as well as Bernard-Lazare, strongly protested (*La Loi et les Congrégations*, 1902).

Appropriately enough, it was in the long introduction to Israel Zangwill's *Chad Gadja* (1904), of which the *Cahiers* published the first French translation, that Péguy declared war on the modern world in the shape of its two intellectual pillars, Taine and Renan, accused of having dehumanised the humanities, one by his reductionist methodology and the other by his vision of the world.[9] All this discussion goes far beyond Zangwill's tragic tale of a young Jewish intellectual uprooted from his traditions by just such philosophies which gave him a sense of pride in his distant past and made him feel ashamed of the nostalgia he still felt for his abandoned childhood religion. He ultimately ended the conflicts within himself by committing suicide. And yet the links are self-evident between 'le Zangwill', as Péguy came to call his introduction, the first of many subsequent attacks on the pretensions of modern philosophies of history, and Zangwill's modern Jewish tragedy. Péguy was so moved by the latter that he thought it disrespectful to subject it to the explanatory approach favoured by literary historians or critics of the Taine school. Nothing was said about the author or the work: the tragedy was left to speak for itself.[10] Some time later, André Spire, the Jewish writer and poet, set out to enlighten the *Cahiers'* readers about the unknown author whose story had caused such a stir. He did so in a delightfully ironic fictional piece entitled *Israel Zangwill* (1909) which, though it gave a minimum of information about the English writer, concentrated on showing the impact made by *Chad Gadja* on French Jewish readers.[11] In the story, Zangwill's tragedy moves to tears even a hardened assimilated Jew holding high State office. For an hour or so the latter remembers that he is Jewish. The effect of *Chad Gadja* on Spire was lasting.

Against the 'Mission completed' view of development, basically a biological concept according to which civilisations are born, flourish, make their contributions and are then replaced and possibly surpassed by their successors, Péguy gradually developed a theory of his own, that of unique and irreplaceable voices eternally resonating in concert. Israel's voice was that of history and justice. The lesson it had to teach was that of survival; its mission was to provoke 'inquiétude', to prevent a self-satisfied world tempted to rest on its laurels from falling asleep. The theory of unique voices finds one of its most forceful expressions in yet another polemic accompanying the sad tale of an alienated modern Jew at odds with himself.[12] In *Bar Cochebas* (1907) the Tharaud brothers depict the fate of a middle-European Jewish student inspired by his reading of Corneille's heroic drama *Le Cid* to avenge his father's honour. Only in his case there can be no happy ending, for he operates on a different moral code. Having killed the man who had insulted his father, he, unlike le Cid, has to live with murder on his conscience. Unable to do so, he kills himself. Once again, Péguy's widely ranging and digressive reflections on the ways of the modern world are seemingly unrelated to the simple story. In fact, they provide a general and profoundly philosophical context to a specific example of cultural disorientation. There is, moreover, an interesting difference in tone and perspective between text (the story) and context (Péguy's reflections) in that the anti-semitically inclined storytellers tend to mock the little Jew who aspired to be le Cid. Péguy, for his part, reflects with some sadness, perhaps remembering the rupture in his own life, on the painful disorientation caused by the aspiration to be, or to appear to be, somebody else.

What, then, was the solution to the Jewish Question? Ideally, the modern world would have to be re-humanised, re-vitalised. But that was a long-term prospect. In the immediate and on a practical level, the solution clearly lay with Jewry itself. If it wished to survive, to prove its vitality and play its role for the good of all, it had to assume and assert its identity, to let its voice be heard. With the Dreyfus Affair as an example Péguy contrasts two survival strategies which form part and parcel of the much wider concepts of *mystique* and *politique*. The latter were not confined to the Jewish community. France and the Catholic community practised similarly opposing strategies, but it is in the Jewish context that they are most sharply focused in *Notre Jeunesse*. First, Jewish *politique*. It involved an almost disastrous peace strategy consisting of silence, in public; of lying low until the storm has passed, not attracting attention, a readiness to sacrifice the innocent Dreyfus in order to protect the community from the anti-semitic fire and to prove to all and sundry its loyalty to France. This may well have been an act of wisdom, albeit of a short-sighted kind which values immediate interest, short-term survival, before everything else, notably justice, Israel's calling.

Péguy is critical of all types of *politique* mentality, though in the Jewish case he allows two extenuating factors. First, the desire for peace must be forgiven in a people whose skin bears the scars of centuries of persecution. *Notre Jeunesse* comprises the most moving pages arguably ever written to explain and excuse the Jewish fear of persecution. All the same, it would have been a disaster in the long term if that fear had prevailed. Fortunately, and this is the second extenuating factor, *politique* will not ultimately triumph, or so Péguy liked to believe, because in the end Israel will follow the prophet, thereby fulfilling its role.[13]

The prophet in this instance was Bernard-Lazare, the embodiment of Jewish *mystique* which generated an entirely different survival strategy. Instead of waiting for the storm to pass or relying on the goodwill of others to right an injustice, he moved heaven and earth to have one Jew's innocence recognised. Indeed, he *created* the Dreyfus Affair by transforming the original case, which no one initially wished or dared to re-open, into a national crisis of conscience – one of those soul-searching crises which obliged the country, or at least liberal opinion, to re-examine cherished beliefs, to question its confidence in respected institutions. By his action, Bernard-Lazare and those who followed him saved Republican democracy, and the very soul of France, from eternal shame and sin. He also saved Jews all over the world from a new, secular symbol (Dreyfus) of treachery to replace Judas. Last but not least, he saved the life of an innocent man. Here was the only kind of survival strategy that really counted, the only far-sighted moral solution to the Jewish Question.

Notwithstanding Bernard-Lazare's self-professed atheism, he personified for Péguy the vital continuity of Israel's prophetic voice, a voice which, he insisted in *Notre Jeunesse*, was uniquely Jewish in its consuming passion for justice and sense of people, its disregard for temporal authorities of all kinds if they went against the dictates of conscience. In short, the Jewish prophet, the ideal sort of Jew, was an exemplary agitator in perpetual tension and motion – precisely the kind of Jew others feared, not least of all the Jewish establishment.

After his return to Catholicism in 1908, Péguy's philo-semitism became more problematic, in large part because it lost its previous wholeness which included his friends as well as their history and traditions in the name of which they defined themselves as Jewish. To a certain extent, Péguy could identify with those traditions, notably the prophetic traditions embodied by Bernard-Lazare. They filled a spiritual void, providing a badly-needed anchorage for the uprooted Catholic ill-at-ease in the atheist world in which he had chosen to live. Once Péguy had re-rooted himself in his history and traditions, the situation changed – not that the reborn Catholic was any less faithful or devoted to his Jewish friends on a personal level, but he inevitably came to see and judge their heritage, the old law, from a Christian perspective. The resulting tensions might be termed the Jewish–Christian question, and this re-opened issues already settled in the context of the Jewish question by the postulate of unique voices, each of which maintains its resonance without being displaced or replaced by the other.

The first signs of strain and of Péguy's efforts to liberate himself from constraints, mostly expressed in vague, ambiguous understatements, appear in *Notre Jeunesse*. Israel has not yet lost its uniqueness, still less is it belittled, as it will be subsequently, by way of justifying its completion in Christianity. But there are pointers in that direction, notably in some of the 'we–they' differences – Christian–Jewish contrasts according to which charity is the highest virtue in Christendom; a passion for justice rules the Jewish world. Christians are saved by their saints, Jews by their prophets. Read in the light of later texts, this apparently simple statement of an accepted difference between the self and the other takes on another meaning: we know that Péguy thought of Christ as the last of the prophets and the first of the saints ushering in a new and richer world. Interestingly enough, Bernard-Lazare, the exceptional Jew, is perceived as a prophet with saintly qualities. Indeed he becomes a Christ-like figure in his rejection of the old *lex talion* (an eye for an eye) and his calm forgiveness of the wrongs done to him by the Jewish establishment. More strikingly still, the latter's *politique*-inspired conduct, justifiably criticised in connection with the Dreyfus Affair, is given not only a long history but an illustrious precedent in the fleeting allusion to the long Jewish experience of betrayal and willingness to hand over the innocent. The great majority of Jews are prepared, observes Péguy, 'to buy peace by handing over the scapegoat, to pay for a precarious peace through some handing over or other, some betrayal, some shameful act. It knows what it is to hand over innocent blood'.[14] I hasten to add that such asides, generally attenuated in some way as soon as they are uttered, do not represent the writer's considered view of Jewish responsibility in Christ's death, as we shall see presently. But they may well have served the purpose here, as do the 'we–they' contrasts, of helping to distance the Catholic, to loosen ties which had become theologically irksome. Much the same could be said of the relationship with Bernard-Lazare, who disappears from Péguy's works after *Notre Jeunesse*. The acknowledgement of spiritual debts in a stirring tribute freed Péguy from a dazzling and now inhibiting image, all the more inhibiting as Bernard-Lazare was a very Jewish Jew and one, moreover, with more than a little hostility towards Catholicism.

The first Christian work, which actually precedes *Notre Jeunesse* by six months, *Le Mystère de la charité de Jeanne d'Arc* (1910), is remarkably free from strains and stresses in its lyrical promotion, through the voice of the heroine and the poet's *alter ego*, of the Jewish people from Christ-killers to Christ-bearers, the race chosen to give birth to the Saviour and privileged to be the eyewitnesses to his life.[15] Responsibility for his death lies with the whole of humanity. It is apt, and perhaps not altogether accidental, that the public announcement, so to speak, of the poet's return to his childhood faith comprises an unequivocal repudiation of the charge of deicide, the murderous consequences of which the young dreyfusard had witnessed with consternation.

Similarly unproblematic is the recognition of the Jew in Jesus, a Jew among Jews. Péguy may have been helped in this respect, as has been suggested, by some of his friends.[16] It is certainly the case that Bernard-Lazare had planned a major work on Jesus the Jew, with the aim of placing his teachings within Jewish sources to the point where the latter would render the teachings of the New Testament superfluous.[17] The little we know about Eddy Marix, whom Péguy regarded as an outstanding prophetic mind on a par with Bernard-Lazare and to whom he dedicated one of his most original Christian works (*The Porch of the Mystery of the Second Virtue*, 1911), would hint that Marix, too, was looking for 'the pure Jewish tradition' disentangled from Christian distortions. Péguy clearly did not go down that path, but the idea of a

Jewish Jesus in the prophetic tradition – a revolutionary, rebel, dissenter and heretic taking to task the rich and the powerful and envisaging the liberation of the slaves in this life – may well have appealed to Péguy, contributing perhaps to the elaboration of an original theology of hope from which hell and damnation and all they imply are banished.

Israel's relationship with Christianity proved to be an altogether more complex matter and the poet's frequent meditations on the subject testify to a struggle against, but ultimate acceptance of, a fairly conventional view, albeit expressed in a poetic language all his own. Péguy was no doubt exceptional for the times in his respect for the Old Testament and an unambiguous recognition of Christianity's Jewish (as well as pagan) roots. However, it is also clear, at least to me, that he saw their fruition in Christianity.[18] His was a legitimate Christian stance, but one which was difficult for him to express bluntly in the conventional way without contradicting in some measure his previous theory of unique voices and, more importantly perhaps, ruffling Jewish sensibilities, separating himself from his Jewish friends who could not follow him and whom he made no attempt to convert. Hence the imaginative efforts in *Le Mystère de Saints Innocents* (1912) to draw together the Old and New Testaments without diminishing the independence or value of one in favour of the other. For this purpose a variety of devices is used. The juxtaposition of parallel events, each unique in its context but occurring twice, once in Jewish and once in Christian history, is one such linking device. Most effective, perhaps, is the elaborate development of imagery drawn from nature and architecture. Thus, for example, the majestic avenue of poplar trees, the latter standing for the prophets, which leads to the castle (Christ or Christianity). One has to pass along the avenue before reaching the castle, but the avenue retains its majesty and value independently of the castle. Ultimately, however, this view of the relationship proved difficult to maintain. The image discussed above is broken in the end by an explicit value judgement in favour of the New Testament on which an extra dimension is conferred. 'For the old testament is a line / But the new covers a surface'.[19] The poplars of the avenue do not have the solidity of the oaks in the castle's park. Similarly, the Joseph–Jesus parallel, after having been explored at length for its affinities, ends in a contrast decidedly unfavourable to the material concerns of the Old Testament as distinct from the spiritual values extolled by the New. Joseph's sacks of corn saved the people from starvation but Christ's teaching provided sustenance to the spiritually hungry.[20]

Notwithstanding such signs of the direction in which Péguy was moving, the following work, *Eve* (1913), comes as something of a shock in its almost triumphalist solution to the Jewish–Christian question, complete with some blunt denigrations of the losing side. This long epic poem presents a spiritual history of mankind from a Christian perspective, with the unusual theological scenario of Eve being Christ's mother, as she is the mother of all humanity. Eve stands for the whole of the old, pre-Christian world, including, and at times more specifically, for Israel. She has no voice. Christ is the sole speaker and although he shows respect and affection for his poor old mother, he also draws an uncomfortably anti-Jewish antithesis between the sterility of the old world which denied him and the fecundity of the new, positive world which he ushered in.[21] For all Péguy's original theology, which included, it is generally held, some strikingly Jewish components, one cannot help wondering whether he was not in the end carried away by the dynamics of the 'we–they' contrasts, driven back to the uncomplicated, uninhibited rhetoric of his early education, albeit one dressed up in, and to some extent masked by, beautiful poetry.

An even bolder Jewish–Christian confrontation, more directly denigrating to the Jew, and this time to the modern Jew, occurs in *La Note Conjointe* (1914), the last work, interrupted by the war in which Péguy died. The main purpose of *La Note* was to defend the Jewish philosopher Henri Bergson, whom Péguy regarded as his 'maître', against attacks from all sides, including, from within the *Cahiers*, the assault on Bergsonian intuitionism by the Jewish rationalist Julien Benda. The latter, then, was bound to come under Péguy's polemical fire. But why the dispute should have inspired a Jewish–Christian comparison, and one so unflattering to Jewry, ostensibly represented here by Benda, is not clear.[22] The reason lies, I suspect, with Bernard-Lazare – who is not mentioned – and with Péguy's need to settle accounts with the friend before departing for the war from which he had a premonition he would not return. In his last uncompleted work, *Le Fumier de Job* (which Péguy apparently intended to publish), Bernard-Lazare had drawn a similar comparison in which everything was to the Jew's advantage. He is an energetic revolutionary, in love with life, rational, with a long tradition of literacy behind him, free from any sense of sin. The Christian is the opposite:

> The little Jew has behind him thousands of years of civilisation. He belongs to a people which for centuries has been able to read and still reads.
> The Jewish ideal: the man who can read.
> The Christian ideal: the idiot. *Beati Pauperes Spiritus*.
> What remains to the Jew? Optimism and hope, a frantic hope.
> The Hebrew language has twelve verbs to express joy and states of joy, active and passive.

The tuff, the rock is optimism, a love of life, the belief in its beauty and excellency, a fundamental disbelief in the immortality of the soul. This is why the race is strong –
Messianism and socialism
Not believing in life after death, in having to give an account after death, limiting all retributions to this life, consumed, moreover, by an instinctive passion for justice, the Jew was bound to place on earth the reign of the Messiah and the realisation of justice and happiness in this world. He placed paradise in the future–
Thus, he naturally came to socialism–
The Jew has no sense of sin, he has an idea of sins, violations of the divine law, but not of sin engendering moral evil.[23]

Péguy takes up most of these points and reverses them in favour of the Christian. A sense of sin, for example, generates anguish and a life-enhancing *inquiétude*. Previously associated with Israel's mission, *inquiétude* now becomes part of the Christian's revolutionary temperament. On the question of literacy, he agrees that the Jews have been reading from time immemorial, and, moreover, they are solemn readers – they read the Law. Just the same, he is not at all certain whether the innocence and simplicity of his illiterate grandmother are not preferable. He ends up by glorifying ignorance, for the letter kills, whereas Bernard-Lazare had extolled the Jewish thirst for knowledge, starting with Adam and Eve. What Péguy does is to transfer the prophetic and revolutionary qualities he admired in Bernard-Lazare and Jewish *mystique* to Christianity (and to himself). Israel, an 'exhausted race', is left only with the desire for a peaceful life and the capacity to endure patiently – in short, with *politique*. One could argue of course that the highest spiritual tribute Péguy could have paid to his Jewish friend was to graft his spirit on to Christianity, although it is regrettable that the prophet had to disappear in the process, his role ended. It must also be said that it is a measure of his respect for the memory of Bernard-Lazare that a man of Péguy's fiery temperament had not previously responded, at least publicly, to anti-Christian sentiments which he must have found deeply wounding.

In conclusion, let me recount an anecdote which demonstrates Péguy's reluctance to be separated from his Jewish friends. He told one of them of a dream he had had in which they were all dead and feeling immensely happy and free, with all their problems resolved. At one point it looked as if his Jewish companions were going to leave him. They were returning to the bosom of Abraham, they explained laughingly. 'Don't do that,' Péguy said. 'Come to Paradise, it is more amusing there. And you came.'[24]

NOTES

1. Charles Péguy, *Notre Jeunesse* (1910), *Oeuvres en prose complètes*, III, Bibliothèque de la Pléiade, (Paris: Gallimard, 1992), 55–83; 93–5; 145–6. All references to Péguy's prose works will be to this edition (Robert Burac) which comprises a great deal of biographical and historical background material. See also Burac, *Péguy, la révolution et la grâce* (Paris: Laffont, 1994).

2. Gershom Scholem, *On Jews and Judaism in Crisis*, quoted in Annette Aronowicz, *Jews and Christians on Time and Eternity. Charles Péguy's portrait of Bernard-Lazare* (Stanford, CA: Stanford University Press, 1998), p.151. Bernard-Lazare died in 1903, at the age of 38, after having spent much of his short life fighting for truth, justice and the rights of the oppressed, from Captain Dreyfus to the ghetto masses in Eastern Europe to Christian Armenians, Catholic schools and anarchist writers in France. Ever since his death, Péguy had intended to draw the portrait of this exceptional figure who embodied, for him, the prophetic spirit. After several attempts, abandoned because he felt unequal to the task, polemical circumstances finally obliged Péguy to produce in *Notre Jeunesse* (1910) a shortened version of the grandly conceived work. A combination of factors, (a) attacks on Bernard-Lazare in the right-wing press, unleashed by the inauguration of a monument honouring him as the first dreyfusard, and (b) the welcome extended by the same press to the newly converted Péguy assumed to be a penitent dreyfusard, made a reply imperative. And Péguy rose to the occasion. Incomplete though it is, the portrait as it stands is a splendid piece of writing which captures in marvellous depth the very essence of a real-life hero, an ancient prophet living in modern times. However, since Péguy did not come to know Bernard-Lazare intimately until the last years of the latter's life when he was battling against cancer, the portrait focuses on the dying prophet, and also on the Jew at ease with his history and people rather than on Bernard-Lazare's prior struggle to achieve that ease. That struggle, of which Péguy knew though he had not directly witnessed it, may well have been of importance in his own spiritual journey. See Nelly Wilson, *Bernard-Lazare: Antisemitism and the Problem of Jewish Identity in Late Nineteenth-century France* (Cambridge: Cambridge University Press, 1978), 'Amitié de Péguy et de Bernard-Lazare', *Bulletin de l'Amitié Charles Péguy*, 13 (Jan.–March 1981), Jean-Denis Bredin, *Bernard-Lazare* (Paris: Fallois, 1992).

3. Below are listed some of the major contributions to the general subject of Péguy and the Jews: Pie Duployé, *La Religion de Péguy* (Paris: Klincksieck, 1960), esp. pp.409–73; Jules Isaac, 'Israel dans l'oeuvre de Péguy' (1950) reproduced in *Expériences de ma vie, Péguy* (Paris: Calmann-Lévy, 1959), pp.344–65; 'Les amitiés juives de Péguy', in *Expériences de ma vie, Péguy* (Paris: Calmann-Lévy, 1959), pp.304–11; Edmond-Maurice Lévy, 'Mes souvenirs de Charles Péguy', *L'Amitié Charles Péguy, Feuillets*, 175 (March 1972); Lazare Prajs, *Péguy et Israel*, (Paris: Nizet, 1970); Wladimir Rabi, 'Israel', *Esprit*, 8–9 (Aug–Sept 1964); Jacques Viard, 'Prophètes d'Israel et annonciateur chrétien', *Revue d'Histoire Littéraire de la France*, 2–3 (March–June 1973). See also several contributions on Péguy and the Jewish world in *La réception de Charles Péguy en France et à l'étranger* (Orléans: Centre Charles Péguy, 1988).

4. Péguy, *Toujours de la grippe* (1900) *Oeuvres en prose complètes*, I, Bibliothèque de la Pléiade (Paris, Gallimard, 1987), 464–5.

5. Péguy, 'Le Ravage et la Réparation' (1899), *Oeuvres en prose complètes*, I, Bibliothèque de la Pléiade (Paris, Gallimard, 1987), 264–5.

6. Péguy, *Toujours de la grippe* (see note 4), 453.

7. Among them, to name only a few: André Spire, Edmond Fleg, Georges Delahache, Elie Eberlin, Robert Dreyfus, and, of course, Bernard-Lazare. Among the *Cahiers*' numerous reports on world-wide oppression figure prominently those dealing with the persecution of Jews in Romania, Russia, Poland and Algeria. Quite apart from their intrinsic value, these documentaries and the on-the-spot investigations often involved, point to an altogether new sense of solidarity as well as a new strategy: the appeal is to public opinion and to solutions other than the practice of charity or quiet behind-the-scenes interventions traditionally favoured by Jewish organisations.

8. Péguy, preface to *Juifs* by Georges Delahache (1901), *Oeuvres en prose complètes*, I, Bibliothèque de la Pléiade (Paris, Gallimard, 1987), 854.

9. Péguy, introduction to *Chad Gadja* (1904), ibid., 1396–451. The edition of the Complete Works reprints only Péguy's texts and not those of his contributors originally published in the *Cahiers de la Quinzaine*.

10. Ibid., 1396-7, 1450.

11. André Spire: 'Israel Zangwill', *Cahiers de la Quinzaine*, 11.5 (1909), pp.6–15.

12. Péguy, 'Cahiers de la Quinzaine' (1907), *Oeuvres en prose complètes*, II, Bibliothèque de la Pléiade (Paris: Gallimard, 1988), 657–673. See also in the same volume 378-9.

13. Péguy, *Notre Jeunesse* (see note 1), 50–55.

14. Ibid., 51.

15. Péguy, *Le Mystère de la charité de Jeanne d'Arc* (1910), *Oeuvres Poétiques complètes*, Bibliothèque de la Pléiade (Paris: Gallimard, 1948), pp.7–163.

16. Burac (see note 1), p.216.

17. Wilson (see note 2), pp.260–64.

18. For a different view on this point and on those discussed later see, *inter alia*, Viard and Aronowicz (see notes 2 and 3 above).

19. Péguy, *Le Mystère des saints innocents* (1912), *Oeuvres Poétiques Complètes*, Bibliothèque de la Pléiade, (Paris: Gallimard, 1948), p.421.

20. Ibid., pp.394, 417.

21. Péguy, *Eve* (1913), *Oeuvres Poétiques Complètes*, Bibliothèque de la Pléiade, (Paris: Gallimard, 1948), pp.724-5.

22. Péguy, *Note conjointe sur M. Descartes et la philosophie cartésienne* (1914), *Oeuvres en prose complètes*, III, Bibliothèque de la Pléiade (Paris: Gallimard, 1992), 1288–305.

23. Bernard-Lazare, *Le Fumier de Job*, ed. by Philippe Oriol (Paris: Honoré Champion, 1998), pp.71–82.

24. Quoted in *Signes du Temps* (Sept. 1964).

Liberalism, Anglo-Jewry and the Diasporic Imagination: Herbert Samuel via Israel Zangwill, 1890–1914

DAVID GLOVER

Through better education, cheap posts, and a widespread Press, the attractions of new countries are nowadays more fully understood in the old. With the new safety and cheapness and comfort of sea voyages, the chief of the earlier hindrances to migration have disappeared. Men realise the advantages of migrating, and at the same time find it easier to migrate. The consequence is a vast and continuous flow of population, probably more vast, more continuous, more widespread in these times than at any previous period in the known history of mankind.

Herbert Samuel[1]

Generous in its sympathies, expansive in its vision, Herbert Samuel's portrayal of a world whose fortunes would increasingly turn upon the willingness of modern nation-states to embrace mass migration still stands as one of the boldest and most prescient statements on this vexed topic ever to have appeared in print. Indeed, Samuel's spirited optimism is all the more remarkable when one considers its date of publication, for his essay on 'Immigration', from which this brief epigraph is taken, was published in *The Economic Journal* in September 1905, barely a month after the 1905 Aliens Act had received the Royal Assent. This was, as is well-recognised from today's longer-term perspective, 'the first legislation which gave the British government general powers to refuse entry', a move arising primarily in response to 'the large numbers of Jewish refugees fleeing persecution in Tsarist Russia'.[2] As a British Jew and rising Liberal parliamentarian, Samuel had fought hard against the Tory-sponsored Bill and the essay grew out of his involvement in the unsuccessful struggle to prevent it from becoming law, some of its passages originating in speeches and interventions he had made in the House of Commons debates. Nor was this the only chastening historical irony Samuel had to bear. By the time the Aliens Act had come on to the statute book in 1906, the Liberals were once again in power and, as a newly appointed under-secretary at the Home Office, Samuel found himself required to administer the very law he had so strenuously campaigned against. The questions with which he had begun his 1905 essay – 'What kind of immigrants are desirable? How far should the State regulate immigration?' – must surely have returned to haunt him during these early years of government.

Implicit throughout Samuel's essay is the notion that, insofar as it touches on the freedom of individual movement, immigration represents a special challenge to liberal political philosophy – indeed, Samuel bemoans the fact that writers like Bentham or John Stuart Mill make no mention of this subject. But Samuel too had ignored immigration in his otherwise admirably thorough treatise on *Liberalism: An Attempt to State the Principles and Proposals of Contemporary Liberalism in England* (1902), to which his article in *The Economic Journal* might be regarded as a hasty appendix. Why this oversight in a book dedicated to demonstrating the ethical superiority and political feasibility of Liberalism's social mission? After all, the question was hardly new. Agitation against Jewish immigrants had been on the increase since the 1880s and Samuel's essay makes reference to a long history of 'Acts restricting immigration and imposing disabilities on aliens' stretching back to the sixteenth century (323). Samuel points towards a partial answer when he observes that the problems associated with immigration 'may be repellent to politicians on account of their practical difficulty', though his subsequent discussion makes it clear that he believes these difficulties to be largely illusory (317). However, the linking of repulsion and impracticality in Samuel's diagnosis seems to me to be suggestive of liberalism's own limitations in the face of those local, communal and sometimes irrational forces that lie outside the scope of the cosmopolitan progressivism that initially inspired Samuel's decision to seek a career in politics from a relatively young age. In this essay, therefore, I want to explore some of the blind-spots that impaired Samuel's attempt to modernise his party's thinking – some of the weaknesses in his conception of what liberalism, and particularly the new, socially responsible liberalism, could be.

At one level one might expect these weaknesses to be a product of the tensions between a universalistic political philosophy and its specifically English adaptation, a tension that is perhaps signalled by the subtitle to Samuel's *Liberalism*. And, as I hope to show, this division of emphasis did indeed create real problems in matching Samuel's principles to his proposals. But behind this contrast lies another, more intractable area of difficulty, that of Samuel's Jewishness and its relationship to his wider political convictions. Samuel's entry into the Cabinet in 1909 has often been described (not least by himself) as the first appointment of 'a practising Jew' to such a post (since, as Samuel reminds us, Disraeli was a convert to Christianity) and this was evidently a source of great pride to him, particularly in later years.[3] However, as Samuel also makes clear in his own *Memoirs*, his relationship to the faith was always complex and at the age of 21, much to his mother's consternation, he gave up 'the profession of Jewish beliefs' altogether; although he did not divest himself of his synagogue membership, he only attended services thereafter on 'formal occasions'.[4] While this apostasy was only temporary and was subsequently eclipsed by a turn towards Zionism that seems to have begun around 1914, it is undoubtedly the case that 'his religious ideas were tempered by a rationalist, scientific humanism', exemplified by the books on philosophy that he started to publish after losing his parliamentary seat in 1935.[5]

Samuel's ambivalence towards Judaism in the years leading up to the Great War helps to account for one of the curiosities of the 1905 essay on immigration. For, though its occasion was the passage of an Act directed chiefly against Jews, Samuel's detailed discussion of the condition of 'aliens' in England makes hardly any mention of the fact that these 'Russians and Poles' were Jewish or that they were in flight from persecution as Jews. Even in the Commons debates his remarks on the plight of Jews tended to be confined to precise rebuttals of his opponent's anti-semitic prejudices, salted with the odd rhetorical flourish, such as his pointed reminder that Lord Beaconsfield had come from 'alien' stock and that the Bill would 'exclude such families as his'.[6] Because of Samuel's reticence on this subject, I propose to come at his political thought from a somewhat oblique angle, placing it in apposition to that of an Anglo-Jewish figure of a very different stamp who put Judaism and the life of the Jewish community at the heart of his literary and political work: the novelist, playwright and journalist Israel Zangwill. My hope is that a careful and necessarily selective deployment of Zangwill's writings from the same period should help to illuminate the dilemmas that Samuel's liberalism was finally unable to surmount, for the latter's career was coextensive with its crisis and decline. If 'the Liberal Party owed its survival as a distinctive, albeit attenuated element in the British political spectrum' to Samuel's leadership, it is no less true to say that he presided over its demise.[7] The tragedy of Samuel's New Liberal programme was that it had been designed to protect the party from precisely those forces of political competition to which it ultimately succumbed.

Part of the methodological attraction of such an unusual pairing is that Herbert Samuel (1870–1963) and Israel Zangwill (1864–1926) occupy opposite ends of what is almost the same conceptual space, representing the two faces of late nineteenth-century radicalism. This is as much revealed by their public personae and personal histories as by their contrasting careers. Samuel was the austere, coolly meticulous parliamentarian, a rather pedantic master of detail and procedure, the suave embodiment of governmentality: twice Home Secretary (1916 and 1931-32), first High Commissioner of Palestine under the post-war British mandate in the early 1920s, chair of a number of major committees including the 1926 Royal Commission on the Coal Industry, chair and then leader of the Liberal Party at the beginning of the 1930s during the period of National Government, Samuel was, in the words of *The Times*, 'one of the most eminent Liberals of his day'.[8] As someone brought up within 'the secure Victorian haute bourgeoisie ... [and] able to devote himself to politics, philosophy and travel, untroubled by the need to establish a career and earn a living', he was a man who was born and groomed to rule in every sense.[9] Israel Zangwill, by contrast, came from a desperately poor family in Whitechapel, the eldest son of five children, his father a Russian refugee from the 1840s who made a precarious living as a trader in second-hand clothes. A restless and at times a puzzlingly mercurial figure, Zangwill was an exceptional scholar who graduated with triple honours from London University before starting his working life as a schoolmaster. However, he soon found his true vocation as a man of letters and quickly moved from teaching into journalism, specialising initially as a satirist and humorist, then making a solid reputation with his bestselling fictional portrait of London's East End, *Children of the Ghetto* (1892), a novel that earned him the title of 'the Jewish Dickens'.[10] Although he continued to publish stories and plays throughout the Edwardian period, by 1908 he had ceased to see himself as a writer and devoted most of his energy to political work. Zangwill's fluctuating political stances on the Jewish question were often intensely controversial. His meeting with Theodore Herzl in 1895 brought him into the Zionist fold, but in 1905 he broke with official Zionism to set up and lead the Jewish Territorial Organisation (ITO) whose aim was to secure a homeland for the Jewish people wherever a suitable place could be found. This move put him at odds with the bulk of the Zionist movement, and the beginnings of a reconciliation between the two organisations had to wait until the Balfour Declaration in 1917. Zangwill remained a major, if frequently uncomfortable, political figure until his death in 1926.

Despite the enormous difference in their social origins, Zangwill's literary successes did occasionally bring the two men into contact. When Samuel chaired a joint Select Committee on stage censorship in September 1909, Zangwill was called to give evidence, along with other prominent writers such as John Galsworthy and G.K. Chesterton. And, at a less formal level, there were points at which their social circles intersected: Zangwill was a good friend of the poet Nina Davis, who married the Jewish geneticist Redcliffe Salaman and whose son Arthur became the husband of the Samuels' daughter Nancy.[11] After the death of Nina's father, the noted Hebrew scholar Arthur Davis, Zangwill was invited to give the first memorial lecture in his honour to the Jewish Historical Society in 1918 and, when this was published a few months later as *Chosen Peoples*, Samuel contributed the foreword.[12] Yet their political views, and indeed their political temperaments, were more often than not sharply opposed, with Zangwill's own liberal beliefs showing distinctly socialist and communitarian sympathies, even tending towards what Samuel must have regarded as an irresponsible extremism on certain issues – everything that the latter had sought to defend liberalism against. Samuel, for example, was cautious to the point of evasiveness in his treatment of the question of women's suffrage in his *Liberalism*, since he believed that this issue had the potential to divide the party at a time when it needed to be united around a platform of social reform.[13] Zangwill, however, believed that the women's struggle was a powerful revolutionary cause and was prepared to defend the actions of those male feminists *avant la lettre* like Samuel's nephew Hugh Franklin who were ready to resort to violence when necessary.[14] 'Revolutions are not made with rose water,' Zangwill told a reporter for *The New York World*.[15]

There is a sense then in which these two men could be said to have lived their lives 'in perfect interindependency', each shadowing the other, constitutional rectitude pitted against extra-parliamentary rhetoric, literary evocation unsettling the patient labour of statistical documentation.[16] In what follows, I will focus on two key aspects of Samuel's political formation between 1880 and 1914 for which certain of Zangwill's fictional writings provide a useful optic: the class content of Samuel's Liberal revisionism and its origins in local politics; and secondly, the part played by notions of race in his arguments concerning immigration and empire. In conclusion, I shall briefly consider the relationship between these two issues and the question of Samuel's rather belated espousal of Zionism, at least when compared to Zangwill's more immediate though somewhat turbulent engagement with the movement.

East End Memories, East End Fictions

What were the sources of Samuel's liberalism? What made him a political being? Looking back over his youth in his 1945 *Memoirs*, Samuel had no doubt as to the answer: life in the metropolis. And, since the *Memoirs* draw quite heavily upon Samuel's own records, this is an explanation that must be taken seriously. Although he was born in Liverpool, Samuel's earliest memories were of London, where his family moved in December 1871 when his father decided to become an active partner in the family banking firm of Samuel & Montagu. The *Memoirs* commence with an unforgettable tableau of London in the 1870s as a site of extreme opulence and equally extreme poverty. Both were everywhere in full view, from the 'little processions of hungry-looking men', singing of their lack of employment as they marched along the West End streets collecting money from the passers-by, to the sight of Queen Victoria driving through Hyde Park in a horse-drawn carriage, her well-to-do subjects on either side curtseying and raising their hats as she went past. These recollections are intended to set the tone of the book, to foreground the manifest ways in which the world has moved on, to remind the reader of all those modern amenities that are now taken for granted. In the 1870s London was without electric light, underground travel or motor vehicles. It had no cars, buses, taxis, telephones, cinemas or even bicycles ('except the high "penny-farthings"'), and in winter it was 'frequently' crippled by heavy 'black fogs', the notorious London 'pea-soupers' that had since become almost a distant memory. And on every corner the child Samuel might glimpse the street urchins who were his down-at-heel mirror image: 'ragged boys ... selling papers, ready to hold a horse or carry a bag; in a fog to light people home with torches' (1).

Already this socially-aware urban observer anticipates the self-portrait of Samuel the meliorist, a man who has lived through and helped to bring about an era 'of great social progress – the fruit of liberty of thought, the spread of education, the inventions of science and the growth of democracy', a list that recalls the similar citation of 'advantages' that occurs near the beginning of the 1905 'Immigration' essay (297). However, this momentary recovery of lost time is more than merely an inventory of reasons to be politically cheerful, for it also serves as a prologue to Samuel's account of the boyish idealism that drew him into politics in the first place. The opening chapter slides effortlessly from 'Parentage' to 'Boyhood' to 'Social Conditions' as the centre of metropolitan gravity shifts from Samuel's home in Kensington Palace Gardens to Whitechapel and the 1889 London Dock Strike, an event indelibly associated in his indignant 18-year-old mind with the injustices that sparked the French Revolution a hundred years before. Samuel contributed to the strike fund, but it was less the possibilities of collective action that stirred his youthful imagination than the 'shameful conditions' that he encountered in the East End slums: 'room after room where men, women and children were at work at high pressure –

tailoring, cabinet-making, matchbox-making or fur-pulling (6). In Samuel's memory it is from this point on that he resolves to try to enter Parliament 'and to take part in social legislation' (7). Turning his back on the Conservatism represented by the 'large portrait of Disraeli' that his mother had placed over his bed, Samuel began to gravitate towards his lifelong commitment to the Liberal Party (3).

There were of course personal and practical connections that drew Samuel to London's East End too. His uncle Sir Samuel Montagu (later Lord Swaythling), as well as being a prominent banker, was MP for Whitechapel from 1885 until 1900 when he stood as a candidate in Leeds and lost his seat in the 'khaki election'. And in January 1889 Samuel's elder brother Stuart, with the support of his uncle, embarked on a political career of his own by standing as a 'Progressive' candidate in the first London County Council elections, part of a loose coalition of Liberals, socialists, and the occasional renegade Tory. Samuel, who had just left school, threw himself into helping his brother to canvass local voters and it was from 'the accident of my brother's candidature' that he first became acquainted with the indignities of East End life 'as I went from slum to slum and from one block of tenements to another, and talked to the people' (6). This was the year that Samuel went up to Oxford where he continued his political work for the Liberals and also took part in the campaign to recruit rural labourers to the new general union organised by the dockers' leaders Tom Mann and Ben Tillett. Writing to his mother in April 1891, Samuel described a 700-strong village meeting addressed by Ben Tillett at the end of which 'I jumped on the big packing-case that had been our platform and led three cheers for "Tillett and the Union", which must have been heard over half the country'.[17] Just over a year later, in the summer of 1892, he was back in the East End helping his uncle retain his Whitechapel seat in the general election.

Many of these episodes are discussed in the *Memoirs* where one gets a vivid picture of the extent of Samuel's early radicalism – assisting in setting up 'little co-operative stores in workmen's cottages', talking at length with Tom Mann, organising support meetings – though Samuel is adamant that these activities 'had nothing to do with Socialism', since he was never convinced of the need for public ownership of the means of production (16–17). Nevertheless, it is striking how much Samuel's preoccupation with problems of social class and social inequality seem to obscure the importance of other social issues. Though Samuel keeps returning to London's East End, there is scarcely any mention of the increasingly Jewish character of the Whitechapel district, nor of its ethnic composition more generally, a recognition which is also largely absent from Samuel's private papers from the period, the 1905 Aliens Act notwithstanding. This is surprising on several counts. In sheer numerical terms, this was the period that saw London's Jewish population's near-threefold rise from around 46,000 in the early 1880s to 135,000 by the turn of the century, as a result of the pogroms in Russia and Eastern Europe. According to one estimate, 120,000 of these, or slightly less than 90 per cent, were located in the East End.[18] It is true that in political terms the effect of this demographic change was not as great as the figures by themselves would suggest, since their alien status prevented many recent immigrants from exercising the right to vote. And this was particularly the case in the London County Council elections where the franchise was very tightly drawn. In 1889, consequently, only about a third of the East End electorate was Jewish, a factor which perhaps explains the intensity with which the LCC seat was fought in Whitechapel.[19] For tactical reasons Sir Samuel Montagu was keen to play down the prevalence of anti-semitic prejudice there when he gave evidence to the Royal Commission on Alien Immigration in 1903, 'except in very, very few instances'.[20] But it is clear that immigration and settlement were major issues in the politics of the period, both within the Anglo-Jewish community and without. Thus, in July 1891, only three months after Samuel had enthusiastically raised three rousing cheers in appreciation of Ben Tillett's oratory, the union leader was on the platform of another well-attended meeting, this time organised by the Tory democrat Lord Dunraven, to promote the newly-founded Association for Preventing the Immigration of Destitute Aliens.[21]

This is not to say that the wider dangers of anti-semitism pass unmentioned in the *Memoirs*. At a later point in the book Samuel is caustic in his denunciation of the 'empty ideas of race and destiny' that inspired the German National-Socialists, emphasising 'the enormous mischief that may be done by men who launch, and their followers who accept and apply, ideas that are evil' (273). Against such 'fanaticism' race and ethnicity may be legitimate sources of pride, an attitude that – as I have already noted – clearly informed the value Samuel ascribed to his own political achievements, despite the religious doubts he experienced in his youth, and that was also to influence his support for Zionism. On the other hand, Samuel's pleasure in his successes sometimes shows signs of a rather different racial imagination. In his explanation of why the North Riding constituency of Cleveland elected him as its MP in 1902, Samuel singled out not only those climatic, industrial and economic conditions that favoured Liberal allegiances, but also praised 'the large element of Norse blood in the people' for producing 'a more prosperous and a more independent-minded population' than that of traditionally Conservative South Oxfordshire, where he had fought and lost in 1895 and again in 1900 (38). Instructively, Samuel had discovered that 'the outwardly charming villages of Oxfordshire' hid extremes of poverty reminiscent of those he had previously observed 'in the squalid slums of Whitechapel', including 'the sweated home industries' that he had once thought could only be found in the city (15). Given that sweating was often associated with Jewish immigrants in the 1890s, part of the subtext of his recollections is a critique of the dominant prejudices of that period.[22] Against such a background, however, Samuel's rationalisation of his electoral victory in the north sounds a distinctly odd note, reintroducing a racial geography of economic and political behaviour that seems to reverse the implicit thrust of his earlier observations and hinting at a darker side to his apparently straightforward brand of social progressivism. What then was the precise role played by race and ethnicity in Samuel's political thought in this period?

Before turning more fully to Samuel's views on race and empire and their relationship to his first attempt to set out what he took to be the fulcrum of modern liberalism in 1902, I want to look for a moment at Israel Zangwill's East End fiction, reading it as a kind of corrective to Samuel's omissions. At first sight, such a comparison seems simple enough. Where Samuel was reluctant to particularise the hardships experienced by the Jews he had met in Whitechapel, Zangwill's most famous book *Children of the Ghetto* could be said to provide a rich ethnography of the lives and livelihood of 'a peculiar people'. According to this argument, Zangwill gives us the full flavour of the East End Jewish community, its soup kitchens, its trade union meetings, its jokes, its rituals and its entertainments, as well as its internal conflicts and its proto-Zionist dreams. Indeed, Samuel himself once suggested that novels might serve as 'useful lesson-books' for politicians, and so help to fuel the demand for 'justice' and for social reform. 'A good novel is better than a pamphlet,' he insisted, and 'stories are more effective than statistics' because 'they clothe facts in the dress of personality, and bring them to us in a garb to which we are accustomed.'[23] Zangwill, however, has an appreciably different notion of the lessons that literary realism has to offer and his view of fiction is, not surprisingly, far less instrumental and far more exploratory than that of Samuel. In *Children of the Ghetto*, the novel's ethical dilemmas stem from the inexorable erosion of the ghetto's communal and spiritual values under the impact of liberal modernity, together with the absence of any real substitute for the beliefs and solidarities that are inevitably being lost. And these are problems upon which Samuel's brand of parliamentary meliorism can have little purchase. Worse still, in remedying the ills of the ghetto, they threaten to destroy its achievements.

Thus, when Zangwill writes in the novel's 'Proem' that the 'faults [of these ghetto-dwellers] are bred of its hovering miasma of persecution, their virtues straitened and intensified by the narrowness of its horizon', his judgement is at variance with the kind of defence of the Jewish community that was to become commonplace over the course of the following decade, particularly in the hands of politicians like Samuel or Montagu.[24] Zangwill is, for example, willing to find a provisional good even in those practices that were anathema to Samuel. Thus Zangwill's portrait of the sweater Bear Belcovitch is deliberately set against the representations of the parasite with the 'protuberant paunch' and 'greasy smile' that appear in 'Parliamentary Blue-Books, English newspapers, and the Berner Street Socialistic Club' (84). Instead we are shown a man who now lives much more poorly than he had once lived in Poland, who has had to see his family going hungry, and whose business activities provide others with a means of subsistence. Nor does Belcovitch ever refuse 'to become surety for a loan when any of his poor friends begged the favour of him' (93). In short, Belcovitch is a devout and, by his own lights, a humane individual. Ironically, it is the sweater who provides employment for the trade union activist Simon Wolf after he has been 'thrown over by the labour party he had created' (444).

But, as Zangwill keenly appreciated, the tragedy of the ghetto is that it has no future, despite the nostalgia it engenders in the memories of those characters like Esther Ansell who leave only to be drawn back to it – which is surely why Esther must embark for the United States (however temporarily) at the novel's close. To this 'slow breaking-up [of the ghetto] in our own day', the world of West End Jewry – precisely the world of Samuel and his family – can offer no solution.[25] Fixated upon assimilation, with the Reform Synagogue as its 'centre of culture and prosperity', West End Judaism is part of the problem: 'cold, crude and devoid of magnetism', a spiritual and ethical desert (415). If 'the Jew has mixed freely with his fellow-citizens', these 'indiscriminate social relations' have 'only become possible through a religious decadence, which they in turn accelerate' (323). Significantly, the relationship of Kensington to Whitechapel in the book is, at least in part, one of power and manipulation. As the poet Melchitsedek Pinchas scathingly reminds 'the great Jewish labour leader' Simon Wolf, 'de whole wealthy West-End stood idly by with her hands in de working-men's pockets while you vere building up de great organization' (258-9). When the striking East End workers abandon their dispute and accept a compromise, it is because of an intervention by the stockbroker Gideon, the local MP, 'unceremoniously elbowing Simon Wolf out of his central position' on the Strike Committee (269). According to Meri-Jane Rochelson, the figure of Gideon was modelled on Whitechapel's MP at that time, Samuel's uncle.

The story of the strike is an illustration of Zangwill's concern with the decline of the ghetto's moral order, the degeneration of 'ancient piety in the stress of modern social problems', showing the impact of cultural and political forces that the East Enders are powerless to halt (263). Yet one of the weaknesses of the novel is that, in his tight focus upon the vicissitudes of this 'peculiar people', Zangwill largely eschews consideration of the wider, non-Jewish world that formed the matrix for those 'modern social problems' within which both East End and West End Jewry were, in their different ways, so thoroughly enmeshed. Apart from the glimpse of an occasional figure, like that of the Goldsmiths' housekeeper Mary O'Reilly, gentiles are conspicuous by their absence from *Children of the Ghetto*. So, to fill out the novel's insights into exactly how and why the ghetto was being transformed, it is necessary to augment Zangwill's 1892 classic with another text which first appeared in book form in the same year, a novella written, so to speak, with the author's other hand, *The Big Bow Mystery*.

Originally commissioned by the London evening daily *The Star*, *The Big Bow Mystery* was serialised over a two-week period from 22 August to 4 September 1891. It has attracted little attention from Zangwill scholars; not entirely unjustly, for it is undeniably among the author's more lightweight performances, hastily written 'in a fortnight – day by day' as an ephemeral entertainment.[26] Yet if its construction is formulaic – a variation on the classic locked room mystery of the type pioneered by Edgar Allan Poe 50 years earlier – its setting and characters are not. As its title implies, *The Big Bow Mystery* is placed cheek by jowl with Whitechapel, in that adjacent district which was something of a centre for anti-alien agitation. Indeed, in his history of the 1905 Aliens Act, Bernard Gainer notes that the struggle to introduce such legislation 'began in earnest' with the election of Captain J.C.R. Colomb as Unionist MP for Bow and Bromley in the 1880s.[27] At the same time, it was an area in which socialism had 'gradually built up a certain strength' and this co-presence of radicalism and conservatism in local politics is as much a part of the book's atmosphere as the ubiquitous mist and fog that shroud Bow's mean streets.[28] Throughout *The Big Bow Mystery* Zangwill so interweaves politics and everyday life that the reader can never be sure whether or not the murder around which the novel revolves is somehow politically motivated, an interpretation heavily suggested by the juxtaposition of a victim who is a gentleman philanthropist dedicated to the uplift of the working classes and an accused man who is a leading trade unionist. To heighten this effect, the ragbag list of suspects contains socialists and radicals of various hues, not to mention such colourful and unlikely types as the victim's impressionable landlady, a pair of rivalrous detectives and a dilettante poet who works as a newspaper leader writer. Even Mr Gladstone is included among the *dramatis personae*, putting in a brief and characteristically solemn appearance at a curiously 'non-political gathering' that provides a climactic moment in the unravelling of the mystery (88).

As these clues suggest, *The Big Bow Mystery* is, in Julian Symons' shrewd verdict, 'much more nearly a parody than has been acknowledged'.[29] However, the target of this parody is not simply the detective genre *per se*. For Zangwill's satire only begins to make sense if one returns to the journalistic context within which his novella was first produced. *The Star*, founded in January 1888, was expressly 'intended to be the Radical Evening organ for the Metropolis', supporting Irish Home Rule and other advanced Liberal policies on its 'uncompromising' editorial pages. On the other hand, in order to help advertisers 'to reach the middle classes and the masses', the paper relied heavily upon popular crime reporting and gossip columns.[30] The Whitechapel murders were, predictably, an early example of *The Star*'s more sensational coverage and Ripper narratives continued into the 1890s.[31] By the end of its first year of operation *The Star* had reached a circulation of 50,000, ran to five editions daily, and could confidently declare itself a 'phenomenal success'.[32] *The Big Bow Mystery* was positioned ideologically – that is to say, humorously – in the teeth of this winning formula.

Symptomatically, *The Big Bow Mystery* refers both to the novella's working title and to a newspaper headline *inside* the narrative: as the plot progresses 'evening posters' ominously proclaim that 'The Bow Mystery Thickens' (34). Moreover, in the newspaper serialisation (though not in the book), *The Star* is identified as the first paper to put the cause of the victim's death on its placards, 'for the satisfaction of those too poor to purchase', a citation that ironically blurs the line between fact and fiction, just as – so its critics might have been forgiven for thinking – London's own self-styled radical evening daily often did (23). And in another pleasingly mocking touch, Zangwill also has *The Star* jumping to erroneous conclusions by assuming that this is a case of suicide rather than murder. Nevertheless, these playful flourishes are more than artful jokes to delight the reader at the editor's expense. For as the mystery unfolds it becomes increasingly clear that the press is not so much an ingredient in the story but in fact supplies the medium or frame within which the entire story is emplotted, since it turns out that the motivation behind the crime and the confession that finally provides its solution are both intricately bound up with popular renown and a desire for self-promotion. As *The Big Bow Mystery* builds towards its climax, the avalanche of letters, telegrams and petitions to the Conservative Home Secretary protesting the condemned labour leader's innocence becomes a spectacular media event anxiously focused upon Downing Street with an 'ever-augmenting crowd' amongst whom 'newsboys were busy vending their special editions', while reporters 'clutching descriptive pencils' eagerly awaited any 'whisper of a reprieve' (140). Yet the tale ends on a severely deflationary note when Grodman, the curiously-named scientific investigator who has been adopted as the people's champion confesses to the murder in order to prevent his rival from wrongly getting the credit for having solved the mystery.[33] Having achieved the fame he always desired for committing the perfect crime but shocked when he discovers that his confession was unnecessary, Grodman takes his own life. It only remains for 'the working men who had been standing waiting by the shafts of the hansom' ready to pull the detective triumphantly back to Bow to carry his dead body away on a stretcher (157). The cycle of publicity is now, at last, complete.

The Big Bow Mystery was not the only detective novella in which the sealed and ultra-private interior of the locked-room mystery is turned inside out, amplified by the attentions of the press into a metropolitan, if not a national, *cause célèbre*. Edgar Wallace, perhaps learning a trick or two from Zangwill, also re-imagined the locked-room mystery as a kind of political theatre in *The Four Just Men* (1905), using the passing of anti-alien legislation as the pretext for a popular fictional puzzle. Yet what makes Zangwill's text distinctive is the way in which he relentlessly sends up not merely the tics and foibles of his lower-class characters, but the sentiments and prejudices that animate their popular politics, no matter what their ideological persuasion. So stalwarts of the Bow Conservative Association like the small grocer and jury foreman Sandy Sanderson, who regards the philosopher 'Shoppinhour' as an 'infidel writer' (38), are pilloried alongside the radical free-thinking cobbler Peter Crowl, 'a Vegetarian, a Secularist, a Blue Ribbonite, a Republican, and an Anti-tobacconist' who can regularly be seen haranguing the Sunday morning crowds on Mile End Waste, 'a small, big-headed, sallow, sad-eyed man', his hair 'thinning rapidly on top, as if his brain were struggling to get as near as possible to the realities of things' (55–6). And their shibboleths and slogans fare no better. The movement to raise a mass petition on behalf of the arrested labour leader Tom Mortlake reads like a satire of such radical causes as that of the Tichborne claimant, a symbol of oppression and a test of 'fair play' to his working-class supporters.[34] To Peter Crowl, the very thought that Mortlake might be guilty brings tears to his eyes, seeming to call into question his most deeply-held political convictions. 'The Cause of the People', he intones pathetically when Mortlake looks certain to hang, 'I believe in the Cause of the People. There is nothing else' (139). To deliver the requisite degree of shock, the exact quantum of poetic injustice, Mortlake's arrest takes place in the middle of a commemoration ceremony at the Bow Break o'Day Club organised to mark the public unveiling of a portrait of the murdered philanthropist. If conservatives and socialists are temporarily brought together at this stirring event, which puts Mr Gladstone and the proletarian hero Tom Mortlake on the same stage in a room abuzz with loud huzzahs and the noise of song, there is no mistaking the satirical portrait of a popular radicalism as an unreflective and empty-headed emotionalism that emerges here. But, should the reader have happened to miss the point, Zangwill underscores it by defending the apparent impropriety of introducing 'Mr Gladstone into a fictitious scene ... on the ground that he is largely mythical' (11).

By juxtaposing popular politics and sensational crime *The Big Bow Mystery* is essentially reproducing the texture of the world adumbrated by *The Star*, but the novella does so in such a way as to call into question the paper's view of things. The aggregate effect then is seriously to unsettle the highly charged solidarities invoked in *The Star*'s editorial pages, showing them to be shallow or too easily swayed, gulled by its own rhetoric. But in satirising the newspaper, Zangwill's novella also points towards a more troubling aspect of *The Star*'s pursuit of sensationalism. Early on in the story references are made to the still-unsolved Whitechapel murders, a reminder of how ruthlessly the paper exploited this particular news item. However, the truth was more brutal than Zangwill, as a contributor to *The Star*, could openly admit. As Judith Walkowitz has shown, in its reports of the Whitechapel murders *The Star* tended to pander to and inflame its readers' worst prejudices by linking the Ripper's crimes to the Jews. Thus, at the height of the murders, *The Star* helped to produce a hue and cry around the sinister nocturnal figure of 'Leather Apron', alleged to be 'a Jewish slippermaker by trade', lending credence to the so-called 'Jacob the Ripper theory' which in turn encouraged the 'denunciation of Jews at the inquests' and led to 'widespread intimidation of Jews throughout the East End.'[35] Problematic stories about Jews continued to appear in *The Star* around the time of *The Big Bow Mystery*'s serialisation – reports discussing 'the Buying and Selling of Jews in London', for example – but there is also evidence that pejorative representations of the Jew were being contested.[36] The day after the final instalment of *The Big Bow Mystery*, *The Star* published a letter by a Mr Michael S. Isaacs attacking a prominent London magistrate for 'his libellous abuse so persistently showered upon us ... when dealing with Jewish witnesses'.[37] Nevertheless, such complaints indicate that, among Jewish readers of the paper, the workings of the law could not always be relied upon to guarantee a measure of justice or protection. Advanced radicalism might boldly proclaim 'the Brotherhood of Man', but as the murderer in *The Big Bow Mystery* acidly comments in Social Darwinian fashion, 'the brotherhood of man was to the ape, the serpent, and the tiger' and the only real form of mutual recognition that existed was the 'peculiar sympathy' between the stalker and his prey (150).

Liberalism, Utilitarianism, and the Politics of Immigration

Zangwill's suspicion of modernity – his worries about its effects upon the Jewish community, and his fears about the malleability of the new collective allegiances of trade and class – was hardly likely to commend itself to *The Star* whose official view was much closer to Samuel's insistence upon the favourable prospects for change in the short and medium term. When the paper reviewed Samuel's *Liberalism* in February 1902, it praised the book for helping 'all Liberals to realise how many things they agree about and how few things they disagree about', which was precisely Samuel's intention.[38] Samuel clearly did believe that it would be possible to unite the party around a platform of social reform that would be acceptable both to its seasoned supporters and to the newer social constituencies cultivated by papers like *The Star*: in short, to bridge the emergent divide between old and New Liberals, to reconcile the individualist and collectivist strains in Liberal thought.

   Liberalism is briskly forward-looking from the outset. Even Samuel's statement of first principles seems ahead of its time. His claim that 'it is the duty of the State to secure to all its members, and all others whom it can influence, the fullest possible opportunity to lead the best life' could well be read out of context as a line from a modern liberal theorist like Ronald Dworkin.[39] Defined as a matter of individual preferences – since 'no two men, indeed, would agree' on what constituted 'the best life' – this 'one essential doctrine' of liberalism is necessarily predicated on 'a policy of social reform' in order to attain certain goods that pertain to every life, such as 'health' or 'material comfort' and ought therefore to be addressed collectively as part of the general welfare (4–8). In other words, the issue that structures so much of the book's argument is a deeply Edwardian concern with what was coming to be called 'the Social Problem', described by J.A. Hobson in his 1901 book of that title as the search for 'the best means of minimizing social waste or, conversely, of maximizing social satisfaction'.[40] In practice, consideration of 'the Social Problem' often came down to a discussion of the terms on which the

interests of organised labour could be fully incorporated into the nation
state, one of the pressing reasons why liberalism needed to take stock and
redefine itself. For if the party did not, there were those who were ready
and willing to step into the breach. Samuel noted, somewhat defensively,
that the reader would already have 'within reach a dozen handbooks
describing the principles and purpose of Socialism' and he was personally
well-acquainted with these ideas (xv). As a young man he had taken part
in the debates among Liberals and Socialists held under the auspices of the
Rainbow Circle – where he had first heard J.A. Hobson speak – and its
secretary Ramsay MacDonald had gone so far as to invite him to join 'the
infant [Labour] Party' in August 1895.[41] In the Rainbow Circle and
elsewhere Samuel had also come into contact with prominent Fabians
like Sidney Webb, Graham Wallas and George Bernard Shaw, and
though he was never convinced by their views, they played a formative
role in shaping his thinking. Consequently, a key aim behind his 1902
reformulation of *Liberalism* was to see off the socialist challenge, to
produce a distinctively *liberal* brand of collectivism.

But Samuel did not regard the contest between Liberals and Socialists
in purely ideological terms. In this he was aided by the tendency among
some of his fellow Liberals to present 'the Social Problem' as lying
outside the sphere of political representation *per se*, since – in Winston
Churchill's somewhat disingenuous characterisation – 'the main
aspirations of the British people are at this present time *social* rather than
political'.[42] What mattered, therefore, was how the increasingly manifest
inequalities in popular life chances were to be managed. If British
democracy was at risk it was because of the immense gulf between the
multitude of 'misfortunes that can happen to a man without his being at
fault in any way, and without his being able to guard against them in any
way' and 'the mighty power of science, backed by wealth and power, to
introduce order, to provide safeguards, to prevent accidents, or at least to
mitigate their consequences'.[43] Despite his concern to articulate Liberal
first principles clearly and comprehensively, the notion that social
problems were susceptible to eminently practical solutions that
transcended party differences seems to have appealed greatly to Samuel
and he often sought to dissolve real political disagreements into technical
or organisational issues. It is on these grounds, in what must now appear
as an astonishingly naïve move, that Samuel attempted to demonstrate
that divisions of opinion about the Boer War were actually disputes
about matters of fact rather than political principle. Of course, Samuel's
politics had definite ideological limits of their own – as I have just shown,
he was very careful to distance himself from the embryonic Labour
Party. However, he undoubtedly believed that his political horizons were

set by what he felt to be the art, if not the science, of the possible. In his eyes it was precisely *because* other, more preferable political solutions were available that the idea of wholesale nationalisation could be dismissed, and not simply because of arguments about the status of private property.

At first sight Samuel's stress upon practicalities comes as something of a surprise – after all, he had himself insisted that 'the trunk of the tree of Liberalism is rooted in the soil of ethics' (6). And it has been cogently, and in part correctly, argued that Samuel's political theory was 'strikingly close to that of [the Oxford social philosopher] T.H. Green', at least insofar as it took as its starting-point Green's view that the role of the State was to act as the final guarantor of individual self-development, underwriting a version of 'positive liberty'.[44] Thus the maintenance of our rights as subjects could be seen as vital to the elaboration of a common moral consciousness, a common good whose recognition 'is the essence both of morality and political obligation'.[45] But despite this ethical inspiration, Samuel's liberalism departed considerably from the spirit of Green's work in his willingness to resort to utilitarian political arguments in resolving practical political problems, arguments that Green's philosophical Idealism was largely designed to discredit – though Samuel's departure that may have been influenced by Hobson's claim that such a shift was in fact an unavoidable feature of Green's own thinking too.[46]

A 'sound imperial policy' was integral to Samuel's view of modern liberalism and he was always reluctant to allow the Tories to reap the political benefits of empire simply because some sections of his own party were 'out of touch' with what he regarded as 'the true, sound Imperial spirit'.[47] Accordingly, the justification of empire in *Liberalism* is a prime example of Samuel's no-nonsense utilitarian manner, proffering a balance sheet of imperialism's advantages and disadvantages, including its effects upon the home country. Here is a specimen checklist from the chapter on the 'Advantages of Empire':

> Turbulence is replaced by peace and stagnation by progress, and native governments that often possessed every element of badness, are exchanged for a rule which, if alien, is probably the most efficient that mankind has yet developed. To the Indian, the empire has brought relief from the race wars, the religious wars, the dynastic wars, the plundering expeditions and brigandage which were formerly the rule in almost all parts of Hindustan. He is subject to law instead of to the capricious tyranny of princes. Famine and plague are sometimes forestalled and largely relieved.

And not least among the boons conferred on India is the opening of new lands to give room to her crowded populations (319).

On the credit side are efficiency, progress, and the rule of law: solidly traditional liberal virtues. But beyond these, Britain is becoming the solvent of India's own 'social problem', producing what one might see as a species of demographic justice by intervening in the health, habitation and environment of the 'native' population. At this point Samuel is beginning to think the idea of empire in terms of what Foucault called 'biopolitics', that is the attempt 'to rationalize the problems presented to governmental practice by the phenomena characteristic of a group of living human beings constituted as a population: health, sanitation, birthrate, longevity, race'.[48] And for such an endeavour the utilitarian calculus was indispensable.

The same style of reasoning informs the majority of Samuel's individual analyses of specific topics throughout the book, even where the issue under discussion might seem to discourage such treatment. Consequently Samuel's analysis of the proper relationship between religion and the State follows the same basic model as his actuarial defence of empire. Here Samuel upholds the principle of disestablishment (as opposed to disendowment) not solely on the basis of a right to 'religious equality', but because he is able to cite empirical evidence to show that separating Church from State does not have the destructive consequences so often ascribed to it. For 'in all the self-governing colonies of the British Empire, and in the United States as well', the absence of a national church has not led to moral decline (215–16). Of course, the question of religious toleration returns the reader to liberalism's *raison d'être*, its protection of the opportunity to choose the good life for oneself, an opportunity that surely is hindered if there is a substantial asymmetry between the various churches. But, once having argued for the desirability of religious pluralism, Samuel prefers to pass over such ramifications, so crucial to the problem of assimilation, in silence. Though this is the only chapter in the book in which the Jewish faith is mentioned, it is confined to a footnote about numbers.

Biopolitics and religious pluralism: together these twin themes take us to the limits of English liberalism in this period and in the years that followed. Indeed, one could plausibly argue that it was only when forced to respond to the agitation around the Aliens Bill that Samuel began directly to confront the issues of anti-semitism and Jewish migration, issues whose importance was intensified by the heightened conflict between Liberals and Conservatives in the run-up to the 1905 election. The timing of what was to be the climacteric of the anti-alien movement does much to explain why Samuel failed to tackle immigration in his 1902 book of 'principles and proposals'. And his shocked reaction to the renewed anti-alien campaign suggests that he had underestimated its resilience in the parliamentary arena and even that it took him by surprise. It was, he told members of his constituency in his weekly newsletter of 29 June 1905, 'one of the most futile, unworkable, and oppressive ever introduced in modern times into Parliament'.[49] But by then the Bill had already reached the Committee stage.

Samuel's strategy in his 1905 essay for *The Economic Journal* was to show that what he called the 'vast and continuous flow of population' belonged among the great sea-changes of modernity besides which the recent arrival of 'the aliens in East London' was a mere drop in the ocean (334). In so doing he brings out the truly global dimensions of the diasporic condition in the twentieth century:

> Project the imagination to some point from which we can embrace in a single bird's-eye view the inter-movements, in the past as well as in the present, of the various races of the world among one another. We shall see at different periods many civilised communities planting here and there small colonies of their citizens, afterwards to be absorbed in the populations around them; we shall see from time to time spasmodic migrations of hordes of conquering barbarians; we shall see also little bands of pioneers, like the Spaniards and Portuguese in South America, the English in North America and Australasia, founding primitive settlements which are destined to develop into great States. But not until we turn our eyes to our own age shall we see so broad a current of peaceful migration, steadily carrying a million persons from one continent to another year after year, and at the same time so many separate streams slowly but continuously modifying the ethnological character of so many different countries (318–19).

Like some unstoppable 'force', this dynamic tidal motion – 'intermingling, ousting, blending, changing' – 'is now powerfully at work moulding the future of vast portions of the world' (319). Yet if this swelling tide is the harbinger of a new era, it is not only economically productive and positively inter-racial, but also curiously secular and benign, at least in relation to the phenomenon with which Samuel was wrestling.

As with the earlier treatise on *Liberalism*, and no matter how far-sighted his vision might be, Samuel's reliance upon utilitarian modes of political calculation and his long-standing belief that the empire could be 'an engine of enlightenment and the spread of civilisation' are not without their difficulties.[50] For, despite his stress upon the primarily non-violent nature of these changing patterns of migration, it is clear that the imperial approach to race and citizenship is a source of conflict which utilitarianism is by itself unable to resolve. For example, when reviewing the question of whether the resettlement of Indians or Chinese in different parts of the empire is desirable or not, Samuel finds that he is confronted by a series of hard cases in which the political claims of subjects and colonists may be sharply at odds with each other. And in these instances we see the hydraulic metaphor of currents, flows and streams upon which Samuel relies so heavily beginning to drift towards the same discursive structures as those of his opponents. So, while he meets the anti-alien arguments about the swamping of local labour markets by foreign workers with withering criticism, Samuel is unable to avoid slipping into the selfsame rhetoric. The net benefit of importing Chinese workers or Indian traders into a given colony will only be defensible 'so long as the process is not on a large enough scale to threaten the predominance of the white race' (336). Similarly, after comparing the experiences of Britain and the United States and pointing to the relative success of the latter in assimilating very large numbers of immigrants in the previous two decades, Samuel enters a cautionary note: 'there is in nations what chemists would call in liquids a saturation point, beyond which infusions can no longer be absorbed' (333). The racial underpinnings of this caveat are made still more explicit in the essay's penultimate paragraph where Samuel argues that it might be necessary to disregard the threat to liberty imposed by restrictions on entry in cases of 'economic pressure' or because of 'a great adulteration of the national stock' (338).

How was it possible for Samuel to maintain a position that was at one level implacably hostile to the anti-alien lobby, yet simultaneously not only made significant concessions to it, but also shared much of its vocabulary and characteristic tropes? One answer is that Samuel's rhetoric simply reflects the continuing prestige within political economy and social philosophy of styles of reasoning derived from the biological sciences and mechanical engineering. However, Samuel's accommodation to his opponents' arguments was also considerably enabled by his repudiation of the doctrine of rights, as sketched out for example in T.H. Green's *Lectures on the Principles of Political Obligation* (1885), despite the influence that other aspects of Green's work had exercised upon him. In the 1905 essay on 'Immigration' Samuel stirringly invokes the 'great humanitarian, cosmopolitan movement of the end of the eighteenth and the earlier part of the nineteenth centuries, with its belief in the essential equality of man and his natural rights'. Yet, in a striking *volte face* he is no less forthright in dismissing the whole notion of rights as a relic of 'some transcendental political dogma' fundamentally incompatible with modernity. 'No political scientist nowadays believes in the doctrine of natural rights', Samuel insists. A nation may have what he vaguely calls a 'duty to the world at large', but the only valid 'test' of any political measure is the extent to which it contributes to the 'well-being of the society concerned'. It follows that 'if the admission [of alien immigrants] results in appreciably lowering its own civilisation, in degrading the standard of comfort of its people, in lessening, therefore, its influence for good on other nations, then surely its duty to the world, as well as its duty to itself, would justify exclusion' (319–21).

Now Samuel was never entirely consistent on this point. He could in certain circumstances refer to rights, like the 'right of asylum', as if they were indisputable. In his speech to the Commons in May 1903 attacking the horrific abuses visited upon the indigenous peoples of the Congo Free State by the agents of King Leopold of Belgium, he stoutly proclaimed that there were 'rights of liberty and of just treatment [that] should be common to all humanity'.[51] And perhaps in the light of such harrowing atrocities no other language of redress was possible, for the cause of 'Congo Reform' was one of the great humanitarian campaigns of the Edwardian era.[52] Nevertheless, in the same speech Samuel also made it perfectly plain that he 'was not one of those short-sighted philanthropists who thought that the natives must be treated in all respects on equal terms with white men'.[53] Once again, a balance had to be struck between the civilised and the barbarous, between those factors that promoted the moral health of the nation and those that would bring about its decline. And two years later he did not shrink from drawing a similar conclusion on an issue much closer to his heart. 'Although to estimate the qualities of a people is a hard task', observed Samuel in his best utilitarian manner, 'it must be attempted in dealing with this group of immigration questions' (334).

In the debate on the 1905 Aliens Bill, Samuel accepted that no nation could afford the additional burden imposed upon it by the arrival of large numbers of criminals and paupers, but then proceeded to dispute whether empirically these were 'the true facts' in this instance.[54] Not only were the numbers of alien paupers, criminals and the insane lower than those in the home population, but there was no evidence to suggest that the arrival of Jewish immigrants had led to the 'displacement of skilled English labour' nor proof that they made 'bad citizens'.[55] On the other hand, signs of assimilation – always the touchstone of Samuel's argument – were readily apparent. In particular, Samuel noted that 'although many of the Jewish Reservists in Russia and Poland are refusing to fight in the

Far East', in the Boer War 'the Jewish population of England lost a larger proportion of their number in the field than the rest of the English nation'.[56]

Strategically, Samuel's arguments sought to position Jewish immigrants firmly within the progressive mainstream of English culture: far less of a social problem than the anti-alien lobby would want to claim, bringing valuable skills and new jobs to the British economy, and already manifesting their loyalty to their country of adoption. In sum, 'they are usually sober, industrious, domesticated, quick-witted, eager for education', at one with, and in some respects superior to, the country's urban working classes. Any 'faults' they may be said to possess 'are the outcome of the lives they have been compelled to live elsewhere'. It is to be expected 'that in the better conditions in England' these flaws will be 'in time discarded' and therefore that 'the net result of their presence' will finally be to the nation's advantage (334, 339).

But what if the balance sheet should prove indeterminate? In the 'Immigration' essay Samuel at least recognises the possibility of a stalemate, conceding that 'the counts in this indictment and the heads in this defence are all of them equally true' (334). In such situations Samuel proposed that the safest political rule of thumb was 'to err on the side of liberty' (339). But what happened to that rule if the calculus went against the hapless alien? One of the great strengths of Israel Zangwill's writing in the Edwardian period was his willingness to take on this eventuality and to think seriously about its consequences. Just as *The Big Bow Mystery* satirises the social base of late-Victorian popular radicalism, so a number of his stories and essays published after 1900 seem to work to exacerbate the political difficulties that dogged Samuel's avowedly inclusive liberalism. If many of Samuel's arguments from the debates on the 1905 Bill now read like a species of apologetics, a reasoned defence of 'Why Jews Succeed', then Zangwill's essay bearing this title is obstinately and refreshingly designed to show why they do not.[57]

Failure and loss are thus among the central themes of Zangwill's last completed book of fiction, the diverse collection of stories called *Ghetto Comedies*, published in 1907, which provide an ironic commentary on the kind of claims made by Samuel.[58] Far from positing an idealised Jewishness or a Jewishness that can take its rightful place within a modernising narrative of progress, the figures in Zangwill's text are often used precisely to problematise what it means to be a Jew. As if to emphasise this point, several of the stories deal with the Jew as a problem within representation, featuring an artist as storyteller or chief protagonist, primarily (though not always) Jewish, and usually working in the visual arts. The themes of the stories are strikingly and appropriately topical: anti-semitism, the perils and pitfalls of assimilation, Zionism, and the plight of the East European refugee.

Among the most topical is 'Anglicization', a tale with Dreyfusard overtones that might almost have been written as a riposte to Samuel's vaunting of the role played by Anglo-Jewish soldiers in the Boer War. Simon Cohn, the son of a successful Jewish tailor enlists in the City Imperial Volunteers and on his return home falls in love with Lucy, the sister of a non-Jewish man whose life he has helped to save during a night patrol in South Africa. But Simon discovers that her father 'has just joined some League of Londoners for the suppression of the immigrant alien'; and then, a little later, he finds that she will not marry him because he is a Jew.[59] The shifting identifications and disidentifications, like the cross-cutting ironies to which they lead, are unrelenting: Simon's mother is shocked that Simon does not want a Jewish girl, yet is outraged when Lucy refuses him; Simon thinks himself thoroughly assimilated, but learns that he could never be anglicised enough for the woman he desires; Mrs Cohn believes the war has brought about a 'friendship' between the races that is 'sealed in blood' (78), while Lucy thinks it 'only natural ... that after shedding our blood and treasure for the Empire we should not be in a mood to see our country overrun by dirty aliens' (82). In a bitter denouement that gives the lie to Samuel's comfortable assumptions about the civilising effects of imperial 'greatness', Simon's happiness and self-respect are destroyed by the fruits of the very patriotism he had thought would erase his own sense of difference.

A parallel realisation can be traced in the pages of 'The Jewish Trinity', the story that immediately follows 'Anglicization' in *Ghetto Comedies*. But this time the conflict is more damagingly located within Anglo-Jewry itself. In 'The Jewish Trinity' the sculptor Leopold Barstein falls in love with the daughter of Sir Asher Aaronsberg, a prosperous manufacturer and former MP, only to find his path barred by prejudice of an even more insidious kind than that experienced by Simon Cohn. Leopold moves in the opposite direction to Simon: his love for Mabel Aaronsberg leads to a new and surprising absorption in his ethnic identity, for he thought that he had long since 'parted company with Jews and Judaism' (89). His growing preoccupation with the 'mystery of race and blood' inspires in him a sympathy for 'the idea of a national revival of his people' and his visits to 'the slums and small synagogues of the East End' helps to give shape to his Zionist aspirations and brings him into contact with the nationalist movement (99). Yet when he speaks to Mabel of his dream of their settling in Palestine after the marriage she is horrified. 'One couldn't breathe,' she tells him. To live 'entirely among Jews' would be to live in a 'great Ghetto!' (104). Her father's position is equally dismissive. Zionism is, in Sir Asher's eyes, a 'narrow tribalism', a political impossibility which, if it were ever to achieve its goals, would 'undermine all the rights we have so painfully won in the West' (113). Leopold furiously responds that the price of emancipation in denial and self-hatred has brought into being a 'Jewish trinity' in which 'the Jew's a patriot everywhere, and a Jew everywhere and an anti-Semite everywhere': 'three-in-one and one-in-three' (115).

Like Simon Cohn, Leopold Barstein discovers that he cannot be other than a Jew, yet the terms on which he may embrace this identity seem to lead to an impasse. This awareness proves to be enormously fateful for him. Unable any longer to regard himself as 'a cosmopolitan artist', his love for Mabel Aaronsberg and with it his attachment to Zionism seem to lead nowhere – or rather, to new forms of estrangement, to a disenchantment with his own people (92). Perhaps not surprisingly, there is an odd and oddly comic sequel to this tragedy. When we come across Leopold again later in the book we find him 'sitting in his lonesome studio, brooding blackly over his dead illusions'. In 'the aftermath of his East-End Zionist period' he has become the recipient of a plethora of begging-letters from Jewish ne'er-do-wells down on their luck, those 'Luftmenschen' whose firm belief in providence guards them from harm, but also guards them against success, figures who (as the story will show) continue to amuse and exasperate him (225). Reluctantly, Leopold becomes a guardian angel to one of them, but like the Luftmensch he too could be said to live a life in abeyance. Against this awkward sense of deferral Zangwill was to turn to the 'practical politics' of 'territorialism', the search for 'a land of refuge' for the Jews that was inspired by Zionism but not confined to Zionism.[60]

Zionist Horizons: A Coda

Unlike Israel Zangwill, Herbert Samuel came late to an active and intellectual engagement with Zionism. According to the Memoirs, it was not until Turkey had entered the war on the side of Germany in 1914 that Samuel turned his attention to the future of Palestine as part of a renewal and possible resolution of the Eastern Question. Though the full story of his delayed involvement lies outside the scope of this essay, some of the reasons behind Samuel's initial lack of enthusiasm for this cause will already be apparent. In the first place, Samuel's own relationship to the Jewish faith had undergone a sustained period of doubt from which he seems only gradually to have emerged. Perhaps partly because of this, he seems to have been reluctant to particularise the social and political problems faced by Jews as in any way distinctive or unique to them, and the whole tenor of his commitment to a programme of reform as the *differentia specifica* of contemporary liberalism led him to concentrate on seeking non-socialist solutions to what he saw primarily as questions of labour and class. Nevertheless there is an important connection here. For if Samuel's apostasy made him less susceptible to the emotional and political appeal of Zionism, then the profound social and cultural distance that separated him from those largely migrant constituencies that formed the bedrock of Zionist support meant that there was little likelihood of his identifying with the kinds of sentiments and schemes advanced by a figure like Theodor Herzl. So, although members of Samuel's family were among those who met with Herzl on the occasions when he visited London, this link seems to have had no appreciable effect upon Samuel's thinking. The contrast with Zangwill, whose life was changed forever by his contact with Herzl, could scarcely be greater.

Search as one might, there are no *Luftmenschen* to be found in the annals of Samuel's Edwardian statecraft, no itinerant 'class of beggar students and rabbis and nondescript Bohemians'. In Samuel's preferred political economic discourse the 'alien' is always a productive labourer, to be classed with other workers of the same ilk as a factor of production that typically counts as 'a multiplier' rather than 'a divisor'.[61] Against this utilitarian bent, Zangwill's emphasis – at least in the period up to 1914 – was upon the human tragedy of the diasporan experience. His quasi-statistical description of the Jewish people in 'Why Jews Succeed' as 'eleven millions of human atoms scattered incoherently through the world, devoid of any common territory or common power, unable to concentrate their force in any desired direction' was, paradoxically enough, intended to provide the opening premise for an approach to Jewish suffering and hardship that lay outside the domain of economic calculation, one that addressed the question of how such a dispersed mass of unfortunates might at last find the moral and intellectual resources to transform themselves into political subjects. In Zangwill's eyes, the attraction of an exclusively Jewish settlement in East Africa, an idea that had grown out of negotiations between Herzl and Joseph Chamberlain when the latter held the post of Colonial Secretary, was that it held out the promise of inaugurating the long process of political transformation he envisaged.[62] Not so for Samuel. When asked his opinion of the prospects for such a scheme in an interview for *The Jewish World* in 1903, Samuel's response was guarded and somewhat non-committal. While judging the area 'eminently suited for agricultural development', he stressed its 'commercial isolation' and warned that East Africa was no place 'for a parasitic class'. In any attempt to weigh favourable against unfavourable factors, 'the character and qualifications of the would-be settlers' must necessarily remain an open question.[63] In short, he refused to be drawn.

One of the significant lines of disagreement between Samuel's position and that of Zangwill's turned upon the issue of rights. As we have seen, Samuel regarded the whole issue of natural or human rights as anachronistic, at best a purely rhetorical device and at worst a self-deluding fiction that provided no assistance in the hard task of political book-keeping. For Zangwill, however, rights were not simply entitlements or claims that could be lodged against the political and legal order, demands for redress or restitution; they were also the vehicle through which groups or movements were able to come to a new self-consciousness of their position and aspirations. The desire for 'freedom and equality' could become the 'driving spirit' that would 'found not only a colony, but an object-lesson in civilization'.[64] His critique of the achievements of the settlements in Argentina sponsored by Baron de Hirsch was precisely that their economic successes made their lack of 'autonomy', 'their failure from the political point of view the more heartrending'.[65] And in his anatomy of nationalism in 1917, Zangwill went on to argue that there were no less than 'five kinds' of 'human rights at issue for any free race': 'civil, religious, cultural (including linguistic), political, and national'. As the Great War began to edge towards its grim conclusion Zangwill came to believe that 'the problem and ideal' was 'how to maintain the virtues of tribalism without losing the wider vision' and risking a 'world [that was anything] other than a free area for mutual migration and economic exchange'.[66] If that final phrase recalls 'the wider vision' of Samuel's own essay on 'Immigration', Zangwill's sense of what he once called the 'ebb and flow in popular politics' with their volatile allegiances and contradictory identifications is worlds apart from the kind of bloodless rationalism characteristic of Samuel's liberalism, and his critique recognises that anti-semitism can become deeply embedded in the most radical or ostensibly urbane formations.[67] This was an acute source of difficulty for Samuel: some of the least comprehending pages of his *Liberalism* are those that try to argue that jingoism and 'false patriotism' are anathema to the modern liberal outlook since they are 'opposed to the well-being of the world' (352).

How then could Samuel have come to espouse a version of Zionism – indeed to have formulated a policy that brought the eventual foundation of Israel a step closer? This was hardly likely to have been due to a belated appreciation of the importance of 'cultural rights' or a shift in his understanding of politics, though – oddly enough – I do want to suggest that Samuel's 'conversion' owes something to Zangwill. In his *Memoirs* Samuel reminds his readers how heavily preoccupied he was in the

Edwardian years with the practical concerns of party and office, securing a political base and building a political career. There was, he writes, 'plenty to do elsewhere' without becoming entangled in a movement that appeared to be but a 'distant ideal' (139). Yet Jewish affairs continued to intrude. The rise in 'alien' immigrants arriving in Britain in 1906 after the abortive Russian revolution the previous year intensified the problems the Home Office faced. Samuel was insistent that 'political or religious refugees were not to be refused admission' and moved to reinforce the 1905 Act's provisions on asylum, the sole legislative gain that the Liberals had been able to salvage from their parliamentary defeat.[68] And on a more personal level, Samuel found himself implicated in the anti-semitic invective that was a defining feature of the Marconi scandal.

Bernard Wasserstein notes that 'Samuel's reading in the period before 1914 included very few books on Jewish religion or politics', with the exception of those he read while researching 'the alien question' and Disraeli's novel *Tancred*.[69] But we do know that he read Zangwill and even thought enough of his ideas to copy out a phrase from an essay of Zangwill's in his book of quotations. The phrase characterised anti-semitism as a 'dislike for all that is unlike' (that is, as 'an expression of the universal tyranny of majorities') and it appeared in 'The Return to Palestine' published in *The New Liberal Review* in December 1901, in which Zangwill argued that 'anti-Semitism has been the greatest pioneer of Zionism, the one most directly operative both in the foundation of the present Palestinian colonies and the provocation of the great Zionist movement led by Dr. Herzl'.[70] Moreover, as Wasserstein also notes, in the years that followed Samuel was in 'occasional' contact with the ITO, 'the breakaway group from Zionism' that Zangwill led.[71] Though slight in themselves, these facts help to fill out Samuel's assertion to the astonished Zionist leader Chaim Weizmann in 1914 that he had been taking an interest in the ideas of the movement over the years. Now, with the entry of Turkey into the war, Samuel believed that a return to the Jewish homeland was no longer a 'distant ideal'. For the 'probable' break-up of the Ottoman Empire meant that the geopolitics of the region had changed utterly and that 'the re-establishment of the Jewish State', 'the centre of a new culture', had become a real possibility. Once again, Samuel's notion of cultural uplift relied chiefly upon a utilitarian rationale, rather than an appeal to 'ancient' rights: by providing an example of the unfettered achievements of the Jewish people *within* modernity, the new Palestine would encourage Jews everywhere to raise 'their character' and demonstrate 'their usefulness to the peoples among whom they lived'.[72] Yet what ultimately made such a move thinkable was the power and influence of the British Empire whose might could provide the military and economic backing for this process of nation-building, bringing Palestine into the imperial orbit as a protectorate or annex. In arriving at this sobering appraisal Samuel was again appealing to that 'sound imperial policy' which he had first put forward on the hustings at the turn of the century, a policy that was perhaps more indebted to an appreciation of Disraeli's stance on empire than to a close reading of *Tancred*. It is not the least of historical curiosities that Zangwill, whose oscillating relationship to Zionism was dogged by misfortune and miscalculation, should have provided a bridge between Samuel's own refusal of Zionism and his subsequent endorsement of it.[73]

NOTES

1. Herbert Samuel, 'Immigration', *The Economic Journal* 15 (September 1905), p.317; all subsequent page references will be given in the main text.
2. Teresa Hayter, *Open Borders: The Case Against Immigration Controls* (London: Pluto Press, 2000), p.69.
3. Bernard Wasserstein, *Herbert Samuel: A Political Life* (Oxford: Clarendon Press, 1992), p.111.
4. The Rt. Hon. Viscount Samuel, *Memoirs* (London: The Cresset Press, 1945), p.18; all subsequent page references will be given in the main text.
5. Jaime Reynolds, 'Herbert Samuel', in *Dictionary of Liberal Biography* ed. by Duncan Brack et al. (London: Politico's, 1998), p.319.
6. *Parliamentary Debates: House of Commons,* 4th series, CXLV (2 May 1905), col.731.
7. Wasserstein (see note 3), p.viii.
8. *The Times,* 6 February 1963, p.15.
9. Reynolds (see note 5), p.319.
10. The phrase seems to have originated in Israel Abrahams' review of *Children of the Ghetto* in the *Jewish Chronicle,* 14 October 1892.
11. I am indebted to Professor Todd Endelman for providing me with this information.
12. Israel Zangwill, *Chosen Peoples: The Hebraic Ideal versus the Teutonic,* with a foreword by the Right Hon. Herbert Samuel and an afterword by Israel Abrahams (London: George Allen & Unwin, 1918). Samuel's foreword is a short appreciation of Arthur Davis's work.
13. For an outline of Samuel's reasoning on this topic, see his letter to his wife Beatrice on 9 November 1901 instructing her on how to debate the question of women's suffrage with her friends. (*House of Lords Record Office* HS A/157/82). As Wasserstein points out, Samuel did not change his views until after the First World War when, having been impressed by 'the part played by women in the war effort', he successfully moved a resolution to allow women to serve as MPs in October 1918. Wasserstein (see note 3), p.232.
14. Hugh Franklin was imprisoned for a number of offences including attacking Winston Churchill with a dog whip for his treatment of the suffragettes in the 'Battle of Downing Street' in November 1910, as well various acts of political vandalism. While in prison in 1913 he went on hunger strike and was forcibly fed. On Samuel's outraged reaction, see Wasserstein (see note 3), p.125. Zangwill's support is discussed in Meri-Jane Rochelson, 'Israel Zangwill and Women's Suffrage', *Jewish Culture and History* 2.2 (Winter 1999), p.10.
15. 'The Fighting Suffragettes are Right, says Zangwill', *The New York World,* c. 20 Nov. 1909, Israel Zangwill Clippings File, New York Public Library.
16. Samuel Beckett, *Mercier and Camier* (London: John Calder, 1973), p.102.
17. The letter is quoted in Wasserstein (see note 3), p.17.

18. Geoffrey Alderman, *Modern British Jewry* (Oxford: Clarendon Press, 1992), pp.117–18.

19. For a discussion of this point, see Wasserstein (note 3), pp.11–12.

20. *Minutes of Evidence taken before the Royal Commission on Alien Immigration*, II (1903), col.17077.

21. Israel Finestein, *Jewish Society in Victorian England: Collected Essays* (London: Vallentine Mitchell, 1993), pp.210–11.

22. Though this critique was commonplace among the wealthier sections of Anglo-Jewry at the turn of the century it was hardly disinterested. By construing sweating as a national problem, politicians like Samuel were not only defending the less fortunate members of the Jewish community, but also attempting to minimise the opprobrium visited upon themselves through the anti-semitism such problems stimulated in the public mind. See Eugene C. Black, *The Social Politics of Anglo-Jewry 1880–1920* (Oxford: Basil Blackwell, 1988), pp.39–40.

23. Herbert Samuel, 'Novels Still To Be Written', *The New Statesman*, 5 July 1919.

24. Israel Zangwill, *Children of the Ghetto: A Study of a Peculiar People* ed. by Meri-Jane Rochelson (1892; repr. Detroit: Wayne State University Press, 1998), p.61. All subsequent page references will be given in the main text.

25. Israel Zangwill, *Dreamers of the Ghetto* (London: Heinemann, 1898), p.vii.

26. Israel Zangwill, *The Big Bow Mystery* (1892; repr. New York: Carroll & Graf, 1986), p.11; all subsequent page references will be given in the main text.

27. Bernard Gainer, *The Alien Invasion: The Origins of the Aliens Act of 1905* (London: Heinemann, 1972), p.166.

28. Gareth Stedman Jones, *Outcast London: A Study of the Relationship between Classes in Victorian Society* (Oxford: Clarendon Press, 1971), p.348.

29. Julian Symons, *Bloody Murder. From the Detective Story to the Crime Novel: A History* (Harmondsworth: Penguin, 1985), p.87. Over the years *The Big Bow Mystery* has variously and ingeniously been read as a coded statement of Zangwill's artistic credo (Scheick), as 'a parable of ethnic marginality' (Rochelson), and as a mirror image of political Zionism (Eisenzweig). See William J. Scheick, '"Murder in My Soul": Genre and Ethos in Zangwill's *The Big Bow Mystery*', *English Literature in Transition* 40 (1997), 23–33; Meri-Jane Rochelson, '*The Big Bow Mystery*: Jewish Identity and the English Detective Novel', *Victorian Review* 17 (1991), 11–20; and Uri Eisenzweig, 'Zionism and Detective Fiction: A Case in Narratology', *Telos* 60 (1984), 132–40.

30. *The Newspaper Press Directory 1888* (London: C. Mitchell & Co., 1888), pp.32, 210.

31. For a late example of Ripper-style reportage, see *The Star*, 13 February 1891, p.3.

32. See *The Newspaper Press Directory 1889* (London: C. Mitchell & Co., 1889), pp.44, 222.

33. Meri-Jane Rochelson has pointed to the possible Yiddish derivation of Grodman's name as meaning 'straight' or 'right' and suggests that it provides a red herring for Jewish readers: Rochelson (see note 29), p.17. However, there is little else in this text that accents this connection.

34. For an analysis of how this famous case of legally disputed inheritance (1871–72) became the vehicle of popular political aspirations lasting until the early 1880s, see Rohan McWilliam, 'Radicalism and Popular Culture: The Tichborne Case and the Politics of "Fair Play", 1867–1886' in *Currents of Radicalism: Popular Radicalism, Organised Labour and Party Politics in Britain, 1850-1914* ed. by Eugenio F. Biagini and Alastair J. Reid, (Cambridge: Cambridge University Press, 1991).

35. Judith R. Walkowitz, *City of Dreadful Delight: Narratives of Sexual Danger in Late-Victorian London* (Chicago: University of Chicago Press, 1992), pp.202–7.

36. See *The Star*, 30 April 1891, p.3.

37. See *The Star*, 5 September 1891, p.2

38. 'What We Think', *The Star*, 24 February 1902.

39. Herbert Samuel, *Liberalism: An Attempt to State the Principles and Proposals of Contemporary Liberalism in England* (London: Grant Richards, 1902), p.4; all subsequent page references will be given in the main text.

40. J.A. Hobson, *The Social Problem* (1901; repr. Bristol: Thoemmes Press, 1996), p.17.

41. See MacDonald's letter to Samuel reproduced in the *Memoirs* (see note 4), pp.26–7
42. 'The Approaching Conflict' in Winston S. Churchill, *Liberalism and the Social Problem* (London: Hodder & Stoughton, 1909), p.237, my emphasis. Although this volume is a collection of Churchill's speeches 1905–09 the ideas he puts forward are profoundly indebted to debates that had been set in train prior to the turn of the century.
43. Ibid.
44. See John Bowle, *Viscount Samuel: A Biography* (London: Gollancz, 1957), pp.37–41. For an excellent study of T.H. Green's ideas, see Melvin Richter's important book *The Politics of Conscience: T.H. Green and his Age* (1964; repr. Bristol: Thoemmes Press, 1996), especially pp.339–42.
45. Richter, *The Politics of Conscience*, ibid., p.233.
46. Hobson, *Social Problem* (see note 40), pp.4–5. In his book of quotations Samuel endorsed the notion that the 'basis of ethics' was essentially 'utilitarian, because virtuous acts are those which are useful to society'. *House of Lords Record Office* HS E/33/514.
47. See Samuel's address to the Reading & County Liberal Club as reported in the *Reading Observer*, 15 December 1900 in which he argued that the Liberals' weakness on this question had effectively sold the pass to the Tories. Samuel's liberal imperialism was among the most heavily criticised aspects of his book on *Liberalism*: he was taken to task by the *Speaker*, the *Daily News*, the *New Age*, and the *Labour Leader*.
48. Michel Foucault, 'The Birth of Biopolitics' in *The Essential Works of Michel Foucault 1954–1984. Volume 1: Ethics, Subjectivity and Truth*, ed. by Paul Rabinow, trans. by Robert Hurley et al. (Harmondsworth: Allen Lane The Penguin Press, 1997), p.73.
49. Herbert Samuel, 'Magical Number – 20', *North-Eastern Daily Gazette*, 29 June 1905.
50. Part of Samuel's rationale for 'a sound imperial policy' as cited in the *Reading Observer*, 15 December 1900 (see note 47).
51. *Parliamentary Debates* 4th Series, CXXII (20 May 1903), col.1297.
52. See Adam Hochschild, *King Leopold's Ghost: A Story of Greed, Terror and Heroism in Colonial Africa* (London: Macmillan, 1999). It should be noted that Samuel's reaction was conditioned by his own 'enlightened' brand of liberal imperialism and that it also reflects his economic interests in the region. His 1904 Diary shows him regularly attending meetings of the West African section of the London Chamber of Commerce.
53. *Parliamentary Debates* 4th Series, CXXII (20 May 1903), col.1297.
54. *Parliamentary Debates* 4th Series, CXLV (2 May 1905), col.726.
55. Ibid., cols. 726–30.
56. Ibid., cols. 731–2.
57. Israel Zangwill, 'Why Jews Succeed', *The New Liberal Review* 3 (May 1902), 471–81.
58. Zangwill seems to have begun thinking about this book in late December 1902. See the letter on Jewish life as a tragic-comedy, quoted in Maurice Wohlgelernter, *Israel Zangwill: A Study* (New York: Columbia University Press, 1964), p.298.
59. Israel Zangwill, *Ghetto Comedies* (London: Heinemann, 1907), p.80; all subsequent page references will be given in the main text.
60. See, for example, the essays 'A Land of Refuge' (1907) and 'Territorialism as Practical Politics' (1913) in *Speeches, Articles and Letters of Israel Zangwill* ed. by Maurice Simon (London: The Soncino Press, 1937).
61. Zangwill, 'Why Jews Succeed' (see note 57), p.471. The terms 'multiplier' and 'divisor' are taken from Arnold Toynbee and are quoted in Samuel's 'Immigration' (see note 1), p.321.
62. For a full account of this episode, see Robert G. Weisbrod, *African Zion: The Attempt to Establish a Jewish Colony in the East African Protectorate 1903–1905* (Philadelphia: The Jewish Publication Society of America, 1968).
63. 'The Proposed New Settlement', *The Jewish World*, 4 September 1903, p.472.
64. Zangwill, 'A Land of Refuge' (see note 60), p.245.
65. Ibid., p.242.
66. Israel Zangwill, *The Principle of Nationalities* (London: Watts & Co., 1917), pp.40; 89–90. In an alternative formulation he describes 'the problem' to be that of 'how to preserve the brotherhood of Israel without losing the brotherhood of man'. Ibid., p.89.

67. Israel Zangwill, 'Jewish Colonial Trust' (1908) in *Speeches, Articles and Letters* (see note 60), p.279.
68. Wasserstein (see note 3), p.90. For a good account of the implementation of the 1905 Act, see Jill Pellew, 'The Home Office and the Aliens Act, 1905', *The Historical Journal* 32 (1989), 369–85.
69. Wasserstein (see note 3), p.204. Wasserstein gives Samuel's reading of Disraeli's *Tancred* an important, if somewhat hypothetical, role in the development of his Zionist allegiances. In fairness, it should be noted that Samuel was jotting down snippets from *Tancred* into his book of quotations in 1904, though the significance for him of phrases like 'All the great things have been done by the little nations' may as easily have been linked to the British as to the Jews. *House of Lords Record Office* HS/33/330-1.
70. *House of Lords Record Office* HS E/33/287. See also, Israel Zangwill, 'The Return to Palestine', *The New Liberal Review* 2 (December 1901), p.616.
71. Wasserstein (see note 3), p.203.
72. Samuel, *Memoirs* (see note 4), pp.140–41. All the above quotations are taken from Samuel's extensive notes on a conversation with the Foreign Secretary Sir Edward Grey on 9 November 1914 and cited at length in the *Memoirs*.
73. Zangwill was quick to pick up the significance of Samuel's new position. 'I hear Lloyd George and Herbert Samuel have become Palestinians' he wrote in a letter on 8 January 1915. See Joseph Leftwich, *Israel Zangwill* (London: James Clarke & Co., 1957), p.236.

The Representation of Jews on Edwardian Postcards

ESTELLE PEARLMAN

The significance of the postcard as a social document, providing a vivid record of attitudes and values of the past, is becoming increasingly acknowledged with the publication of books, catalogues and articles that explore the great variety of subjects they portray. From 1959 onwards, when Richard Carline presented the first review of the history of postcards as a 'branch of art',[1] there has been a phenomenal revival in the hobby of postcard collecting, particularly in the United States, England and France.

It is in this popular method of communication – 860 million postcards passed through the Post Office during one year in the Edwardian era[2] – that we find pictorial representations of Jews that depict a caricatured, often comic image of 'a people apart'.[3] Postcards in the main were published for profit. If they were to be a commercial success it was imperative that their message should be immediately understood, making them a medium in which illustrators routinely deployed stereotypical images. The characteristic stereotype of the Irish is a heavy drinker, the Scots, a frugal nature. Stereotypical images of Jews target appearance, manner and characteristics, but this portrayal is frequently executed through the mode of humour. From 1904 onwards some 125 publishers in England and Scotland produced more than 300 different designs of postcards depicting Jews. Postmarks show that these cards were available in areas other than those where Jews settled. The appearance of the Jew on postcards is invariably grotesque, the manner ludicrous and a constant theme is an immutable, avaricious, devious character.

An important consequence of the publication of postcards is that stereotypical and seemingly hostile images of Jews became easily and widely available to the British masses who were able for the first time to purchase, in the form of a 'comic' postcard, negative portrayals of perceived traits and behaviour of Jews who were immigrating to Britain during the late Victorian and Edwardian periods. The continuity between Victorian and Edwardian representations was heightened by early Edwardian publishers' reproduction or adaptation of drawings by Victorian artists, such as Phil May.

Like caricatures by Thomas Rowlandson and William Heath during the eighteenth and nineteenth centuries, early twentieth-century postcards on the theme of Jewish financial gain commonly feature specific aspects such as a hooked nose and biblical names to reinforce the identity of the subject as a Jew. Linguistic ridicule together with jibes at the propensity for using expressive gestures is another device frequently used on pictorial postcard representations to identify and stereotype the Jew (Figures 1 and 2). In his study of anti-semitic stereotypes in popular culture between 1660 and 1830, Frank Felsenstein suggests that by the middle years of the eighteenth century the habit of ridiculing the broken English of Ashkenazi Jews was already established.[4] A mezzotint printed and sold by Carrington Bowles in 1792 entitled 'I've Got de Monish' is an early example, which shows the substitution of hard and soft consonants – the 'd' for 'th' – and the toning down or flattening of sibilants – 'sh' for 's'.

One of the most popular themes on early postcards is the trade of pawnbroking. In his history of pawnbroking, Kenneth Hudson writes that he knows of no other significant aspect of British life that has been so consistently ignored by those who make a living by reflecting, analysing and criticising society.[5] Historians such as G.M. Trevelyan, E.P. Thompson, G.D.H. Cole and Raymond Postgate, as well as writers of the 1920s and 1930s like George Orwell and J.B. Priestley, have been silent on this important aspect of English life. But Hudson is also guilty of an omission. He did not, in the course of extensive research and great enthusiasm for the subject, unearth the huge range of pawnbroking postcards, many of which depict Jews. In the course of his research Hudson came across the common assumption that most pawnbrokers are Jewish, charge extortionate rates of interest and are receivers of stolen property on a large scale. To what extent do postcards confirm this assumption? Whilst there are many varieties of postcards depicting those who patronise the pawnbroker, from every social class, from toffs to drunkards, Jews are never shown as users of the services of pawnbrokers. Postcards also show that 'Uncle', as well as being the euphemism for pawnbroker, could also mean Jew, as suggested by the obese character tapping his grotesque hook nose and captioned 'Your affectionate Uncle'. Names such as Cohen, Goldstein and Levy are used as another means to identify the pawnbroker as a Jew, as well as the distortion of biblical names: Isaac becomes Ikey; Moses, Mo.

'A Crystal Receiver' (Figure 3) appears to confirm the eighteenth-century dubious reputation of the Jew as a receiver of stolen property,

FIGURE 1

Published by Inter Art [1398].

FIGURE 2

I should shay sho!

Published by Inter Art [3429].

alluded to in a verse which includes the line: 'Since they of stolen things are oft receivers'.[6] The style of the Crystal Receiver postcard, published almost a century after Charles Dickens wrote *Sketches by Boz*, is also a reasonably accurate reflection of his description of the early nineteenth-century pawnbroker as 'an elegantly attired individual' with 'curly black hair, diamond ring and double silver watch-guard'.[7]

Paradoxically, Jews themselves published caricature representations of themselves on postcards both in Britain and abroad. Such postcards also portray stereotypical racial characteristics, in particular the hooked nose. The promotion and purchase of these images by Jews, with their long history of persecution and social marginalisation, may suggest a form of idiosyncratic acceptance and self-irony through which 'in-group' identity is affirmed.

Caricature representations of Jews were published on postcards in 1905 by J.A. & A.A. in the United States. The postmarks show that they were circulated in New York, where the majority of immigrants settled, and also Philadelphia. The stereotyped features of the hooked nose and exaggerated gesticulation are depicted, but these cards, bearing bold Yiddish captions (sometimes with pale print English translations in parentheses) were produced by Jews for Jewish consumption. This is confirmed by the caption 'Mazel Broche Und A Grosse Mispoche' [May Your Troubles Be Little Ones] on a postcard depicting parents with a troupe of young children, all of whom have hooked noses.

The situations featured on the postcards published by Jews for the market outside Britain tend to focus on their experiences, rather than hostility. Some examples from the United States are the embarrassment of the foul smell of smoked fish ('Was Fur A Geschroche') to being discovered eating non-kosher food ('A Koscher Zettel – Du Kannst Chaser Essen') to bankruptcy ('Machuleh is Trumpf!') (Figures 4, 5 and 6). The Jews of Warsaw were another group able to find humour in adversity. Postcards published by C.W. with Hebrew captions were printed in Germany for Polish Jews. There is pathos in the humour illustrated on these postcards when the theme of the 'wandering Jew' is evoked by the depiction of Jews searching the globe with a microscope and telescope for sanctuary (Figure 7), when they are able to find amusement in being refused entry (Figure 8), and finally when they are able to laugh at the fantasy of elderly Talmudic scholars attending the performance of a can-can dancer, so outrageous and contrary to Yeshiva values (Figure 9).

In Britain, Joseph Asher, a German Jew, published postcards from 1904 onwards, under his name and also that of E.S. London (Empire Series) and Kismet Series.[8] Asher employed the artist Donald McGill who

FIGURE 3

Published by Photochrom [2266].

FIGURE 4

WAS FÜR A GESCHROCHE
SMELTS (SMELLS)

FIGURE 5

A KOSCHER ZETTEL

(HAM! YES? NO?)

DU KANNST CHASER ESSEN

Copyrighted 1915 by J. A. & A. A.

FIGURE 6

MACHULEH ıs TRUMPF!

(*BUSTED*)

Copyrighted 1905 by J. A. & A. A.

FIGURE 7

Published by Central [2108].

FIGURE 8

Published by Central [2114].

FIGURE 9

במקום בית-מדרש להבדיל

Published by Central [2106].

produced postcards that, unlike those published in the United States and Warsaw, feature Jews as devious characters, as the butt of ridicule, and as grotesque. The 'Funny Parrots' series bears the name of Joseph Asher and shows a cat eyeing a parrot with the words 'Well now, I suppose that must be a Jew Chicken!!' (Figure 10). The popularity of this card is suggested by a later version captioned 'Bet he's a non-Aryan. Just look at his Beak'.

The fact that Asher published postcards which portray the Jew disparagingly raises questions which are difficult to answer. I would suggest looking to the music hall culture of this period. Discussing Edwardian life, Paul Thompson points to an atmosphere of tolerance in the popular culture of music halls and cinemas, its evasion of political and religious disputes and its fatalism.[9] On the other hand, the music hall was a place where the occasional stereotype of the Jew could be found. It is known that the postcard artist Donald McGill was a frequenter of this popular Edwardian form of entertainment.[10] It is possible that here he and other postcard artists found inspiration for their caricatures. A photograph postcard of Harry Rogers as a Jew wearing a false beard, moustache and eyebrows, who appears with his partner Katie Weston, claims that they are 'the renowned Hebrew Comedy Duo' (Figure 11). Harry Rogers also appears together with a cross-dressed character on a series of postcards which appear to be a grotesque parody of Jewish 'romance' in the form of tableau scenes (Figure 12). These postcards were published by Alexander Bloom (a Jew known locally as the King of Postcards) who also specialised in music hall song sheets.[11]

On 10 January 1913 the *Jewish Chronicle* published a letter of protest from 'C.S.T.' complaining about 'the self-styled "Hebrew" character comedians and the growing tendency to caricature the Jew and show him off in a most obnoxious light to his Gentile neighbours'. There is no record of support for the writer and there appears to be no adverse comment or even acknowledgement of hostile pictorial representations of Jews available on postcards in everyday circulation at the time. Were postcard representations accepted by Jews because in the main they were comic portrayals? Alternative accounts are suggested by the observations of the Fabian historian and social researcher Beatrice Webb, who, in her chapter on the Jews of London's East End in Charles Booth's *Life and Labour of the People in London*, marvelled at how the Jew from Eastern Europe 'suffers oppression and bears ridicule with imperturbable good humour', remaining silent 'in the face of insult and abuse'.[12] Similarly, Gerry White's study *Rothschild Buildings* records the memories of 'Jack' of his employment at Whiteley's Store in London in 1913: 'Oh, they were very anti-Semitic – yes, oh yes. Specially two or three in the

FIGURE 10

Published by Joseph Asher & Co. [A1194].

HARRY   KATIE

ROGERS & WESTON

THE RENOWNED HEBREW
COMEDY DUO.

FIGURE 12

ON THEIR HONEYMOON

Published by East London Printing Co.

warehouse. But it just went out one ear – I had to keep the job – went in one ear and out the other. Just took no notice of them.'[13]

An obsession with the existence of a Jewish conspiratorial plot was evident in the publication during the 1920s of a series of postcards by The Britons, an anti-alienist organisation.[14] A despondent face, wearing a warrior's helmet bearing the word Briton is shown on top of a harp played by a smirking, obese, hooked-nosed character surrounded by money-bags, beside whose foot a crushed John Bull sinks into the ground. This postcard, festooned with pawnbroker signs to reinforce the message, is entitled 'Jews Harp' (Figure 13). The harp is a symbol of power and by showing the Jew plucking the harp on which appear the words 'dope, tobacco, oil, the press, heat, politics, finance, theatre and film, chemical industry, gold, silver, art, law, food', the postcard suggests that Jews are working for control and domination in every sphere. In 1927 the Honourable Percy Hurd MP was the recipient of a postcard which bears the caricature of a portrait of what appears to be a Jewish Boadicea beneath the caption 'Britannia Rules the Waves', in which two obese Jewish gourmands respond with the words 'Yeth, but we rule Brittania' (Figure 14). Once again pawnbroker signs are employed to both symbolise and reinforce the message of Jewish interest in power. The nationalist, racist message of the postcards issued by The Britons is the threat of a Jewish plot for world conquest and control.

The hostility depicted on the demonic donkey postcard 'Cent per Cent' and on those published by The Britons is in a different category from that on the majority of British postcards (Figure 15). Whilst it should be acknowledged that postcards of this nature are relatively few in Britain, they do alert us to the need to explain the varieties of hostility depicted on postcards. The theme of the Jewish conspiracy for world domination can be regarded as 'a modern, secularised version of the popular medieval view of Jews as a league of sorcerers employed by Satan for the spiritual and physical ruination of Christendom', and forms part of the discourse of political anti-semitism.[15] In contrast, Jews have been denigrated in pictorial representation by their misuse of language and incongruous accent, as Felsenstein argues, and this is a method whereby a perceived potential threat from a stranger is diminished.[16] One might also look to theories of humour. One theory of joking emphasises its capacity to negate social power by denying the propriety of the behaviour of the people who form the butt of the joke.[17] What jokers do, or, in the specific case of 'comic' postcards, what the joke does, is to form an excluding relationship with the subject; and thereby the butt of the humour, the Jew, is degraded and constructed as inferior. People who form the butt of humour are constructed as not fully accepted members of the community,[18] a theory confirmed by the publication on 'comic' postcards of immigrant Jews.

FIGURE 13

FIGURE 14

FIGURE 15

Published by O.C. [300].

To what extent do the portrayals of Jews on postcards accord with the view of historians and social commentators regarding attitudes towards Jewish immigrants? The postcards help fill some of the gaps that J.A. Garrard, J.H. Robb and Colin Holmes refer to, in acknowledging the problems of accumulating evidence on the extent of anti-semitic attitudes to immigrants.[19] Unsympathetic images on postcards appear to contradict A.T. Lane's view that immigrants were depicted as refugees from economic, political and religious oppression and that one of their strongest defences was that they were overwhelmingly poor.[20] Lane takes the view that British liberal traditions of offering asylum to the persecuted gave Jews a form of protection against anti-semitic attacks, which would be condemned as disreputable. But the portrayal of the Jew on postcards as an untrustworthy stranger indicates how anti-semitism was sustained at the same time as liberal attitudes. Alan Lee suggests that the failure of anti-alienism (interpreted here as anti-semitism) to gain political credence before 1914 was related partly to the fact that in British working-class culture there was no fundamentally hostile image of the Jews for politicians to exploit.[21] Similarly, whilst Colin Holmes highlights specific aspects of hostility encountered by Jews he denies that there was overt public expression of this hostility.[22] The evidence of Edwardian postcards counters both these views. Kenneth Lunn, in contrast, identifies links between organisations, journals and individuals in the pre-1914 period and the activity of the inter-war years, to suggest a continuity of thought within a tradition of British anti-semitism.[23] Alan Lee's unevidenced presumption that the Jew functioned like the Scot, the Welsh, the Irish and the Yorkshireman as a convenient butt for ethnic and related jokes, is confirmed by looking at postcards.[24] Indeed, whilst rightly noting that it is difficult to assess such influences, Lee suggests that it would be unwise to underestimate their effect on responses to the Jews. In June 1909 the *Daily Mail* published the impressions of a German journalist residing in the North of England, which asserted that the Jewish population was law-abiding and contributed towards the general prosperity.[25] But the journalist noted what he termed a 'slumbering anti-Semitism feeling, not outspoken, sometimes indefinite, sometimes denied, but in spite of all there it is'. The caricatures and texts that appear on postcards at this time confirm this impression.

The Edwardian anti-alienist Arnold White wrote that 'whoever frames an indictment against the quality of some of these poor creatures is laid open to the dreaded charge of anti-Semitism. Nobody can honestly do it without being called anti-Semitic all over the world, thus gaining a reputation which in these days spells ruin to most people.'[26] On the contrary, it did not spell ruin for postcard publishers. Davis postcard publishers, who specialised in producing souvenir postcards of pre-1909 Oxford college life, show no reticence in expressing antagonism towards Jews.[27] In 'The Oxford Pageant' not only is the stereotype of the usurer reinforced in the 'historical' representation of the Jewish quarter as an enclave of moneylenders (three pawnbroker signs in close proximity) but the hooked-nosed Jews are portrayed in the black and white print as importuners (Figure 16). The accompanying text constructs them as a threat to the dignity of an important tradition of one of the most noble and revered institutions in the land – 'A procession of the University passing near the Jews' quarters is ridiculed and interfered with by the Jews in different ways'.

In accounting for Edwardian anti-semitism, Paul Thompson emphasises contemporary notions of racial superiority, whereas Jose Harris suggests that it inveighed against Jewish immigrants not on ethnic grounds but because Jews were perceived as exemplifying the early Victorian virtues of capitalist accumulation at a time when there was a shift to values of patriotism and public spirit.[28] These differences of attitude between Jew and Gentile are stereotyped in two different postcards of the same seaside scene which reveal quite different fantasies: The beer drinker looks at the sea and thinks 'Ah, if only it was beer', while the Jew thinks of a business proposition: 'Rebecca! If all that vas beer and it vas ours, vat a lot of money ve could make selling it at 8d a pint.' Jewish 'comic' postcards with their unashamed emphasis on the Jew who is driven by material gain, seem repeatedly to echo in a popular form the sentiments of Beatrice Webb, who portrayed the Jewish immigrant as the incarnation of the Ricardian rational-economic man – rootless, privatised and 'deficient in the highest and latest development of human sentiment – social morality'.[29] The postcard (postmarked 1909) of a café monopolised by Jews who are not using it as an eating house but rather for playing dominoes, beneath a sign 'Notice to Domino Players – You must have one cup of coffee every 3 HOURS', may be seen as symbolic of England taken over by those with no allegiance, a concept confirmed by the caption 'OUR CAFÉS. England for the English. I Don't Think' (Figure 17).

Prior to their expulsion from England in 1290 Jews were portrayed in negative visual images. The 'Jewish nose' caricature, originally a device for allusion to evil, prevailed after Jews were permitted to re-enter England under Cromwell in 1656, and became a motif symbolic of devious financial dealings by financiers, avaricious profiteers and usurious embezzlers in the engravings of Georgian artists. Linguistic ridicule and the use of biblical names can be traced to the Georgian period, and jibes at the propensity for expressive language and ostentatious display to the

FIGURE 16

THE OXFORD PAGEANT.

SCENES IN THE JEWRY, 1268.—A Procession of
the University passing near the Jews' quarters is
ridiculed and interfered with by the Jews in different
ways.

ISAACSTEIN

Published by Davis.

FIGURE 17

Published by Tacon Bros.

nineteenth century.[30] All these elements became stereotypical signifiers of Jews in pictorial representations on early twentieth-century postcards, implicitly engaging with the contemporary controversy over Jewish immigration.

NOTES

1. Richard Carline, *Pictures in the Post* (London: Gordon Fraser, 1971) p.7.
2. A.W. Coysh, *Dictionary of Pictures Postcards* (Suffolk Antiques Collectors Club, 1996), p.9.
3. The *St James Gazette* referred to the Jews as '"a people apart". Long as they may live among us they will never become merged in the mass of the English population'. 4 April 1887, cited by G. Alderman, *Modern British Jewry* (Oxford: Oxford University Press, 1992), p.120.
4. Frank Felsenstein, *Anti-Semitic Stereotypes: A Paradigm of Otherness in English Popular Culture, 1660–1830* (Baltimore and London: Johns Hopkins Press, 1995), p.53.
5. Kenneth Hudson, *Pawnbroking* (London: Bodley Head, 1982), p.18.
6. Mayer E. Rabinowitz, *The Jew as Other* (New York: JTSA, 1995), p.49.
7. Charles Dickens, *Sketches by Boz* (London: Hazell, Watson & Viney, n.d.), p.141.
8. Elfreda Buckland, *The World of Donald McGill* (Dorset: Blandford, 1984), p.88.
9. Paul Thompson, *The Edwardians* (London: Routledge, 1992), p.249.
10. Buckland (see note 8), p.18.
11. Anthony Byatt, *Picture Postcards and their Publishers* (Malvern: Golden Age Postcard Books, 1978), pp.18–19.
12. Beatrice Webb in Charles Booth, *Life and Labour of the People in London*, quoted in S. Lindemann *Esau's Tears* (Oxford: Oxford University Press, 1997), p.365.
13. Gerry White, *Rothschild Buildings* (London: Routledge, Kegan Paul, 1980), p.244.
14. This organisation was founded by fourteen people in July 1919 as a 'society to protect the birthright of Britons and to eradicate alien influences from our politics and industries'. Gisela C. Lebzeltzer, quoted in *British Fascism* ed. by Kenneth Lunn and Richard C. Thurlow (London: Croom Helm 1979), p.41. The prime mover was Henry Hamilton Beamish, a man obsessed with the idea of Jewish world conspiracy. Readers of the journal *Jewry ueber Alles* published by The Britons (1919–25) were informed 'with Jewry the tribe is the unit, with White people every adult is a responsible individual; a Jew is not an individual – he is only a bit of his tribe'. Another notorious source of these ideas was the publication which appeared in Britain after the First World War known as *The Protocols of the Elders of Zion*, originally published in Russian in 1903. A new translation of the *Protocols* by Victor Marsden, a reporter for the *Morning Post*, was published in 1920 by The Britons and became the standard English edition. In 1963 The Britons Publishing Company bought out its 82nd impression. See *A Lie and a Libel: The History of the Protocols of the Elders of Zion*, ed. and trans. by Richard S. Levy (Lincoln: University of Nebraska Press, 1996), pp.xii, 33, 41, 63–5.
15. N. Cohn quoted in Colin Holmes, *Anti-Semitism in British Society 1876–1939* (London: Edward Arnold, 1979), p.13.
16. Felsenstein (see note 4), ch. 3.
17. Susan Purdie, *Comedy* (Brighton: Harvester Wheatsheaf, 1993), p.5.
18. Ibid., p.127–38.
19. John Garrard, *The English and Immigration* (Oxford: Oxford University Press, 1971), p.79; Holmes (see note 15), p.264.
20. A.T. Lane 'The British and American Labour Movements and the Problem of Immigration 1890-1914' in *Hosts, Immigrants and Minorities* ed. by Kenneth Lunn (Folkestone: Dawson, 1980), p.363.

21. Alan Lee, 'Aspects of the Working-Class Response to the Jews in Britain 1880–1914' in Lunn and Thurlow (see note 14), p.111.
22. Holmes (see note 15), p.266.
23. Kenneth Lunn, 'Political Anti-Semitism before 1914: Fascism's Heritage?' in Lunn and Thurlow (see note 14), p.23.
24. Lee (see note 21), pp.107–33.
25. Oscar T. Schweriner, *Daily Mail*, 28 June 1909.
26. Holmes (see note 15), p.149.
27. Coysh (see note 2), pp.77–8.
28. Thompson (see note 9), p.182; Jose Harris, *Private Lives Public Spirit: An Overview of British Society 1870–1914* (Oxford: Oxford University Press, 1993), p.237.
29. Harris (see note 28), p.17.
30. See Felsenstein (note 4).

Notes on Contributors

Bryan Cheyette is Chair in Twentieth-Century Literature in the English Department at the University of Southampton. He is the author of *Constructions of 'the Jew' in English Literature and Society* (1993), *Muriel Spark* (2000), editor of *Between 'Race' and Culture* (1996), *Contemporary Jewish Writing in Britain and Ireland: An Anthology* (1998) and co-editor of *Modernity, Culture and 'the Jew'* (1998).

Nadia Valman is Research Fellow at the AHRB Parkes Centre for the study of Jewish/non-Jewish relations at the University of Southampton where she directs a research project on Jews and literary representation. She has published a number of articles on Jews and Victorian literature and is currently completing a study of the figure of the Jewess in British literature of the nineteenth century.

Nils Roemer teaches Jewish history at the AHRB Centre for the study of Jewish/non-Jewish relations at the University of Southampton. His forthcoming publications include a book on Jewish historiography and popular culture in nineteenth-century Germany (Wisconsin University Press, 2004). He is currently engaged in a book-length study on the question of local memory and destination culture in Worms, Germany.

Michael Galchinsky is Associate Professor of English and Director of the Program in Jewish Studies at Georgia State University. He is author of *The Origin of the Modern Jewish Woman Writer* (Wayne State University Press, 1996) and editor of *Grace Aguilar: Selected Writings* (Broadview Press, 2003).

Jefferson S. Chase is a writer and journalist in Berlin. He was formerly Lecturer in German at the University of Nottingham. He is the author of *Inciting Laughter: The Development of 'Jewish Humor' in 19th Century Culture* (DeGryter, 2000) and the translator of the Signet Classics edition of Thomas Mann, *Death in Venice and Other Stories* (Signet Classics, 1999).

Florian Krobb is Senior Lecturer and Head of the German Department at the National University of Ireland, Maynooth. His publications include three monographs on German-Jewish literature: *Die schöne Jüdin: Jüdische Frauengestalten in der deutschsprachigen Erzählliteratur* (Niemeyer, 1993); *Selbstdarstellungen: Untersuchungen zur deutsch-jüdischen Erzählliteratur im*

JEWISH CULTURE AND HISTORY

neunzehnten Jahrhundert (Königshausen & Neumann, 2000); *Kollektivautobiographien/Wunschautobiographien: Marranenschicksal im deutsch-jüdischen historischen Roman* (Königshausen & Neumann, 2002).

David Forgacs is Professor of Italian at University College London. His research interests are in modern Italian cultural history, the mass media and cinema. His recent publications include *Rome Open City* (BFI Film Classics, 2000) and new editions of *L'industrializzazione della cultura italiana (1880–2000)* (Il Mulino, 2000) and *The Antonio Gramsci Reader* (Lawrence & Wishart, 2000).

Marilyn Reizbaum is Professor of English at Bowdoin College, USA. She is the author of *James Joyce's Judaic Other* and numerous essays on Joyce, as well as co-editor with Kimberly Devlin of *Ulysses – En-gendered Perspectives: Eighteen New Essays on the Episodes*. She writes comparatively on Scottish and Irish literatures, and her current project, from which this essay comes, is *A Genealogy of Jewish Degeneration*.

Edward J. Hughes is Professor of Modern French Literature and Head of the French Department at Royal Holloway, University of London. His most recent book is *Writing Marginality in Modern French Literature* (CUP, 2001), and his current research includes an investigation of Proust's representation of social class, in particular the articulation of class conflict.

Until her retirement, **Nelly Wilson** was Reader in French at the University of Bristol. Her research interests have centred on the crisis provoked by the Dreyfus Affair in French cultural life, notably in Republican, liberal and Jewish circles. Her publications include a study of *Péguy* (Bowes and Bowes, 1965) and a pioneering work on Bernard-Lazare, *Antisemitism and the Problem of Jewish Identity in Late Nineteenth-century France* (CUP, 1978; expanded French translation: Albin-Michel, Paris, 1985).

David Glover is Senior Lecturer in English at the University of Southampton. His books include *Vampires, Mummies, and Liberals: Bram Stoker and the Politics of Popular Fiction* (Duke University Press, 1996) and *Genders* (Routledge, 2000; co-authored with Cora Kaplan). He is currently working on a cultural history of the 1905 Aliens Act.

Estelle Pearlman has worked with the Jewish Women's Network on a number of publications on women and Judaism.

Index